WITHDRAWN

Class A

Class A

BASEBALL IN THE
MIDDLE OF EVERYWHERE

Lucas Mann

Pantheon Books · New York

Library of Congress Cataloging-in-Publication data
Mann, Lucas.
Class A : baseball in the middle of everywhere / Lucas Mann.
p. cm.
ISBN 978-0-307-90754-7
1. Minor league baseball—Iowa—Clinton—History.
2. Clinton (Iowa)—Social life and customs. I. Title.
GV863.I8C556 2013
796.357'640977767—dc23 2012034683

www.pantheonbooks.com
Jacket image used by permission of the Clinton Baseball Club, Inc.
Jacket design by John Gall

Printed in the United States of America
First Edition
2 4 6 8 9 7 5 3

For my parents

CONTENTS

AUTHOR'S NOTE

I had the great privilege of spending the 2010 season with the players, coaches, and fans of the Clinton LumberKings. This book is a reflection of my experience in that world, the meaning and narrative that I found within. Some names have been changed and some chronology has been altered for narrative clarity.

Class A

1 2 3 4 5 6 7 8 9

The Mascot

I AM LOUIE. Tonight, I am Louie. Tonight, regal and oversized, I am Louie the LumberKing.

I am not a Lumberjack. Lumberjacks are lowly, solitary creatures, and I am not that. I am industry and prosperity. I am hope.

I am nervous.

The mascot's dressing room used to be the umpires' dressing room, tucked under the bleachers on the first-base side of the stadium. Umps have signed the splintering cabinet where my uniform hangs. I think I can make out *"Clinton forever"* still scratched into the wood. And, *"Remember me."* And, *"A stop on the journey."* The journey to the majors. That's what he hoped. That Clinton, Iowa, would turn into a AAA town like Columbus or Nashville and that would lead to Milwaukee or San Diego or even Yankee Stadium. But this is the Midwest League, Class A, the lowest rung of full-season professional baseball. Yankee Stadium is far off.

There's a toilet in the corner, sprinkled with pubic hairs that I think could be both mascot and umpire in origin. There's a tin of mint-flavored tobacco, empty. There's a spit bottle, once a Gatorade bottle, now filled with saliva the color of tree sap.

Replicas of my image are littered everywhere, and they help me, despite the smells and the sight of this rotting cubicle, to buy into my own myth. Promotional postcards with my face saying, *"Fun is always in style, come out to the ballpark!"* A bobblehead of me. I tap my minia-ture ceramic skull, and it nods, comforting. There are cards from chil-dren addressed to me. *"I love you, Louie."* *"Your number one fan forever, Louie."*

I dress late, overwhelmed. I start with the socks, long black baseball socks. The kind that I first put on when I was five, schooled by my father the way I imagine young girls are when it comes time to slide on tights without causing a run. This is one of the earliest tactile memories I have, getting my toes all the way in and then rolling the polyester blend up my leg, feeling somehow armored.

The white pants come next. They're too tight. They're made for small, quick mascots because the ideal mascot is agile and teenage. I suck in, but you can't suck in thighs or ass. I snap the waist closed, and my fat springs it open. I feel my hands sweating. I try again, fumbling, getting desperate. It's Thirsty Thursday, and the house is always decently packed on days when alliteration can be made to signify fun. There're over a thousand out there, quite a turnout in a town with a population that has dwindled to twenty-six thousand people. It's one of the nights when the construction of this place, its self-referential glory, feels legitimate. I'm an important part of this.

The national anthem begins to play as finally, protected with a belt stretched to its last hole, my pants stay fastened and I'm halfway toward a full transformation.

Louie the LumberKing speaks of the past.

Did you know that there used to be more millionaires per capita in Clinton, Iowa, than anywhere else in the country? Did you know that? In the country.

I've heard that a lot since the beginning of the season because it's true and it's nice to say. At the turn of the twentieth century, Clinton was the center of a lumber empire. Millionaires were made here. Thirteen of them, all burly and proud in the portraits they left behind. They became barons of lumber, famous even beyond Clinton, and they built mansions that you could get lost in looming above the center of town. Though the industry and its spoils have long since disappeared, some mansions are still here. A few stand in a regal clump on Fifth Avenue, chopped up over the years into smaller and smaller apartments, odd looking from up close when you see the plastic children's toys on the lawn. One mansion is a museum, rarely visited. One was demolished in the late 1970s, and a department store sprouted in its place. The department store is gone now.

A lot of things are gone. Things downtown closed; some collapsed. Things burned. In 1968 the sociopathic hippie son of a local businessman set fire to nine buildings because he was just so bored. He torched Clinton High School, another town landmark, and it turned to ash blocks away from the opulent homes gone empty.

The longtime fans, the ones I've sat with every game along the third-base line, a group that has dubbed themselves first the Roadkill Crew, then the Baseball Family, remember how high the smoke went. You must have been able to see it from everywhere, along Highway 30 and across the river in Illinois, too. The glow reflected on the water, shifting, glinting, like a puddle of oil on a tar road.

That hippie boy set the most famous fires, but not the last ones. Fans have told me that it feels as if something were always aflame now. When buildings are old, when nobody's watching, anything can be tinder. Some of the fires are on YouTube. The dilapidated apartment with the mother and her two toddlers inside. The ancient white house without smoke detectors. The Lutheran church with flames dancing in the stained-glass windows. Old homes with no life in them, no care for them, so eventually they burn. And people like me, from anywhere, can click refresh, refresh on the videos. Three months ago, there was a string of fires on a single block, simultaneously ruled "not suspicious" and "under investigation" by local authorities. But fires don't matter here and now in the stadium. And neither does ash.

I enter my torso.

I squeeze through the neck hole of discarded high school football shoulder pads. The XXL LumberKings jersey that has been sewn onto this skeleton hangs off me, and when I tuck it into the pants, it gives my top half a superhero's triangular shape.

Now for my head.

My head is made of mesh and wood and cardboard and felt. My head must be two feet in diameter, sturdy and square-jawed, capped with an enormous golden crown. There are fake veins running down my neck to show my intensity. I have a goatee sewn on, thick and black. I look like a suave, royal Paul Bunyan. My mouth is carved into a confident smirk, and when people look at me, they won't know that it's my mouth that I see through, a dual eyesight. I watch the world in front of me and at the same time the lining of my own skull, the scaffolding of my own construction. There's a patch of dried blood inside my chin.

The door swings open, and I'm caught staring into the mirror, stroking my faux beard. It's Mitch.

"You look fucking legit, bro," he says.

"Really?" I say.

"Legit. Trust me. Legit."

He tucks my neck into my shoulders. He stands back. He shoves me hard and says, "You fired up?"

I nod and almost topple forward with the weight of myself.

I am Louie.

When the anthem finishes, I grab my flag. I push through the door. I trip over a hose, only just catching myself on the dirt with the palm of my left hand, right hand still clinging to the banner. I start again. My approximation of a sprint takes me around the edge of the infield. The team limbers up for the crowd. I hold the flag in front of me and try to wave it as I run. I feel my head wobble as I pass Nick Franklin, the star shortstop. A year ago, after he graduated high school, he was given $1.28 million by the Seattle Mariners. Now he's been sent here to Clinton, Iowa, to learn and then move up out of here on schedule. All the LumberKings' players were drafted or signed by the Mariners, and Clinton is just one of the early outposts in their development process. Seattle's largest present investment, though, by a good amount, is young Nick Franklin, and so now he's Clinton's prize, a transplanted, temporary millionaire.

I stop running in front of the Baseball Family, their pocket of seats always full, even on the many Mondays when the rest of the stadium is empty. I see Betty laying out her candies, one by one, measuring the way each piece sits on the concrete wall, close enough to call out to the players, not so close that the candy falls on the field and the game is disrupted by a rogue Jolly Rancher. Next to the Jolly Ranchers are the strawberry suckers in wrappers made to look like real strawberries. And then the packets of Walmart-brand fruit snacks, first the white, then the blue, then the purple ones that taste like flat grape soda.

"When did you start?" I asked her once. "Why did you start?"

"One day, I thought they work so hard out there, they must get hungry," she said. "That was fifteen years ago."

The players remember, she told me. There's a postcard at home from Derek Holland, who is famous now and pitches for the Texas Rangers in front of forty-five thousand people. It says, "Merry Christmas," and is addressed to Grandma Betty. It says he misses the candy.

He was produced here, Derek Holland. In a way. He came here raw and nineteen, and in Clinton, with Clinton, in front of the fans, he was nurtured into something better than what had arrived.

Bill, Betty's husband, keeps his sandaled feet hooked back like a bird's talons, hidden under the shadow of his chair. He's missing two toes, a memento from the years when he worked at Allied Steel, back when steel, along with paper, along with wood, along with plastic, along with corn, catalyzed the town. But Allied left with a lot of other businesses, and left behind 100,000 tons of coal tar blocks down from the riverfront stadium, not cleaned for decades. And long before that, Bill was standing on the work floor when a four-ton beam fell, smashing his foot and resulting in the steel plate that now heats his head in summer.

I realize that I like the eyes on me. I wave my flag, and I can trace gazes drifting back and forth along with my movements. It's every overwrought fantasy I ever got lost in on Little League fields—the simple, pure importance of a body being looked at. It's not me, really, but still, this vehicle that I operate commands attention. And I can't say that being the temporary center of this world that I have made mine for the season, the diamond, the lights, all of it, doesn't make me strut.

On the pitcher's mound, Erasmo Ramírez begins to warm up. He reaches down with his right arm and does one last check of his pants. He's satisfied. There's a perfect crease of polyester folded over onto itself, making a straight line of fabric just below his knee.

A minor-league baseball player has an absurd amount of time in the clubhouse before the game. When Erasmo comes in at noon to lift weights alone, he sits for four hours before batting practice, then another two between when he's done shagging balls and the game begins. How many granola bars can you eat? How many highlights can you watch?

How many times can you scroll down a Facebook page, pausing at pictures of your ex on Venezuelan beaches, barely covered, her teasing eyes so far away? So you have to switch your attention to your look.

Erasmo's pants are tight around his thighs and his ass because he likes his legs. His shirt balloons out, highlighting the hard width of him. He was never as tall as he should have been. He used to sit in dorm rooms at sports academies, in dugouts all around Latin America, wishing for a growth spurt, some miraculous transformation into a young man with an elegant body, long and broad and thin, primed with wide-open spaces to fill up. A transformation that felt earned. Now he's realistic, and he bulks up his squat five-foot ten-inch frame until there's nowhere else to fit the muscle.

On the mound, he rotates his arms in a windmill, and the clumps of muscle on his shoulders pulse. He flicks his glove toward the catcher, which means fastball coming. He exhales and then fills his acne-scarred cheeks with heavy, humid air, a move designed to be intimidating.

Betty taps Bill. "Look at his cheeks," she says. "Isn't that cute?"

Erasmo lifts his left knee slowly, deliberately, watching his pointed foot rise and then setting it down in front of him. He looks for a moment like an overweight ballerina. His movements are remarkable only in how unnoticeable they are. At this level of the minors, you'll see flamboyant young men jerk their legs up near their chins, rock their bodies back, shoot their arms down behind them so that they can whip forward at the hitter. Some stomp around the back of the mound, unhinged, posturing like fighting bulls. Erasmo is boring except for the burst that comes when his foot hits the dirt, a blur of rotation, until the ball spins out at ninety-two miles per hour and burrows into the catcher's mitt.

His favorite part of pitching is the eyes on him.

"Nobody looks at left field," he told me hours before the game as we sat under the Coors Light sign beyond the outfield wall, staring at the freshly mowed grass, shrugging at a plume of black smoke rising into the clouds from somewhere. "Nobody looks at first base; nobody looks at the coach. Everybody looks at me. All these people"—he gestured his pitching hand toward the bleachers that were empty and will always be more empty than he pictures them—"all these people and they see me." He smiled, a soft and young smile, the baby fat that still coats his face bunching under his eyes. Off the field, he is shy. He sits alone a lot. He listens when others have a conversation. Sometimes he laughs. He turned twenty a few months ago and celebrated in the clubhouse by eating a Hostess cupcake from a gas station.

I duck through the gate by third base to mingle in the stands. I'm greeted as both a friend and a celebrity. I hear everybody. Hi, Louie, hey, Louie, Louie, it's you again, Louie, my friend, Louie, I love you, Louie, our wives want to give you a big hug, would you like that, Louie, would you?

The wives sandwich me. I think there's a hand stroking my face for comic effect, but of course I can't feel. Breasts collide with me and conform to my plastic torso.

"You're so stiff," I hear a voice say. And then, "I remember this from when I was a little girl."

A good mascot is mute, so I just nod.

Muteness is key, but that's not the only guideline. I've done my research on my precursors. The need for a mascot's presence is almost as old as the game. The first mascots in professional baseball were also the first black men in white professional baseball, and their forced minstrelsy, the way the audience was allowed to feel wholly superior to them, was considered good luck. "Whenever anything's wrong," the Cincinnati Reds told their fans a century ago, "it is only necessary to rub Clarence's wooly head to save the situation, and call on one of his celebrated 'double shuffles' to dispel all traces of care, even on the gloomiest of occasions." Then there were the Philadelphia A's, who collectively decided that a disabled, hunchbacked batboy was charmed and that the perceived kindness toward such a ludicrous creature would be endearing. Before big moments, fans could watch their boys touch the hump.

And there are still all the Native American mascots, from Redskins to Redmen to Braves to Chiefs. That's a subtle shift, I think, away from pure ridicule. Yes, these mascots are totems of bigotry, but they're supposed to be frightening, coarse and powerful presences that help a team toward a winning identity. The Peoria Chiefs still exist here in the

Midwest League, a rival of the LumberKings. They kept the name but changed the mascot to a lanky, upright Dalmatian dressed in a fireman's helmet.

A LumberKing is more. I might be goofy, but I'm an ideal. I'm no mutated animal or anthropomorphized concept. I'm just a man larger than the rest, always smiling. And I have my LumberKing crown, a sewn-on reminder of a time that nobody alive can remember but everyone talks about as if it could still be here.

Erasmo falls behind the first batter and has to groove a fastball. The result is a line drive that hisses back at him and catches the knuckles on his right hand, tearing the skin with its seams. He gives a yelp and watches the ball ricochet off him into the outfield. For a moment, even looking out of my own mouth, I can see worry in his narrowed eyes. Everything can end so quickly. Danny Carroll, the LumberKings' center fielder, broke a bone in his hand a year ago, and it's not lost on Erasmo that he sits now as much as he plays. That the manager looks irritated or, worse, bored when Danny takes batting practice. A piece of him is flawed. His swing isn't the same.

"Any little thing can go wrong," Erasmo told me once, then gave a falsely cavalier shrug.

A good mascot is supposed to direct eyes away from bad things. Right now, I should jump on top of the dugout and be remarkable, whip fervor from nothing, but I lurk in the stadium walkway, peering out at the LumberKings' best pitcher, as worried as everyone else. BJ, the trainer, presses a towel around Erasmo's middle and index fingers, and he tries not to flinch. Later, BJ will congratulate him on not being a huge *chocha,* just a little one. He will say that the most irritating part of his job is the big *chochas,* the pussies who complain. He will hold his fingers in a narrow diamond by his crotch to emphasize his point.

Erasmo has never complained about anything physical in his career as a baseball player, one that began professionally at seventeen. People seem to like him for that.

"We don't quit in Clinton, Iowa," yells Matt, the mailman, a peripheral but boisterous member of the Baseball Family. He has an extensive list of dos and don'ts for baseball in this town. We certainly don't quit.

We get dirty. We run hard. We play the game right. Each mandate is trumpeted from his seat in the front row, an arm's length away from the players as they trot into the dugout.

"Attaboy, Ramírez," he continues now. And then, as though he is quoting something famous, "Excellent. Excellent. This world rewards tough men."

Erasmo hears him, but he doesn't respond. He knocks his heels against the sterilized white of the rubber, and he goes back to work. Today it's the hard labor of trying to win when it's apparent that whatever odd bit of magic gives a pitcher his best stuff isn't there. He surrenders another single and walks a circle around the mound as though alone. He breathes deep, and he throws the fastball that he wants to throw, boring in on the handle of the bat, eliciting a hollow crack and a weak ground ball to Noriega, the second baseman, but it kicks off his foot and into right field. A run scores, two men stand on base, and Erasmo Ramírez, for the next few minutes, looks petulant and confused and twenty years old. Four runs later, the inning is over, and he walks back to the dugout.

He glances up to the stands. Worn white faces look back at him. When he got called to Class A ball in a place he'd never heard of, Erasmo didn't realize that it would be the same people here each night in this small stadium, that it would be so easy to pick out individuals as they call his name. Sometimes his BlackBerry rings, and it's reporters from the biggest newspapers in Nicaragua. They want to know everything because he's important now. On his laptop screen is an article from just a week ago, telling the nation that Erasmo Ramírez is the best pitcher in a place called Clinton, Iowa, that even in America he has his control. When the readers in his home city of Rivas imagine him, thousands of miles away, basking in all of his accolades and wishes fulfilled, they don't think of this: semicircular bleachers with a few rows of dark green seats, above which it's just metal benches, long and low, with the usual bodies dotted along them at various points like a bored student's pencil marks on a clean page. Green poles rise up between the fans and hold a tin roof that hums when wind blows hard off the river.

If you took a picture of this scene, tinted it sepia, and burned the edges, it would be believable as something pulled from a time capsule of the game, from rubble, from ash. This is a Depression-era building, a WPA initiative, one of thirty-three hundred stadiums built in a two-year sprint, all virtually identical, now mostly gone. The crown jewel of the project, Tiger Stadium in Detroit, was bulldozed into a parking lot two years ago.

I wander through the fans.

Children ask me to sign things. A man named Kevin who has come to the games for twenty-seven years for the sole purpose of dancing the chicken dance in front of a crowd turns to me between innings and announces, "Louie, it's time for the chicken dance." A toddler sitting in the front row reaches out to me, blue tendrils of cotton candy covering his cheeks. He's the son of one of the team's catchers. Born in Venezuela, he's spent ten of his first eighteen months in basement apartments of American houses and in stadiums. I see his mind begin to work on centering himself when he notices me, a landmark for where he is and what's happening. I'm not the portly bee in Burlington or the ear of corn with arms and legs in Cedar Rapids or the stupid firefighting canine of Peoria.

I am Louie, and he is home.

I hold him so that people can take pictures of his little head pressed against my enormous one. People like the way that he's fascinated with me, overwhelmed by me. I like it, too. It's so easy to trust my own significance in the suit and in the stadium, to be sure that he will remember me and remember this whole tableau, always, even if soon he can't quite place the memory. His mother urges him to tell me, "*Te amo, Louie,*" but the boy has been mute since he got here.

By most standards, Erasmo has had a fantastic season, but he's failed to win two of his past four games, due to a combination of opposing players walloping his fastballs for disconcerting home runs and his teammates' inability to score. This quasi-failure has contributed to a change in his demeanor. He arrived as the grinning, agreeable little brother of the locker room, but now his quiet is the sullen kind, even as his team is slowly pulling itself into the play-off hunt. He sucks down fruit cups and wanders around, ending up back in the weight room, staring at himself as he hoists dumbbells over his shoulders, ignoring coaches who tell him that's enough.

Tonight, he wills himself back into the game. In the third inning, he begins to feel his changeup working, a pitch relatively new to him, and he throws it again and again. He gets the massive Dominican prospect Rainel Rosario to freeze and watch a changeup float past him, his legs unsure, his face frantic. Erasmo lets himself crack a quick smile before bouncing off the mound. Brad in the public address booth presses the button that delivers the *ha-ha* sound, like in *The Simpsons*, and everybody laughs at Rainel Rosario.

In the middle of the fifth inning, I judge the miniature John Deere tractor race. Two brothers, four and five, struggle to pedal rusted tires on the grass by the dugout. I hold out my hands as they finally pass me, and I indicate, lying, that the race was a tie. I'm cheered by most for my benevolence and booed by two drunk men with thin facial hair around their jaws and indecipherable neck tattoos. They believe in hard truths.

They throw peanuts shells, try to get them stuck in my crown. Betty comes to my defense. There's a sense of etiquette here, woven into the boring spaces of every home game. For fans who've come year after year, fifteen, twenty, thirty years, seventy home games each year, until thousands of innings run together in memories, all from the same view in the same seat in the same park, there is pressure to represent all of the noble tradition that should be, that is, still here.

"Why on earth would you do that to Louie?" Betty asks these drunken man-children. And they can't answer her. It's the same as when she'll whip her head around toward the sound of fans who've come, it seems, only to feel the rush of insulting the home team. She admonishes them without a word.

The nasty fans aren't crazy. It's intoxicating here—the proximity to the players and their proximity to failure. When I used to sit high up in Yankee Stadium with my father, a heckle could earn you, at best, an agreeing nod from the drunks around you, but the players I irrationally hated were bulletproof. They were so markedly better than me and everyone I knew that even when they failed, there was no power to be found in aiming cruelty in their direction. Here, you can hurt them if you want to. Every voice is distinguishable, and the players listen even as they pretend that they don't.

But the idea among the loyal fans, I've come to believe, is to provide something of the best of yourself. Treat them as though they will be great so that they might remember. And isn't the idea of greatness enough? The closeness to the promise of something extraordinary? The possibility that here, right here where you've always been, you cared for them first, before anybody else decided to give a shit?

The top of the sixth inning is Erasmo's last, and he gets out of it with a series of ground balls. He leaves the mound with his eyes focused on the dirt. The game is tied at four, and if his teammates score in the bottom of the sixth, he'll be in line for a win, pulling the club within a game of a wild-card play-off spot, but that doesn't happen. He tries to be stoic because that is what he always tries to be, but his face hangs disappointed. A win would have helped his stat sheet, something for the Mariner higher-ups to notice. Instead, today has been a wasted day, almost as if it never happened except for the slow, accustomed ache running between his elbow and his shoulder. He trudges to the clubhouse to ice his arm. He passes Betty and Bill and Tim and Tammy and Joyce and Matt and Derek and Julie and Gary and Eileen and Cindy and Angie and Craig and they call to him.

As he drapes a jacket over himself with my face emblazoned on it, Betty yells to him, a burst, almost as if she hadn't intended to say it.

"Do you like it here?" she asks him.

He stops trudging for a moment and turns to her. He forces his face into a smile. He nods his head and looks earnest.

"Oh," he says. "Yeah. It's nice."

He doesn't wait to see the satisfaction on her face, and I don't know if he hears her as she responds, "Well, it's not too big and it's not too small."

The game stays tied until the tenth inning, and I'm exhausted. Those fans who wander into ballparks just to drink and heckle are long gone. There are fewer than five hundred now. The weight of my skull is beginning to hurt, and the wood and hard plastic scrape at my collarbone. I let my head hang and then realize how absurdly melancholy that must look—not a normal person dejected, but a localized Disney character, eight feet tall, with his hands in his pockets and his ever-smiling face tilted toward the ground in despair.

Erasmo is still icing his tired right arm at the elbow and at the shoulder, sulking and eating a granola bar.

"Jiménez," BJ calls to him, but he doesn't respond, because that's not his last name. "Jiménez. Jiménez. Oh, shit, I mean Ramírez."

Erasmo looks up and sees the trainer pointing at the clubhouse TV. A sportscaster is announcing that the best young pitcher in the world, Stephen Strasburg, who was guaranteed $7.5 million before he was even sent to the minors, could need elbow surgery. You never know with a pitcher's arm, the sportscaster reminds the viewers. Things can just disintegrate. Erasmo, whose own signing bonus managed to clear $50,000—a number eaten into by taxes and his agent's cut, which would have been 25 percent at a minimum, the remainder placed in a bank account shared with his entire family—leaves to stand by the left-field fence, just in time to see the winning run for his opponents cross the plate.

He likes to walk home alone along the river. It's amazing, he's told me, that there are no sounds. Maybe a buzzard overhead, or a car passing, or a train. Once the fans drive home, downtown is empty. There is a McDonald's and a Wendy's. There's a barbershop, closed down since before Erasmo arrived here, with a couple of chairs left inside facing each other as though in conversation. There's the pawnshop where he buys DVDs on his days off. There's an abandoned karate studio. There's a discount furniture center. And another. There's a music store. And a Taco John's that sells tacos in sacks of twenty. And a gas station where the attendant always says "See you soon" when you leave. And a bunch of windows that reveal dark, empty rooms, with white paint on the glass that used to say something and still almost does, but it's just faded enough to be illegible.

Erasmo lives in the Lafayette, originally a hotel, then converted into the largest apartment building in a town that hasn't built a new apartment building since 1976. He rides the elevator with a puckered woman who drinks from a two-liter bottle of Coke and seems to be vibrating.

Erasmo holds the door for her, and she raises her eyebrows. She doesn't know that he's a town hero. Nobody in this building does. He says that it's as though when he leaves the stadium, people look through him, as if he were no longer who he just was. And then occasionally someone will come running up to him at the Walmart, pointing, squealing, and it'll be nice for that moment.

He cooks for himself—half a stick of butter into a pan, then three eggs, then the tub of yellow rice he's been saving in the fridge. He mixes it with a fork. His roommates haven't come home yet, three Venezuelans, two infielders and another pitcher, who sleep in an even row with him on the floor of this twenty-by-ten-foot studio. Erasmo eats on his mattress because there's no furniture. His stomach hurts because he still can't get used to eating dinner at midnight. He tries to fall asleep to images of himself, his laptop propped open on his bare stomach, the electric warmth on his skin. He scrolls through pictures of his face in glorious strain, his arm in blurred movement, and it's important to remind himself that others see him like this, too. That men with cameras search him out and he means something bigger than where he is now.

Betty tries to stay positive, but Bill gets frustrated sometimes. Tonight, he waves a hand at the field, at all the players.

"It's like they don't want to win," he says. "Can you believe it, Louie? Playing the game like they don't want to win."

The Baseball Family rises. They touch each other on the shoulders and say, "Damnit, that was a tough one." And then, "See you tomorrow."

Betty collects the remainder of her candy, kisses her son Tim on the cheek, and ushers Bill out to the home they've lived in for forty years. She'll stand on the porch tonight and look at what was the house next door and is now sticks and ash and a couple of pieces of badly singed furniture. She wonders how people can just let things burn. There was a whole life in there, pictures on mantels, bicycles, casserole recipes, things that had existed for so long, burned into nothing.

Bill will fall asleep first while Betty listens to the postgame report on the radio, saying the season isn't over, not yet, no reason to lose faith. After a hundred and some-odd games, the LumberKings are still in the running—a few more wins than losses, stuck in third place, a chance to make the play-offs, and just as good a chance not to.

I tiptoe when I take my first steps of the night, having shed Louie. As though somebody might notice him in my walk or my feet or the shape of my ass, and something will be ruined. My T-shirt sticks to my chest. Everything itches. Mosquitoes flock to my head, no impenetrable shell to protect me now.

I'm so small outside the wearable myth, and when I realize that I'm anonymous, I don't like it. It's gutting, the way things can inflate or shine or reverberate under the lights that look unstable so high up, like skinny children with big heads. Spot-lit when the whole surrounding area is dark.

Nobody knew it was me. That's not true, I couldn't resist and I told some folks, but for the most part I was, as every Louie has been, loved without a moment's question, allowed to mean something. I want that meaning to be more concrete, after all these games, but all I can say for sure is that I feel it.

I think of Betty staring at ashes and how quickly things can be gone. How when a player leaves, somebody else is handed his number, and it's as if he was never here, except for a picture that you might take with him and then ask him to sign. This season will be over soon, very soon if they don't make the play-offs, and everybody who showed up every day to play or coach or cheer will cease to do so. Maybe they'll start up again next year. I begin to drive away, humidity fogging my windshield, and then I stop at the tracks for a train. The stadium is behind me, still glowing, something from a book my father would have read to me a long time ago. In front of me, train cars glide by the same as they always do—faceless black ovals. Company names are printed on the sides of the cars. There are no windows. They are full of raw bulk that I will never see. They mirror one another as they pass, like a flipbook that doesn't tell a story. I watch them, moving, moving, moving, finally gone.

Origins

AT SOME POINT IN THE NINETEENTH CENTURY, a game was first played in which people hit a ball with a stick. That is fact. Then things get fuzzy. My father took me to the Baseball Hall of Fame when I was a boy and stood with me while I stared up at the oil-portrait face of Abner Doubleday, the man called the creator of baseball, enshrined in Cooperstown, the place where the creator supposedly created. He was a perfectly American man, Doubleday, face worn with some sort of perseverance, mustache stiff and thick like firewood. He was a Civil War hero, a generously wealthy man, an avid believer in things like God and goodness. He was credited with the invention of baseball fifteen years after his death when a Colorado miner faked a memory, said that on a dirt patch in a little industrial river town he watched Doubleday draw the game's parameters on the ground with a twig, said that they played it that same day, a moment of pure inspiration.

Nothing is ever so right, of course. Baseball was probably first played in some form by Irish immigrant boys, pegging each other in rank city alleys. And the game only became popular, truly American, when gamblers took to it, when there was profit to be made off the fastest and strongest boy in the neighborhood.

This isn't my own well-investigated information, nor is it any revelation. Everybody who cares about the game knows the lie. I knew it when I was a little boy touching the statue of a false idol, but what I loved, even then, was that it didn't matter. That everyone, it seemed, had recognized the importance of the story that had been made. So awe was still appropriate because it was made to be so.

We can go back, trace a line through all the people who made the game oversized.

Go back to Herbert Hoover: "Next to religion, baseball has a greater impact on our American way of life than any other institution."

Go back further, to Teddy Roosevelt, who dubbed baseball one of the key sports for a "true and manly race."

And even further, to Walt Whitman, certainly no straitlaced statesman: "I see great things in baseball. It's our game—the American game."

But these are clipped soundbites. I've always preferred the hyperbole.

Albert Goodwill Spalding gave the game its best quotation: "I claim that Base Ball owes its prestige as our National Game to the fact that as no other form of sport it is the exponent of American Courage, Confidence, Combativeness; American Dash, Discipline, Determination; American Energy, Eagerness, Enthusiasm; American Pluck, Persistency, Performance; American Spirit, Sagacity, Success; American Vim, Vigor, Virility."

Me, I believe this shit. I do so sheepishly, winkingly, overeducated, often stoned, but still. There is no such thing as comfort in smugness.

I am not a baseball player. I was, or I liked to think that I was, but really I was a person who loved stories and loved to be praised. I was a person who liked to be read to, by my mother, sure, because she was most willing, but more by my father, maybe because it was an occasion, maybe because he sounded different when he read, a happier, more hopeful man. There are memories I have that I do not talk about. Prideful, sometimes giddy memories—watching games, winning games, being watched winning by my father, smiling, by my older brother, still alive. This isn't about that, but it's there. I think it always is. I've realized that I set all of my happiest memories on baseball fields, a fabricated but convenient organization. Yankee Stadium, way up in the bleachers, dizzy from the scope of things; the dirt field by my parents' home; the wilted grass by the East River in New York City where my brother pitched me inside with his fastball, telling me that I was finally worthy when I didn't complain about my hands stinging. All of them blending.

I played baseball in high school, was the best player on a bad team. I played baseball in college, a novelty for everyone in my family of bookish depressives, me especially. I wore my team sweatshirt around campus for a while, and I kept an ice pack wrapped around my extremities as if I had survived some battle, and I limped when I did not have to. I liked that part more than the playing. I smoked a lot of pot and told my stoner friends about my baseball in ways that were not at all true, because really I was the worst one on a bad team and I was so quick to cry on the pitcher's mound while my father looked at his feet in the bleachers, not wanting to meet my gaze or claim me.

I live in Iowa now, far from home in a university town an hour west of Clinton, an hour south of the *Field of Dreams* field, the two-century-old family farm cum national tourist attraction, where you can buy a personalized cap or a fifteen-dollar T-shirt reading, "If you build it, he will come." In my first Iowa winter, I paced circles around my little apartment while my girlfriend rolled tight joints that she said would calm me. I put on those ridiculous boots that my father sent me in the mail to tell me that he still knew the things I needed, and I walked out into the snow while she screamed, *What the fuck?* into the puke-smelling hallway of the building that shook when trucks drove by. I walked through the snow until I felt the soak through my jeans and my hands hurt. I called home and said, "I'm in a field somewhere, I think. I hate this. I can't, I can't . . ." trailing off into a sigh.

It doesn't sound significant enough to say, "*unhappy.*" Or, "*missing something.*" Defective, stunted, overwhelmed—this is my own hyper-bole. My nickname on my college baseball team was Mannchild, but I think that was just a pun and an observation of what a fat, lumbering young man with a scraggly beard looks like. It wasn't meant to get at something deeper, though all of us on the team were stubborn children who had grown too strong and liked to prove so by breaking things.

The Yankees won the World Series a week after the first Iowa snow, and I called home. My father was weepy on the phone. "Your mother is laughing at me," he said. "Maybe I'm crazy, but isn't this kind of beautiful?"

I agreed. It was.

We talked about longevity, about Mariano Rivera, our favorite current Yankee, and about fables. He read me *The Old Man and the Sea* when I was too old to be read to. I perked up for the "great DiMaggio" parts, when fishing is no longer just fishing. Because when the old man fails, there's the great DiMaggio, who would have held the fish longer.

"*How long?*" I wanted to know, and my father told me there was no way of knowing. Just as long as was needed.

I knew I was too old to be read to. Thirteen? Fourteen? I lied to friends who said, *Come out, let's go do something wrong,* after Friday night baseball games. I never said, *I'm too scared to do anything but listen to stories.* I kept my dirty uniform on until right before bedtime and then fell asleep to my father's voice conjuring grown men who cared for nothing but play and honor. We read the same books over and over. Or he read them and I listened. Sure, there was Hemingway and Malamud and Steinbeck, the famous men with all their postwar swagger. But mostly he read from crumbling, yellowed pulp books, the equivalent of romance lit for lonely boys with macho aspirations. Our favorites were John R. Tunis books, popular during his postwar childhood, nearly unheard of in mine. They featured black-and-white morality, nail-biting play-off races, characters with nicknames like Razzle, the Keystone brothers, the Kid. I didn't think about panic, unplaced and unending. I didn't think about my brother the addict buried months before, our last conversation a promise for him to come watch me play. Or how newly small and quiet my father was in front of the TV except for in these moments, regurgitating the books that he read as a boy, one son still willingly enthralled.

When we talk now, my father and I say, "*The great Rivera.*" We both watched a TV special that said Rivera's father was a fisherman and he was a fisherman, too, before he was discovered for his greatness. We watched separately, called the next day—*Did you see?*—and laughed.

My father is a proud man, and I am becoming one, too. We do not like to say out loud that fandom is so important, the most important thing, maybe, because it feels like the filling of a void too maudlin to try to define. To admit its importance is to acknowledge the absence of something else that should be there.

I drove into Clinton for the first time before the players did, early February, when there was black ice on the interstate, upturned vans dotting the shoulder, having skidded and then been abandoned, wheels up in the cold. I drove in along Highway 30, through the sprawl where

I would later be told that the heart of the town had moved to, the row of discount shopping where everything happened—Arby's, Wendy's, McDonald's, Burger King, Target, Applebee's, Lowe's, Kohl's, Walmart. It wasn't a mall, just miles of four-lane sameness, each streetlight a new turnoff to another store. I stared up at how big and gray it all was, muted even under those recognizable signs making promises. You could imagine a baseball field sticking out here. You could imagine driving up to it, the lights bright but never harsh, high above all the unimportant details surrounding them.

I came here because of the parameters that the town and the team had already set up, the heightened phrasing right there on the team's Web site, full of tradition-hearkening and old-timey optimism. I came here because it best fit the stereotype I was looking for. I came to find a place that felt almost unreal, a lovable jock time warp out of a predictable story, the kind that placates. And that was the commodity being sold. LumberKings, first of all. What a name. And then the promises on the Web site: The oldest stadium in the Midwest League, one of the oldest in the country. The only town that was a charter member of the Midwest League that still has a team. Community owned for twice my lifetime. And that final assertion *Professional baseball in Clinton is as much of a given commodity as the mighty Mississippi River.*

I walked into the team's front office, revealing four men in hoodie sweatshirts with one-syllable names—Ted, Nate, Mitch, Dave. I was told that it's a bit of a locker room in here and that I'd love it, the bobbleheads everywhere, the fridge full of Mountain Dew, guys calling out memories and farting at each other across the room. Ted, the general manager, told me he had a boy named Lucas, eleven years old. That sometimes he called him Luke, but mostly just Butch or Wiseass.

Dave, the radio voice, took me on a tour. I followed him with care that felt obtrusive, sticking close.

Touch the stadium facade, granite and cold.

Touch the scratched cement floor of the dugout.

Touch the poles and then look up at the lights.

Touch the foul ball net, touch the metal railing and peel off a chip of paint to reveal the paint that was there before. And then another layer.

Touch the wood of the outfield fence and pull out an authentic splinter.

Walk where the game has been played and will be.

A baseball field in the winter is beautiful, all potential. We stepped out into the snow that covered the infield. I listened to the crunch of our boots. We walked the baselines without exactly meaning to. He gave me the whole spiel, and I loved that it seemed like he meant it. He smiled because he could tell I believed him.

We rely on nothing fancy here. He told me that twice.

Other places have more promotions, gimmicks, scoreboards with little games on them. We're not really a bells-and-whistles operation. I noted my disdain for both bells and whistles.

We are about baseball the way it should be for people who appreciate it. He frowned for some reason.

I told him that's why I had shown up, hungering for a place with an unabashed moral code, an ever-strict emphasis on "*should be*" and "*appreciate it.*" And I think it was true.

We went to the wall with the plaque holding 230 names of men who played at least one game on this field and then at least one in the major leagues. We began to read the names out loud, or I did. Dave smiled and listened to my breathy intonations when I recognized somebody. I imagined that he stood by this wall plenty, would do it when I left. I imagined that he had the wall memorized, a periodic table for a different kind of nerd, the kind I wanted him to be.

George Cisar. John Gaddy. Bert Haas. Stanley Klopp. Lou Johnson. Elmo Plaskett. Most were names that I did not recognize, names that played here before my father ever watched a game, that died before I was born, leaving behind maybe Wikipedia stubs all these years later, saying when they made it to the majors, when they left. And this, these names here in wood, imprinted so that when the red and white paint fades, you'll still be able to run your fingers over them.

"Steve Sax," I said and pointed. Steve Sax: slugging second baseman, onetime member of the Dodgers, Yankees, White Sox, Athletics, .281 lifetime average, featured voice on my favorite *Simpsons* episode ever. When my father broke the news to me that the Yankees had traded Steve Sax, I locked myself in a closet, sat down in a pile of used Little League balls, and wept. It was a memory instantly vivid in front of his name, a clear feeling of hurt and importance that, at the time, was the most I had ever felt anything.

. . .

In the office, we all drank Mountain Dew and shared stories.

Mitch, the director of operations, goatee and backward cap, unnecessary sunglasses resting on his forehead, was the only person with a story like what I imagined it would be, the only one homegrown. He was twenty-three, still lived with his parents five minutes away, had dated half the girls who worked the concession stands. He stayed home for college, Ashford University, part of the 1 percent of students who actually attended the Clinton campus and didn't get their degrees online. This was his first job after graduation; maybe it would be his last. He bartends and disinfects shoes at a local bowling alley, too, but that's only because he has to, not fit to mention as his profession.

Ted Tornow, the LumberKings' general manager, never wanted to be in Clinton. He delivered this information with the hurried reassurance of his absolute contentment in this place, but, yes, he was only here because his old team closed, the stadium instantly reused for junior college football. And traveling carnivals. And country music shows. Butte, Montana, was where he wanted home to be. He liked mountains, had no hankering for corn. He liked the sky out there and confirmed to everyone who asked that everything people said about that western sky, the life-affirming bigness of it, was true.

When Butte lost its team, the local paper ran a scathing editorial about big business and coddled millionaires and the dissolution of the American way.

"Major League baseball demands we provide not just an acceptable place, but a frilly, fancy shrine for its entry-level prospects to perform," the paper wrote. And then, "Phooey."

So the team packed up, and Ted Tornow packed up and left to try again in a place where the sky is also big, but only because there is nothing rising into it. Sky that starts right above your head. In his office now there are pictures of mountains, of his old ballpark, team pictures from all the different little places where he's lived and worked, across the South, out west, now in the middle.

Mostly, we talked about the players who would be Clinton's stars in a few months. I was told things about them, entirely hypothetical. There was no way of knowing who would show up, what familiar faces, what new ones. But no matter. They stay basically the same, just what you want them to be, nice boys, special, yeah, but *real,* too, relatable. I was told that I would be grabbed up like a little brother, though I was older than most of the players. I would get into trouble, but not too much, living out my first, my greatest fantasy in a suspended haze of awesomeness. Ted reckoned that he would walk into the clubhouse some mornings, find me passed out, still drunk, smiling in my sleep, deposited there by giggling players on their way home. There was a happy, nodding silence as we imagined what hadn't yet come, but would, but had to.

"Any other questions?" he asked me, finally. "What else did you notice around here?"

"What's the factory?" I asked. "That one I passed on the way in, by all the messed-up streets? It's huge."

Archer Daniels Midland, I was told. The savior, stretched along the banks of the Mississippi at the south end of town. Or, if not the savior, a damn good start. That sweetener in my Mountain Dew, that federally subsidized 10 percent ethanol in my gas tank, and now that experimental biodegradable plastic bag that sheathes my SunChips—all of it is made right here because of ADM. The roads being all torn up has to do with the rebranding of the area around the factory. The town and the company wanted to project uncluttered industry as the first thing that a hypothetical important somebody sees when Highway 30 turns into Camanche Avenue and enters what is left of downtown. There was a lot of clutter there, Ted told me. A lot of squalor and embarrassment. A neighborhood of old, ramshackle wooden houses with narrow streets weaving in between. Those houses, for the most part, have been bought up, razed. The neighborhood between the factory and the river was bought up by the company so that it could expand. The streets are cracked and potholed, now, nearly deserted. Camanche Avenue, running between the factory and the rest of the town, was cleared of homes by federal and state funding, converted into six wide, straight lanes of traffic running parallel to the train tracks, so that trucks, like trains, could take material in, ship product out, and how could more industry not flock to such a place?

A metal statue of a steamboat rudder, painted bright blue, was dropped onto newly planted grass over newly evacuated land, signifying power, somehow past and future and progress at the same time. And the factory did expand. It is a mile long now, the entire southern tip of a town that is only eight miles long. There are gray box buildings taller than everything around them, one after another, no windows, tanks in between and metal tubes running from one identical section to the next, a smokestack for each section, so that if you stand at the middle of the factory you can't be sure that it ends. And there's a glowing golden storage dome, the largest of its kind in the world, maybe sinister, maybe beautiful, holding sixty thousand pounds of coal waiting to be burned in the service of making things.

"It's sort of like," Ted began and smiled before he got the sentence out. I was acutely aware of the fact that I knew what he was going to say before he said it. The metaphor had been waiting, naked and obvious.

"It's sort of like," Ted began, "*if you build it, they will come.*"

I didn't see the players come into town, but I know they came in the way I did because that's pretty much the only way. Clinton is the easternmost point in Iowa and too small for an airport, so there is only one drive, the drive from Quad Cities International Airport, along Highway 30, through the corn, past the towns of five thousand that make Clinton the largest city in the county, past the factory in the middle of nowhere that makes air fresheners that look like pine trees, past the Wild Rose Casino on the edge of town, where the players are not allowed to go but where some of them will. Mostly they passed cornfields, freshly planted. Later, in August, when the corn is almost as tall as they are, impossible to ignore, some players will say they've never seen so much of one thing. But at the beginning of the season, the crop is just an idea. If the bus had stopped for nature exploration, the boys could have taken pictures of fledgling green stalks barely up to their ankles.

After a night in a hotel, players followed each other to the kinds of apartments that pop up on the edges of any small town. The Venezuelans went to the Lafayette, left a space on the floor of their apartment that Erasmo Ramírez would occupy if he got called up from extended spring training in Arizona. Most of the players ended up in Indian Village, a collection of identical apartments that offered low rent and catalogs for getting TVs on layaway, where they would snicker with one another, as hard young men like to do, at the sight of their stooped neighbors cooking hot dogs on portable grills in the parking lot.

A few had been to Clinton before and hadn't moved up. They knew where to go. Danny Carroll knew where to go. This would be his second full season in Clinton, his third in low-level A-ball. This time, he would live with Ray, a local pastor who smiled a lot and said a good grace, reminded Danny of his father. He had set in his mind months ago that he would live with *people* this time, good people, God-fearing people. There would be no yelling all night or porn shrieks or teammates humping pillows and moaning whenever Danny called home. To live for months in two-room apartments, surrounded by the noise and filth and sin of three or four teammates, was exhausting. He didn't expect to be in Clinton too long either way, is what he said to himself and sometimes out loud. A good month, make them remember that talent, that speed, and then an airplane to the rest of his life.

It's best for the players not to think of the scope of what they're trying to do, but I can't help it. There are close to two hundred other minor-league teams. There are twenty-five men on each of those rosters. After spring training in March, every professional baseball player in every organization is evaluated, ranked, put on a team—rookie ball, Low-A, High-A, AA, AAA, the lucky ones perched above the muck in the majors. And then they're shipped. They're moved in bulk because, no matter what, you need twenty-five to fill out a team. For every one or two prospects on a given minor-league squad that the scouts believe will make it to the majors, there are two dozen working alongside them, faithful or trying to be, a "necessary expense," as the Mariners scouts put it to me in the bleachers and would never put it to them. If you happened to be on a commuter flight to a small place anywhere in America in early April, chances are you were staring at loud, large young men in identical sweatshirts, trying to figure out if they were famous. They weren't.

Danny was drafted 105th out of every baseball player in America in 2007. That is fantastically good. Third round, in fact. There were only three players that the Seattle Mariners bought before him in 2007. He remembers that. After him, there were a thousand others, three days' worth of names periodically spit out on a Web site, until the fiftieth round was over and there were no more picks on the board. But then there's the international players like Erasmo, a group that now makes up nearly 30 percent of professional baseball, all of whom are ineligible for the draft and are signed as free agents. Dominicans, Venezuelans, Japanese, people from littler countries in the Caribbean and Central America that some of the U.S.-born players can't place on a map.

On April 6, players arrived in Clinton, but also in bigger towns dotting the Midwest—Peoria, Cedar Rapids, Appleton, Burlington, South Bend, Dayton, Cherry Lane, Illinois. And in Jackson, Tennessee, and other C-cities of the South. And in Eugene, Oregon; Everett, Washington; Columbus, Ohio; Pittsfield, Massachusetts. And Tulsa and Des Moines and Staten Island. Places with nothing in common except for these tall, broad visitors all sharing a talent and an ambition and maybe a delusion.

In that commotion, Danny Carroll landed back here. His hosts lent him a pickup truck that their son used to drive, an F-150 from the 1980s. He looks like a local boy when he drives it. He knows that's not the best thing to look like. The more people who know you, who say innocently, not trying to be hurtful, "Oh, hi, you were here *last* year," the more you are exposed as stagnant.

I imagine the first day, the way I want to see it. I imagine Danny, with all his unenviable experience, as the calm and knowing tour guide.

"It's not usually so warm here in April," Danny told his teammates when they got to town. And it was true, a sticky seventy-nine degrees shouldn't happen until mid-May.

"One time, in Appleton, it snowed," Danny continued.

There were confused nods. Only one other player, Kalian Sams, Danny's friend and fellow outfielder, could remember back three years in A-ball and verify Danny's story, and he was not particularly eager to advertise that fact.

A lot of the young players had never seen snow. Certainly not the Dominicans and the Venezuelans. And even prospects from Florida and Southern California were not made for such weather. Danny is a Southern California boy, from one of those burned brown towns in the Inland Empire, east of L.A., but now he's entering his third midwestern April and has spent more of his adult life here, working, trying to leave, than back home.

As they left the hotel, somebody asked Danny, the expert, what the big factory was, the one across the street, sort of across the street from everything. Danny was unable to answer because Danny, like almost every player I will meet, had never bothered to find out, had written it off as a constant, unfortunate reality not related to what he came here to do. Some players developed their own theories. The strangest I heard was that horses were being ground into dog food. It was the rotting blood of ground-up horses that accounted for the smell.

Danny gave his best friends a lift home in the pickup, Sams and a catcher named Henry Contreras, called Hank, another one who wasn't as young and loud as the rest of the team. Hank sat in the flatbed and started doing sit-ups, saying that the training never stops. Danny laughed. Sams took a video from the front seat on his phone, Hank's brown face bobbing up and down on the gray background, confused smiles from white people in passing cars. They drove down the one-ways like that.

"Dang," Danny said as he drove.

The scene is dang-worthy, I know. *Dang* is the feeling I had in a moment that I didn't tell Ted Tornow about, when I got lost driving to the stadium that first time, with each new outlet seeming to head to the same gated place, and ended up on a dirt road under smokestacks with truck drivers pointing at the "Private Property" sign and calling me a dumbshit.

The two youngest and richest LumberKings wandered out of the hotel. The Mariners made Nick Franklin the 27th pick of the 2009 draft and then made him a millionaire. Steve Baron was the 33rd pick and got $980,000. Nick and Steve were both from Florida, both had just turned nineteen, and both liked to go fishing with their fathers. They were going to be roommates. One had an Xbox 360. The other had a PlayStation 3. They were confident.

Steve Baron hit the outside air, saw the factory, smelled the smoke, and vomited all over the sidewalk.

It's easier to think of the players as hypothetical ideals. To look at their pictures, read their names and stat lines with virtual distance on BaseballAmerica.com. I know this, standing in the clubhouse before the first game of the season, conspicuous and invisible at the same time. I think of my front-office conversation with Dave and Ted and Nate and Mitch, talking about how these boys are just like everyone we knew growing up. And maybe they are. But in these breathless first few seconds they are only impenetrable, nothing but perfectly filled-out skin.

Danny Carroll is the first one to talk to me, the only one. He saves me.

John Tamargo, the manager, has left me marooned in the center of the green carpet, surrounded by lockers and large strangers. Earlier, in the damp, quiet safety of his office, he told me, "You can poke your head around, you can stay as long as you like, but I ain't going to try to make these boys be nice to you."

"No, sir," I said, the instinct to call any coach "sir" still alive in me.

"They're going to treat you how they treat anybody."

I watched his forearm flex as he gripped a ball. He's fifty-eight, bald, and stocky. He limps from a career as a catcher, waddles really. I stared at the heavy gold of his Rolex.

"Yes, sir."

"I'd recommend you shave the beard or whatever that is."

"Yes, sir."

He walked me down the hall, past the trainer's room with free weights and padded massage tables and a bathtub full of ice, to the locker room. He whistled to his twenty-five young charges and said, "Hey! Shut up!" They did. He said, "This guy's going to hang around and watch you. Any problems?"

There were a lot of shrugs. There were a couple of sneers, glances expressing distrust or disinterest or immediate, silent, physical dominance. This isn't a space where anyone not in the game is supposed to be. There are signs asserting that fact, tacked up next to the required notices about the dangers of smokeless tobacco, which have already been defiled with tobacco spit.

Now, stranded, I raise my hand in a stiff wave to all and then drop it immediately. I shuffle around the room, smiling as though there could be victory in that. I wait for someone to step out of the tangle of bodies and become real, singular. I turn to find Tamargo and see him waddling back down the hallway. This is when Danny Carroll saves me because he knows that it's important to be a good person. He smiles and says, "Hey, dude."

Danny has been standing by himself, making a peanut butter and jelly sandwich. He's wearing compression shorts that would hug the fat of his thighs and ass in place if there were any. He's not wearing a shirt, something I'll come to find is common with him and, upon each quick glance, makes more and more sense. He has a superhero's trapezoidal chin, tempered with goofy ears that stick out and impish eyes. He watches me looking around at how many men and how much noise can fit into one room.

"You look scared," he says and smiles because he's right. "Don't look scared."

I nod and try to appear unimpressed as I scan statuesque bodies in various states of undress, tattoos across the full expanse of backs identifying hometowns or credos, or displaying a glowing Virgin Mary. Nick Franklin's ink dominates his lean, still-growing torso, marking the brand: "Franklin, Est. 1991." Music blasts, never one song, always two, from opposite corners, in competition. Right now Usher is playing with heavy bass from subwoofers in Nick's locker. The Americans are listening to it. Three Venezuelans are trying to turn their iPod speakers loud enough to drown Usher out with Daddy Yankee, a Puerto Rican rapper chanting in Spanish about tremendous asses, but Nick Franklin buys better and newer products than they do, and he will not be defeated.

Nick cups his ear and says, "What? What? Sorry, I can't hear you."

Jose Jiménez, a barrel-chested, left-handed reliever, screams at him in Spanish. Nick shrugs.

Players begin cursing each other bilingually, and I see Danny wince a little, just a twitch of his high cheeks, as "fuck" and "shit" and "cocksucker" are tossed around. He's used to it, though. After two years of pro baseball, he knows that despite the constant cross tattoos and Christ-crediting postgame interviews not everyone went to church three days a week every week for his entire life before getting drafted. Coming out of high school the way Danny did means that clubhouses in strange towns become your first knowledge of life out from under your parents' roof. Instead of Intro to Psychology, he gets this. The former college players talk filthy about keg stands and spring break, about faceless, eager sorority girls. Danny had just turned eighteen when he was drafted, and on that night he knelt right in his living room with the whole family and gave thanks before taking a senior class trip to Disneyland. Danny doesn't tell other people what to do here. He says "gosh" a lot. And "dang." He'll say that things suck when he really means it, when they really do.

It must make him uncomfortable that I'm sticking so close, but he doesn't show it. I realize that my interest might be flattering enough to make me tolerable. Boys get used to attention at a young age when they're faster and stronger than those around them. It's when the attention has gone away a little, I'll discover, that it stops becoming boring or an inconvenience. Danny eats his sandwich in four bites and then goes back for more. The strength coach yells at him for using all the peanut butter.

"Man, you see this?" Danny says to me, weary. "They don't give us any kind of spread down here. I mean, how much is a thing of peanut butter at Walmart?"

"Two bucks?" I venture.

"That sounds like too much," he says.

He gives me a brief, mistrustful glance, eyebrows arched, so I say, "Yeah, totally, definitely, you're right."

I look in his locker. There's his jersey for tonight, the Clinton Lumber-Kings' home whites with green and black trim. There's a black and gray glove that he got custom made to say, *Dan the Man*. There are gray cleats to match his gray glove, Air Jordan brand. There's a Bible with bookmarks in it. A proverb that I don't recognize written on notebook paper. There's a picture of him and a young woman with impossibly white teeth. They're standing on a beach. His arms are around her and she's so small.

"You miss your girlfriend?" I ask.

"Wife," he says. "We got married at eighteen. Crazy, right?"

"Good for you."

"She's a blessing, dude. I walked her home from church when we were fourteen, and she's blessed me ever since. She might be coming out here soon. But I don't think I'm going to be here very long this time, so, you know, she's waiting."

I nod and say, "Totally."

There is a pause as he watches me watch his movements, scanning over his bats and body, his Bible.

"Are you a Christian?" he asks.

"Not really."

He nods, and I clap my hands together for no reason.

Nick Franklin has turned his Usher up as high as it can go. He and some others are dancing in the faces of three Venezuelan players. Danny sighs. He calls them all kids. I ask him how old he is. He just turned twenty-one. He grabs one of the bats leaning against his chair. He holds it out, the wood resting on his upturned palms, such a dainty move with such a solid thing. He shows me his name imprinted along the barrel. The company even made a stamp of his signature and pressed it on there, too, a big, swooping *D* and *C,* with tight, practiced waves running between them.

"Sweet," I say.

"Right?" he says.

"How'd you get that?" I ask because he wants me to.

"Agent," he says. "If you're a top-pick kind of guy, they get you stuff. I was third round."

This is the first of many times that he will tell me this. I will come to find out that it's a calling card in here. Everybody knows where everybody was ranked when the team brought them in. Every player crammed into this room has an agent. Many of them were found by agents when they were still boys. Some of the agents are famous; others are nobody special, a guy from the neighborhood who is good at talking. All of it matters. The players have counted each other's money. Sometimes they overestimate for motivation and because it is exhilarating to feel screwed over. The white players sitting at a makeshift card table fashioned from an upturned bucket glance over at Mario Martínez and Gabriel Noriega, a pair of Venezuelan infielders who were signed around the age when they should have been juniors in high school. The white players assume that there was a big payday involved. They see imported bonus babies. They say, "Damn, I wish I was from Venezuela and weighed 115 pounds and could tie my shoes," looking at the rail-thin, nineteen-year-old Noriega, who has a penchant for rhinestone-studded Ed Hardy T-shirts and diamond earrings.

I leave for air, pretending to have to make a call, and hear the screech of a row of ten-ton train cars hitting the brakes.

The trains that run alongside the stadium parking lot don't go fast. There is no rush. There will always be more. There is corn in these train cars, thousands of ears packed in so tight that it's impossible to distinguish individual kernels. Later, in the stands, I will be told that it looks like gold when the tops of the train cars are opened and the sun hits the product. I walk toward the train now, looking, I guess, for a weak spot, an opening. There are ladders running up the side of each car, but I will never see anybody on them, can't picture hands on the bars. I want to see inside, want to feel like I can know more than what is shown, but the size of everything, all the metal, all the weight, it scares me. Instead, I watch the graffiti glide by, names over the corporate logos, written in small towns on quiet nights when the wheels finally stopped.

The corn keeps running across the state, nearly five million Iowa tons per year, and so much of it stops here to be processed on the banks of the Mississippi. The factory opens up and trains and trucks unload their wares, a process that I have never seen happen, will never see happen, a steel door that I imagine opening in slow silence.

The Clinton facility processes its corn with a wet milling procedure, drawing water from beneath the ground, from eight-hundred-foot wells that go deeper than the city wells. There was grumbling from when the wells were proposed, then allowed, in 2006, residents wanting to know how the company got first dibs on water, but that quieted down eventually. The water comes up somewhere into the middle of the gray windowless buildings, and it meets the corn in vats the size of blue whales. The corn is "steeped," which makes it sound like tea, but that's not at all the case. The corn sits in chemical-aided water heated to exactly 50°C, until the kernels soften, ready to be separated into all their parts.

There're five million gallons of water heated each day. There is corn slurry sitting or heating or processing, always. And the smell that pours out from the smokestacks when corn and water and sulfur dioxide are processed with coal-burning energy, the smell that some still complain about, that most shrug and laugh about, that Steve Baron threw up from, that a local congressman tells me is "toasty and comforting," is accepted as routine, as was last year's Department of Natural Resources warning that the particulate matter in Clinton's air was bordering on unallowable, as is the ominous billowing sky on a heavy production day.

. . .

Back in the clubhouse. I follow Danny into the batting cages, housed next door in a big shed with a twenty-foot-high aluminum roof and no windows. He's holding his bat in his right hand like a club, label out. I think I see him looking at his own name. Last year there was talk about Danny having a bad attitude, which Danny didn't like. He wasn't brought up that way. Some people still think that he's pouty, think that he's soft. When he got hurt for the second time, he started thinking too much, and then he started to get mad because that's what thinking does to you.

How can there be so many bones in a hand, each one breakable? He didn't deserve to break two different bones in the *same* hand, each one at the fifteen-game mark of the season, 2008 and 2009.

"Like it was a curse," he tells me.

I laugh, but then he looks serious.

"No, not really," he says. "I don't believe in curses."

Danny lost a little bit of faith last year, and he doesn't plan to again.

Yesterday he talked to a reporter from the local paper for an article called "L'Kings' Carroll Seeks Fresh Start." He told the reporter that God gave him a gift as a hitter and that he didn't plan to waste it. He told the reporter that God's challenges only make us stronger, that he had become a stronger Danny Carroll. He tells me those same things now because he doesn't know me yet. Because I'm an out-of-shape guy with glasses and a sweaty notebook and baseball players are taught to speak to us all that way, self-assured, sober, noncommittal.

I sit on an upside-down bucket to watch him hit balls off a tee. I listen to the lonely sound of bat on leather as it echoes off the aluminum roof. I find myself surprised, waiting for more. I don't know why I haven't been expecting this scene. Maybe it just seems too ordinary. When I was six, my father put tennis balls on a tee and told me to swing. And I did. Over and over. Hitting the plastic stalk instead of the ball, weeping with fury, my first memories of the game. That's what I did in Little League and in my fluorescent, stinking high school gym. Perhaps part of me expected the chance to revel in awed, nerdy fandom, having access to something beyond what I can relate to. To see feats of strength and technology, some futuristic, performance-training playground, the kind of human laboratory that should be hidden from view. But Danny is alone in black shorts and a black T-shirt, feeding frayed practice balls to himself. This is it. This is what is hidden from everyone, from the players' wives and their babies who totter around the fence outside waiting, from fans who speculate about what on earth could be going on in there. This is the process of making stars or fostering excellence or however else it is put by announcers and PR agents.

Danny tries to make each swing just like the one before it. He doesn't bend his knees much or get much torque. His swing is a leadoff hitter's, a fast slap of the ball, designed for line drives that allow him to start running. He keeps his eyes focused on the wall about sixty feet away from him, as though there is a pitcher there. He takes a high step with his left foot, places it down right about where it had been, and swings. The ball skips off the strip of Astroturf beneath him and gets caught in the mesh at the other end of the room. He grabs another ball and repeats. Repeats again. It's the same motion for a hundred balls or so. His expression hasn't changed.

"What are you thinking about?" I ask him as he stands, hands on his hips, looking at the pile he's created.

He gives me a quizzical look.

"Nothing, dude," he says. "It's bad for you to think in here. I had to learn that. Because I'm naturally thoughtful."

There's a pause as he adjusts his batting gloves.

"That's funny, right?" he says suddenly. "Like your mind has an off switch."

Danny Carroll does this every day but Sunday in the off-season and every day from April to September since minor-league baseball cannot take days off simply because God did. He swings, swings again, hears the same sound, watches balls fly and bounce. He grimaces when he hits them wrong, nods when he hits them right. Repeats. It's a basic movement, one that millions do, it's just that Danny does it more. And he must do it better. But the movement, so short, so ultimately uninteresting, remains the same,

"Should I do another bucket?" he asks me.

"Yeah, yeah, another bucket," he says before I can answer.

"Motivation," he says, maybe to me, maybe to himself, or to no one.

"You ever get tired of it?" I ask. "The same thing all the time?"

"It's just what you do," he says.

I have called Archer Daniels Midland, and there is no fucking way that they'll let me see the factory on the inside. Like everyone, I will have to watch the metal and the smoke from the other side of the train tracks.

"It's just a bunch of pipes leading to more pipes," said the media relations man on the phone. "It would probably bore you. It's nothing too interesting."

"Don't be so modest," I said.

There was crackling silence through the phone because he did not find me funny.

Somewhere in there, the slurry is pumped, all day long, right now even, as Danny and his teammates dress and the sun begins to set, dull pink. It's pumped into something that looks like a contraption that James Bond must escape, but the corn doesn't escape. Toothy discs on long rods spin, and the corn is macerated, separating the germ of the plant, leaving a starch-and-acid milkshake ready to be processed. No more kernels, just mash.

A man who used to work at the factory described the next step as being like a cotton candy machine, but fifty times the size. The slurry is spun in metal mesh colanders. The liquid passes through, and crystals are caught in the mesh. The crystals are the sugar. The liquid moves on, sitting again in glinting blue whale vats, where it's mixed with more enzymes and chemicals, cooked until it ferments and becomes pure ethanol as smoke pours out over the town.

The 200-proof liquor can be treated as anything. It's raw. It can be booze. When the factory was smaller, and owned by a smaller company, you could climb into the freight cars, where there was always a little moonshine runoff pooled at the bottom. Workers bottled it quick and took it home. There's a good chance that the first taste of alcohol Tom Bigwood had, like everyone else who grew up around here, was a table-spoon of fresh corn ethanol. Sometimes he couldn't even swallow it, but he still got hammered drunk anyway, as if the stuff were seeping into his blood through his cheeks, foaming on his tongue.

If the factory works at full capacity, 237 million gallons of ethanol will be exported from Clinton by the end of the year, a sizeable chunk of the 1.7 billion that ADM claims yearly. The baby corn the players drove by on the way in churned into something new and shipped back out along the highways and the railroads and the river.

I stand close to Danny as he changes with the rest of the team before the first game of the season. I'm pressed against the divider between his locker and Hank's. I try not to look down at bare penis, but in a tight room crammed with twenty-five of them, that's a difficult thing to try.

I seem to be the only uncomfortable one, something noted and then exploited by two players whose names I haven't learned yet, who turn and whip their cocks for my benefit like cowboys getting ready to do some steer roping. There is no shame to it. In this place, there is constant, pragmatic exposure and assessment, even of things that should be private. In the training room, there's a thick black cylinder used for shoulder stretching nicknamed in an honest reference to a well-endowed Dominican pitcher who has become locker-room legend.

The players' bodies, after all, are what got them here and what are under inspection. They poke and prod themselves and each other. They compare the diameter of lats, the density of thighs. They grab each other around the neck and squeeze, force each other to the ground in headlocks, the stubble of their shaved chests burning on one another's skin until someone is forced to say stop, please, I can't. They stand on the scale before going home every night and record the number on a hanging chart. There is a small, frantic man named BJ whose only job is to stretch and massage and monitor their bodies. Their bodies are the product.

Some do push-ups to warm their muscles now, popping off the ground, coiling then springing. Most rub baby powder along their thighs and crotches so that the skin won't burn when they slide on their Under Armour. They take stiff medical tape, wrap their forearms with it, then slap the tape to hear the hardness of the sound, "for no reason other than to be cool," Danny says. They pass around aerosol cans to shine their cleats. They line the space between their bottom lip and bottom teeth with tobacco and give themselves brownish-green smiles in the mirror. They smear sun-reflecting eye-black along their cheekbones like warrior paint, even on cloudy days. There is ritual to all of it.

As Tamargo emerges to tack up the first lineup of a season that will include 139 more, the bodies push into a clump by the corkboard dotted with Louie the LumberKing mascot stickers. It's like the cast list for a high school musical has gone up, complete with all of the brutal, overly dramatic weight of high school anxiety, of this moment meaning *everything*. I see Danny holding his fists together, swinging them gently, as though gripping a phantom bat.

There are shouts from players who will play tonight, shouts of "Let's do it boys." And, "First win! Right now!" And, "Let's fuck these faggots up!"

Danny isn't in the lineup. There's someone newer than him, someone he will compete with all season, maybe for the rest of their careers. Matt Cerione wasn't drafted three years ago. He is shiny and unblemished, selected in 2009 from the University of Georgia, a perennial powerhouse, their bulldog mascot seen cavorting on ESPN during the College World Series.

Matt Cerione says, "Game time, bro," and shoves a teammate hard, who then reciprocates. They both smile.

Danny doesn't say much as he walks back to his locker. Just, "Well, I'm gonna have another sandwich." And then, "Dang, I need to clean my cleats." I want to tell him something reassuring, but it would be absurd. This isn't a place of reassurance. This isn't a place where one is supposed to be found seeking validation or giving it freely. Danny stands alone, pushing two fingers into the flesh of his pectoral muscles, reminding himself how little give there is. I watch his torso until the others in the room behind him, some bigger, some darker, mostly the same, begin to run together into a mural of skin. It will be like this every day now for half a year, the hopeful waiting to show their distinction. The way it's been for eight decades, when professional players first showed up in Clinton, arriving on passenger trains that no longer stop here, through the corn.

"Long season," Danny says to me. And then, "God is good."

.   .   .

Tom Bigwood died two weeks ago. It had been a long time coming. He said he was going to make it to opening day, he said no way in hell he wasn't, but then he died of colon cancer. In the same paper that ran "L'Kings' Carroll Seeks Fresh Start," there was a paid obituary for Tom, who was never famous the way Danny could be. It commemorated him as a son, a brother, a friend, a season-ticket holder for thirty-three years.

I sit in Tom's seat, like an idiot.

"You know where you're sitting, don't you?" I'm asked by a woman named Betty, with white hair and a face that looks like a chipmunk Christmas tree ornament that my grandmother used to have.

My silence works as an answer.

"That's Tom's seat."

I look around for Tom.

"Oh no, he's dead. You can stay there, I suppose."

Betty gives a short, sad laugh and then says, "I'm Betty, what're you writing?"

She points to my notebook and I flush, mumbling, "Oh, well, everything seems so interesting here." Betty announces to the whole section that a young man wants to write a book about us. I flush more. A couple of people ask me why in the hell I would want to waste my time like that. Betty says, "Oh, hush." She leans in and tells me that she wishes Tom were here. He could have told me anything. Nobody sat here watching more than him. And he remembered specifics. People. Faces. Games. Betty and some others around me chipped in to buy a season ticket for the empty seat where Tom always sat. It seemed right. And they chipped in to get him a brick on the small walk in front of the stadium. A brick engraved with his name and his favorite saying, "*Instant replay*," called out when something awesome happened and he wished he could see it again. Tom's family got him one, too, so now he's doubly there in the ground as we all walk in to watch.

"Oh, there's Danny," Betty says. She points to the left-field line, where the players are ambling toward the dugout. They all look the same from here. She must have remembered his walk.

As the players get closer, Betty waves to Danny. He trots over and says hi. He looks happy, at least amused. He remembers her. Danny was one of Tom's favorites, she tells me. Tom watched Danny in the last year that he watched anything. But this year, when Danny was at spring training in Arizona, Tom was buried in a cemetery two miles from where he was born. The fans from his section were there, and Ted, and some former players who stayed around the area when their careers ended. They brought LumberKings trinkets to enhance the ambience: a cap, a ball, a pennant, leftover green beads from some beer promotion a few years back.

Betty starts to tell me everything about the Baseball Family, which has a lot of overlap with her real family but is bigger. I am in the middle of the Family. There are Julie, Cindy, Joyce, the one who collects all the baseballs. Bill, Betty's husband. Then Tammy, Betty's daughter, Tim, her son, never moved away. And Deb and Dan and Gary, all of them rolling through shared history with a rhythm at once familiar and still surprising. Dan used to work at ADM, quit a few years ago to go drive a truck. Gary still works there, doesn't want to talk about it. Everyone laughs at that. Then Betty asks what's home for me. I tell her I don't really know. She says, sincerely, to me, this near stranger, in a way that would make me laugh in almost every other situation in my life, "We will take care of you."

Betty watches Danny as he runs to play catch, and I wonder how many players she's seen doing that and if the sheer volume and interchangeability makes each one fade a little. She's smiling because it's opening day and everything's happening all over again, like you can always count on it doing. And Danny is back, a nice boy, full of shiny-eyed, resilient belief.

"Tom said Danny just looked like a ballplayer should," Betty tells me.

And I look at him the way she does for a moment, the way Tom must have. I see the soft youngness of his face. His tanned white skin, his sturdy jaw. I see the way he seems to bounce around the field, his grin. The understated wooden cross hanging off him and the dated earnestness with which he periodically reaches his fingers up to hold it, dutiful and devout, inarguable.

I am not good at faith. Sometimes I find it difficult to think of life as anything other than the loss of things, and I know that sounds big, too big, but it's true. I read that the term "*nostalgia*" originated in a seventeenth-century medical student's dissertation, when he mixed the Greek word *nostos*, "return to the native land," with *algos*, "suffering, grief," to describe the madness of mercenaries who spent all their lives moving and trying to remember. It was classified as a potentially fatal disease. Isn't that crazy? To die from wanting to return. But I miss things that were never mine, want to return to a place, more of a feeling, that never really existed, and doesn't baseball always promise that there was once something more?

The game ends. The LumberKings are 0-1. I didn't really pay much attention to the action. It was a boring game.

"Well, all uphill from here," Tim says.

"Or same old, same old," Tammy says.

Danny pops out of the dugout, walks over. He isn't sweating, nor is he dirty. He smiles and nods. Everyone does, bobbing their chins at the shared expectation of what he might someday be, what it might mean to watch him, or maybe just a much needed breeze that everyone felt at once. I look out at what will always be there at the end of every game, running each one into the next.

There is sky, and there is smoke. There is water beyond that. There are train tracks. There is a parking lot. There is dirt, right in front of us. There is this stadium, the splinters in the wall that we don't look close enough to see. Betty asks if I will be back tomorrow, and I say yes.

Things

A BLOND ELEVEN-YEAR-OLD in too much makeup and her freshly
shined church shoes is standing on the grass of the infield singing the
national anthem. She is the best singer in the sixth grade at Washington
Middle School, as well as in the local youth choir, though judging by one
kid's comments to his father sharing a picnic table with me along the
third-base line, that's debatable. I like her. After she nails the high note
on *proudly*, she gets confident and waves her arms a little in front of her,
sending a spastic, I-taught-her-that jolt into her father, leaning over the
home team's dugout with his camera aimed. She waves toward the diamond in front of her, the center-field fence beyond that. She slashes her
hand through the air on *land of the free* like an auctioneer or an HDTV
product girl. I follow her gestures. There is the flag, yes, it is still there. It
is whipping hard, as loud as her singing, because it's spring in Iowa and
often that means you don't want to go outside, let alone stay stationary,
watching baseball. Next to the flag, panning left along with her fingers,
there is the Lumber Lounge, the VIP area befitting a lumber king, where
private parties pay twenty-five dollars a head for unlimited food and
drink. It carries corporate sponsorship now, technically the Leinenku-
gel's Lumber Lounge. Opposite that, behind the left-field fence is the
Coors Light Picnic Pavilion. And the more family-friendly Dr Pepper
Picnic Garden. In between, the old wooden fence in right center and
left center is covered with advertisements for huge, international companies that claim an outpost in Clinton.

The singing girl points at banners hailing Burger King and John
Deere and Walmart and H&R Block Tax Relief and Motel 6 and Comfort Inn and Miller Lite and McDonald's and LyondellBasell plastics
manufacturing and Ashford University, "Serving the Community for

90 Years!" She warbles a bit on *free* and looks shocked for a moment, big blue eyes suddenly bigger, not understanding how her practiced voice could leap the way it just did. But clapping starts up and saves her so that by the time she hits *brave,* she's owning it, every bit the best singer at Washington Middle.

"How about *that*?" Brad asks us all rhetorically from the public address booth. "The kids in this town . . ."

He leaves us to fill in the adjectives.

More exemplary kids compete for attention with the singing girl, who is now bright red and shivering, from some combination of the adrenaline rush and the cold. Little Leaguers, most of them younger than she is, are proudly displayed in their ill-fitting uniforms, having teetered to their favorite positions along with the corresponding LumberKings, trying to keep up with the players' shadows. They bow during the whole anthem, holding their oversized hats to their chests, solemn and adorable. They seem to understand the crucial sincerity of all of this. The critical boy at my table does not. When the song ends, he says, *"Dad, why do we have to take our hats off for the anthem?"* His father says, "Because people are dying for you *right now.*" The boy falls silent.

I have been sitting in Tom Bigwood's memorial seat for two weeks now, welcomed. The season is still in its infancy, but it feels old already, creaking with routine. I notice that Matt Cerione is in center field instead of Danny Carroll again, sheathed in unnecessary layers of skin-tight thermal wear under his uniform, unsure, it seems, how to deal with the adoring Little Leaguer who wants to hold his hand. Kalian Sams is in left field with a boy so much smaller, so much paler than him, gaping upward with a look that says, *Who is this?* Steve Baron is squirming at catcher next to a husky boy, only eight years his junior and with roughly the same amount of facial hair.

Jimmy Gillheeney, a quiet, precise pitcher from Rhode Island, begins to warm up, and the kids are shooed off the field to tepid applause. From the PA booth, Brad welcomes two visitors from Clinton's sister city.

"All the way from Erfde, Germany"—his pronunciation is, as always, flawless—"here to watch our LumberKings play."

Betty waves to them. Others gawk. The German visitors are plied with American beer and smile politely when asked if they like it. The flag whips. Jimmy Gillheeney throws the first pitch. It is a strike and there is clapping. Betty smiles at her husband, son, daughter, friends, and says, "Oh, good." Beyond the outfield fence, in the parking lot in right field, three teenagers burn garbage. Refuse, some broken planks of wood, some grass debris from a tidying of the infield. They stand around it and smile, threatening to shove each other into the flames to see what happens. They were supposed to finish burning before the game, but they didn't and now there is smoke, like its own flag, drifting toward the river.

There is nothing on the river right now. It is still. The only boat is tied to the dock and has been for twenty years. It was once called the *Omar,* and it pushed freighters down a productive Ohio River. Then it was turned into a party boat during the 1960s. Then Clinton bought it to look like the ones that used to be here. Now it houses summer stock theater.

A man is walking a German shepherd on the path along the river. Two teenagers are making out on a bench, rubbing each other over sweatpants. Down the path, farther away from the field, there is the shuttered historical society that used to be a firehouse. It is open on weekdays from 9:00 until 11:00 a.m. The walls there, the ceiling even, are crammed with pictures of buildings and men and women with huge hats. One long picture shows the smudgy outlines of people dwarfed by a beached boat propeller bigger than all of them. It is there to show the size of the boats that used to churn the river. Sometimes the boats carried people, and sometimes they carried wood. Clinton borders the widest point of the Mississippi, and so you can fit five barges, side by side, from Iowa to Illinois. I didn't know that; Tim and Tammy told me. The rest of the Baseball Family confirmed it in chorus.

There's a wooden sign between the historical society and the banks of the river. It is made to look old, but it isn't. It says, "Clinton, Iowa: Gateway to Opportunity," a reference that could take a passerby all the way back to 1855, right after Clinton was named Clinton. Up until then, it had been called New York, a name adopted by the man who built the first store among the log cabins, believing there must be gold in such fertile soil, that there was profit to be made and a city to build around that profit, and that the town should be named for the metropolis it would inevitably emulate. There are a lot of towns along rivers in Iowa with held-over mottoes from their beginnings. Most have *gateway* in them, or *opportunity,* or both.

Clinton, Iowa, is the middle. The in-between. Railroad men, prospectors, those gambling with family wealth, planned the straightest routes connecting Chicago to the West, probing a still-new country, and Clinton, Iowa, was a stop on one of those routes, the very first place west of the Mississippi. People came to build the bridges and they stayed, made a place from nothing.

The past was always referenced here. Even when the town was only fifty years old and lumber was booming, there was still nostalgia for that simpler beginning, just river and dark earth, all potential. In 1911, Patrick Wolfe, Clinton's first local historian, wrote a wistful eleven-hundred-page ode to what his town once was.

> To the older members of the family, those unpretending old homes are full of sacred memories and tender reminiscences. Every nook and corner about them is filled with shadows and lights of the past wherewith "all houses in which men have lived and died are haunted." Inconvenient, cramped and rugged as they were, about them rests the halo of the fireside, the family altar, the cradle, and possibly the deathbed of dear ones.

Clinton's inaugural railroad bridge was the second to cross the Mississippi, and in the wake of the Civil War it opened up the country. In pictures that people have shown me, their ancestors are standing by bridges, standing on trains, as though a metal giant can be a favorite member of the family, as though they are embracing.

That is Great-Grandpa. He built bridges.

That is the man I was named after. He built trains.

In the stands, as the LumberKings get through the top of the first with no runs, fans tell the German visitors that maybe they're all related, and the Germans say, "*Uh-huh.*" Immigrants from Erfde, after all, helped build the bridges. They came *here,* here specifically, not just to America or even the Midwest, but here, passports stamped with a final destination: Clinton, Iowa, out of every place that Ellis Island could lead to. Once the sound of their hammers on metal rang out along the river. Now a boy rides his bike in lazy swerves, and there is the sound of worn rubber on asphalt, the sound of a dog barking, the sound of wind.

Clinton's first sawmill came in 1855, built by a young businessman who flipped it for a profit in four years. A flood followed. There was Lyons Lumber Company, and then there was Clinton Lumber Company and then Lamb & Sons and then the Joyce Lumber Company and then W. J. Young & Co. Smaller factories squeezed onto the waterfront as well, failing or burning with another one rising before the ashes blew away. Everything was wood and dust and bodies, a thousand bodies in some of the largest sawmills, chopping, hauling, in staggered, synchronized movements like pistons or watch gears. They had their pictures taken seated on logs with the river behind them, rows of identical young men, posed to be proud and unsmiling like a baseball team.

They killed the forests of the north in fifty years, processing trees in twelve-hour shifts until, somehow, there were none left, and fertile Clinton first understood what it was to be impermanent. Almost exactly a century ago, the last lumber was shipped out of this town, and the last office of the last lumber baron closed. Now that building carries a landmark plaque, another itsy reminder of the scope of what used to exist, facing a Domino's and a KFC, the first-floor window welcoming visitors with a neon pink sign that says "Clinton Family Hair Care Center." I like to go to the pawnshop down the street from the ballpark when I'm bored or ostracized from the locker room, to stare at objects that can't glare back. I look for trinkets left over from what was once here, among the jingoistic lighters and the real guns and the toy guns that look the same. I don't find anything.

The now-empty river used to look as if it were made out of wood. It looked like a dance floor for giants. Logs were strung together, pushed south, and you could stand on the factory docks, see the timber come in, and know that it would be shipped in every direction, making cities that hadn't been there before.

The mills had baseball teams. More pictures on more mantels: men in gray wool uniforms with "Lamb" or "Lyons" stitched across their chests, holding bats against their shoulders.

This is my grandfather. He cut three thousand miles of lumber in his life and had a good glove at second base.

. . .

Branch Rickey, then the general manager of the St. Louis Cardinals, started the minor leagues as they are today. He was the first to take local agency out of the baseball formula. He went to small-town owners who owned small-town teams, and instead of buying individual players, homegrown stars, as it had always been done, he bought their land, their identity. He bought his first team in Montgomery, Alabama, quickly built his network into Texas, into Kansas, into Syracuse, New York. He funneled his prospects through all these places, hiding and protecting his investments until the day they played in front of a major-league crowd.

Many, including some of his employees, called the system "Rickey's chain gang." Others evoked colonialism or the grueling factories of *The Jungle*. Bad conditions, low pay, lots of workers with no better option that would allow them to say no.

Rickey preferred organic terms like "grow." Better to grow your own than pay market value. Better to find a good seed, nurture it, own it from the start. The best of his crop would remain his, a few others would be sold off to rival teams for at least a little more money than he paid, and most would be cut, pruned off, the kind of business expense that you plan for and think nothing else of.

Minor-league squads are still referred to as *farm teams*, bucolic, waiting for a clean harvest. Guys like Danny Carroll and Erasmo Ramírez are called, by some, *farmhands*, kids working the fields, nurturing a product that might be worth something. But it's a muddled metaphor. These players are both the laborer and the crop. People wait for them to ripen like coffee or sugarcane.

When the Depression ended and then World War II ended and baseball was still there, fans clambered into local stadiums to see victorious values reflected back at them. But the hometowns didn't harvest the benefits of their local teams. The fans were rooting for a business proposition, one that owed as much loyalty to the company supplying them with players as the loyal thousands who urged them on. Clinton fans cheered for their Clinton Owls before the Owls became the Pirates became the C-Sox became the Pilots became the Dodgers became the

Giants became the LumberKings. In each iteration, the players belonged to someone else.

Branch Rickey was a lay preacher's son, a storyteller, a sermonizer. He spoke of desperation as if it were opportunity. "What is the greatest single thing in the character of a successful enterprise, in the character of a boy, in the character of a great baseball player?" he asked in a speech that would be anthologized alongside Kennedy, Cromwell, Demosthenes. "I think it is the desire to be a great baseball player, a desire that dominates him, a desire that is so strong that it does not admit of anything that runs counter to it, a desire to excel that so confines him to a single purpose that nothing else matters."

Hank Contreras, a catcher who seldom plays, stands and watches the action from the top of the dugout. Erasmo Ramírez, newly arrived, joins him, listening. Hank points to things for him. I watch them watch. Nick Franklin leads off for the LumberKings. He swings at the first pitch and hits a line drive that skids hard on the center-field grass. He rounds first, stops, claps once. The crowd likes him already. He is cocky, not in a supercilious way, but one that seems deserved. We applaud. Tim gives his standard whistle of approval, piercing above the sound of everything else like a train horn out of a terrible old poem.

"Casey at the Bat" is a terrible old poem, but it is a famous, unavoidable reference when talking baseball. It was said with pride, after the poem's release, *Love has its sonnets galore. War has its epics in heroic verse. Tragedy its somber story in measured lines. Baseball has "Casey at the Bat."*

"Casey at the Bat" takes place in Mudville, which is entirely fictional but refers to a town in Massachusetts or California or Iowa, depending on which place you ask. Forget the character of Casey, forget the mounting rhythm of a ninth inning strikeout, the poem's power comes from its combination of intimacy and vagueness. It was set in a field whose crowd roar echoed up mountains, down valleys, in the dells, in the flats. An impossible field that was in the middle of everywhere.

The poem was written in 1888, when Clinton still had its lumber. Two decades later, the first corn-processing plant was built over the ash-softened dirt where one of the last mills burned. More industry grew through the decades. The train car shops of the Union Pacific railroad. And next to that, Allied Steel. And pulled back from the river, a little out of town, smokestack invisible to those of us in the bleachers of the stadium on a clear day, DuPont.

DuPont closed in 2002 and sold its plastics plant to a new company that continued production with more machines, fewer workers. An article in the *Clinton Herald* in 2008, titled "DuPont Adds to Clinton's Industry Hotbed," served, despite its present tense, to commemorate the excellent neighbor, friend, cellophane producer, and employer of fourteen hundred that DuPont once was.

Allied Steel closed in 1984, but its coal-tar corpse remained, 100,000 pounds of riverfront poison, shimmering, almost beautiful.

The train car shops closed, too, in the '90s. The trains stopped stopping; the shops were demolished.

This isn't a town of everything anymore, isn't a town like Mudville, where Casey would have batted, but this isn't a dead town, either. Something new is always built to envelop the absence when the previous thing disappears. This isn't a story about absence at all, just change, ebb, slow erosion. It makes the poignancy that I feel when I look out beyond the field seem unearned, no complete bust to mourn, no newsworthy Ohio ghost town to gawk at. I tell friends in Iowa City, my university town with coffee shops and drag shows, the declining population numbers, and they shrug. I tell family back east, and I don't even hear the exoticizing pity that I want in their voices, just, *yeah, figures,* just, *Oh, sure, I've been to towns like that; I can see it now. That's the kind of place everybody drives through sometime on the way to someplace else.*

On a hill a half mile inland, there is Ashford University, newer and bigger and better than the Franciscan University of the Prairies, the local women's school that could no longer afford to operate and had to sell its tiny brick campus to Bridgepoint Education in 2005, which picked the name Ashford for its new, old school. Ashford has grown. Ashford has seventy-six thousand students, roughly seven hundred of whom attend the campus. The rest, online-only students, have never walked along the riverfront that I'm looking at, past the stadium and the fake lighthouse and the community pool. But they exist, somewhere. They pay. They log on to a home page that references a "peaceful and charming" collegiate experience, "nestled right alongside the Mississippi River."

Next year, The Huffington Post will run an exposé about Ashford, point out the details of its semi-presence that seems so commonplace here. There is a red door in the old brick building that says, "President's Office," but the door never opens. Call the president and your call goes to a room in a corporate mall in San Diego, an office with a glass door that says, "Bridgestone Education Inc." Bridgestone is a publicly traded company worth hundreds of millions of dollars, and how much of the money has been allocated for employment and improvements at the faded brick campus on the hill in Clinton, it's hard to say. There are no students lounging on a riverside campus now, nearby this stadium. I try to imagine them all here, a population nearly three times that of the current town, playing Hacky Sack beyond the center-field fence, the crew team painting synchronized ripples with their oars on the river in the distance.

A week ago, everything was different for two days. Six thousand students and family members paraded through the downtown streets in cap and gown, taking proud pictures by the Mississippi. And basketball legend Bill Walton gave a graduation speech titled "Building a Winning Community" at the new football field that doesn't have a team to play on it. And restaurants and stores and hotels were full. And somebody came up with the exact figure that $652,527 was generated because of one college-town weekend. And soon Ashford University, its CEO on the coast in San Diego, will be awarded Clinton's annual Friend of Tourism Award.

But back to the corn. Always this century's biggest structure in town, Clinton Corn Processing Company grew into the absences along the river, bought out, then handed over in a merger with Nabisco, finally sold to ADM, "supermarket to the world," ready to expand. A few years ago, on a spring day like this, I could have walked away from the stadium, headed south, watched cranes pass me, carrying wrecking balls to be heaved into the wood and mortar of newly empty homes, making space for more factory, the crash echoing off the water and the empty buildings downtown the way a line drive single might echo off Nick Franklin's personally monogrammed bat.

A gap of browning grass borders the river on the south side of Clinton now. It used to be filled by a neighborhood, a school, a church, two bars, people. I drive there sometimes because the Baseball Family told me to, just to see the absence, to imagine what once was, what they describe to me. I meet a few of the residents still left, stare at one man's T-shirt: "South Clinton: The Little Town Inside of ADM." I wonder how much of an impression they can make on the company that their lives feel so entwined with, when ADM factories exist in two other Iowa towns and twenty other states and more than seventy-five countries around the world.

Ever since Clinton was named New York, smoke—the productive kind—could be seen along this patch of riverbank. There are those who brag that Iowa land is the most in use in the country, hardly an acre of it wasted, and Clinton has always been useful. In the beginning, settlers burned husks to make the black dirt even more fertile. And how often did the lumber mills catch fire, one spark from a saw landing on the stacks of wood taller than any buildings around them? And every new factory that has come and then gone took in water from the river, sent smoke into the sky, an almost natural cycle, as if the machines were breathing.

There's smoke now, drifting toward us in the bleachers, thick and viscous continuity. Beyond that, the only part of this scene that looks the same is the stadium. In the old photographs from the first game, May 9, 1937, the fans wore wool suits and derby hats because it was an occasion, but otherwise they could be us now. This place has been deemed a landmark worthy of immunity to change.

A *Clinton Herald* article from that first day boasts of "a field that is one of the finest in the central west" and "a park setting of unusual beauty." But the last line is the most telling, describing a stadium that will long be regarded as "one of the few really ideal baseball plants." *Plants.* As odd as it sounds, it makes sense. It was celebrated not for its personality but for its dimensions and materials: *Concrete walk bordering the stadium bounded with metal fencing at a distance of twenty-five feet . . . forty reflectors, each carrying 1,500-watt globes, mounted on steel towers above the stadium roof . . . playing area covered with special sod obtained at Root Memorial Park . . . built of steel, reinforced concrete, brick and cinder block, the structure is 99 and 9-10 percent fireproof; its permanence is obvious to the casual onlooker.*

A few quasi-remarkable moments play out on this old and permanent field today. James Jones gallops in on a low line drive to right, folds his long legs under himself, and slides along the slick grass, snatching the ball and springing up fast enough to throw out a runner trying to tag at second. Kalian Sams fails to hit a home run, but still massacres an inside fastball foul, sending fans diving away from the kiddie castle beyond the left-field line. And players unveil newly developed congratulatory handshakes at the top step of the dugout, asserting their modernity by slapping palms with impossible speed and variety, winking, leaping and knocking shoulders, a series of overzealous movements so much more worth seeing than a simple handshake. Fans tell stories of the first time they ever saw a high-five, argue over guessed-at dates.

We tell ourselves stories in order to live. Didion wrote that, and I smile to myself, thinking of her oversized sunglasses in the bleachers of a minor-league stadium. She probably isn't a "Casey at the Bat" fan, and she didn't write that sentiment about baseball or Iowa; she wrote it about the 1960s and about California, ideas that seem somehow entirely the opposite of here, shiny, important maybe, but fleeting. And baseball has stories, yes, more than any other game because there is just so much time to talk and remember that the stories can dominate the action. But sometimes *stories* seems like the wrong word to deify. Because it's *things,* structures, materials, and institutions that have survived and can be seen, that make anyone give a shit, that the stories are fastened around. I can read and hear all the stories about what the town once had, stories about the exploits of players who were great here but who I never saw. And they are nice. And we in the stands can tell stories of inflated selves, can all feel warm, all smile when these stories are being told. But what can they give beyond warmth and smiles? Things are the proof.

A plaque with names engraved, un-erasable. The facade of the stadium that looks just as it does in the pictures. Smokestacks spewing evidence that this town still produces. A red door that looks like somebody would open it if you knocked.

As for the teenagers burning things in the parking lot—that might not be legal soon. Clinton is the last city in Iowa to allow its green waste to be torched. Some people say it's unhealthy, all that sanctioned smoke. In a county where the air quality is consistently a topic of conversation, a county just informed that its "physical environment" ranks ninety-eighth out of ninety-nine in the state, where a *USA Today* poll puts its public schools in the bottom 6 percent in terms of the quality of what the students get to breathe at recess, there are many arguments made about what exactly is wrong with the air. How can anyone know? What is wrong is invisible, floating, wind-driven. Are the personal fires to blame, the quick elimination of trash piles in yards? Or is it the umpteenth generation of factory smoke, the burned coal, the chemical residue coating pickups with unexplained silt until the rain erases the evidence?

Burn things that you don't want to save, Tim tells me. It makes sense. What is wrong with that? Clear space for what you truly want to last.

A ball is hit deep to center, and Matt Cerione tracks it. It's still early enough in the season for each movement to carry potential. He is auditioning in front of us who don't matter. He moves well, in feral, bursting steps. There is that top-of-the-roller-coaster moment—something is about to happen. Wall is there, ball is there, Matt Cerione is almost there. What sound will his body make when it hits the wood?

He pulls up with a good five feet to spare, waits for the hollow thunk of ball, not body, against the wall, his nameless back to the crowd. The ball bounces past him faster than he expected. He trots after it, annoyed. With everything, I assume. The cold, the humid gray of the sky, this place, a wall with splinters and Depression-era nails that he is asked to dive into. It isn't wrong to want to protect himself.

He looks like a cowboy, Matt Cerione, which makes his decision not to dive all the more disappointing. He looks, I've heard fans say, like he should be mounted on a steed out there, and those on steeds should probably be fearless, but this cowboy is petulant, un-stoic, and often stands outside the clubhouse talking on an iPhone to his father about how shitty this whole operation is and how the game is rigged anyways and how, fuck it, he should quit and go back to school, and, Dad, are you even *listening?*

Deb yells, "What happened, Marlboro Man?" and it sounds less chiding than it does sincere.

"It's a shame you're here now and not in 1991." I get that a lot. And then, "Where were you in 1991?" I was five, in kindergarten. Those are the stories I should know. Am I listening? Do I want to know? There are so many stories. How can I organize things in my head?

It looked almost exactly like this in 1991. That's where to begin. Everything that happened then played out within these same confines—forty reflectors and 1,500-watt bulbs and twenty-five feet of metal fence and that prime lumber out in center. They were the Clinton Giants then, so the jerseys were different. And the players were different, of course. And the fans, the ones sitting next to me, saying my name and tousling my hair as if they know me, they were different, too. Younger. Not exactly happier, but there was a bouncy, hopeful feeling that has faded some.

The players from 1991 *wanted it.* They *deserved* this space. Those things can still be said with total confidence twenty seasons later, and there is no residue to inspect to prove their truth. I am told about players who saw a town that needed heroes, and, yeah, that sounds corny to say, but, man, it was true. After a third of Clinton's population had cleared out, they saw *this,* this stadium, brick and wood and steel and dirt. They saw that it wasn't going anywhere, and damn if they didn't play as if this place were a church and it were always Sunday.

What happened to the world? Enormous questions are asked as Matt Cerione skulks into the dugout at the end of the seventh, dramatic eye-black smudged on his face, wristbands on both wrists, Air Jordan cleats, Oakley sunglasses perched atop the brim of his cap, not a trace of a stain on the jersey that proclaims him a LumberKing.

It should be pointed out that Matt Cerione's unwillingness to crash into a wooden wall has no bearing on the game. The game ends when Steve Baron swings too late on a fastball, grounds out to the Beloit Snappers' second baseman, and kicks at the bag as he runs by, screaming *fuck* with a cracking voice and ripping his helmet off his head. Baron's teammates look less angry, more bored, and they walk back to the clubhouse. There is little consequence to be found.

But that cannot be said. Remember, this place is community owned.

Julie, proud member of the Baseball Family, who sits next to Betty every game, won a single share of team stock in a raffle once, which she will never sell, not ever. There is pride in that decision. It seems like every year, one of the many companies that buy and sell minor league teams comes sniffing around Clinton. They are always ignored. Tim tells me that nobody will sell, no way. Ten years ago, a national segment on ESPN used Clinton as an example of the kind of town that would soon become obsolete in baseball. The reporter compared it to Lansing, where an investor had moved the team that had been in Waterloo, Iowa, a mirror of Clinton but twice the size. ESPN had a reporter wander around the brand-new Lansing stadium asking people the score of the game they were watching. None of them knew it. The LumberKings are still here, and it's nice to think that everyone knows the score. Just last year, Tim tells me, a rich couple attempted to quietly buy the majority of the LumberKings shares, and they too were turned away, mentioned in a *Herald* op-ed that encouraged shareholders to value history over money, a sentiment rarely extended to residents fighting Archer Daniels Midland as it pulses and grows along the shoreline.

"Baseball ain't ever going anywhere," Tim reiterates. Tim is wearing his 1991 championship T-shirt, still pristine. Tim is an optimist.

"Oh yeah, sure, just you watch," Tammy says. Tammy is Tim's sister. They aren't much alike.

"This is here," Tim tells her, eyes tracing the full expanse that mine have been roving all game. *This.* Brick, wood, steel, dirt.

Danny Carroll heads toward the clubhouse with his teammates. He stops by the Baseball Family to say good night.

"Picture!" Betty says.

He obliges, bat over his shoulder, chest pushed forward, a classic and indistinguishable image. She tells him, "Perfect."

"I bet you would have caught that ball, Daniel," she says, more hopeful than certain. "That one against the wall."

Danny smiles and says, "I dunno."

But he does know. He would never get near that wall. Players are temporary. Perfect bodies don't last, and why sacrifice one here, even though *sacrifice* is as much a presence in the game's lexicon as *foul ball* or *win*. But Danny is a smart guy and one who wants to be loved. He knows who he is supposed to be.

John Updike finished his essay about Ted Williams like this: "The crowd and Ted had always shared what was important, a belief that this boys' game terrifically mattered." Maybe it's a reach to point out that Ted Williams is cryogenically frozen at the moment and that such otherworldly science has been maligned as robbing a legend of his dignity, as though the myth can't quite be fully realized until the thing ceases to be. But I like that he's frozen. That's respect. To be allowed to remain. The idea that it's important to once again see you, touch your face. That you might be able to return and so you can't be over until that is ruled officially impossible. Because what is greater than being deemed worthy of lasting? Really lasting?

Betty and Tim and Tammy and Joyce all keep the program from today's game. I do too. There are all the names of the men we watched: Nick Franklin is there, number 3. And Danny Carroll, number 2. There is a new name, and Betty traces her hand over it before we leave: Erasmo Ramírez, number 50, just got called up from Arizona a few days ago. "What a name," she says. "We'll remember that one," Tim says and his mother laughs, the way she has laughed at his jokes here every year of his life. There is Hank Contreras, number 31, the third-string catcher. They haven't seen him play yet, but there he is, printed, folded, and saved, his name.

These fans were supposed to be an annotation for me. Quick quotes, bits of atmosphere. Maybe that's exactly what they are. They are here. They are always in this place. They believe in its existence. We all scribble the final score. Ten people's hands move at the same time, reaching for scorecards or notepads, all of us grinning at the identical, somehow sensible compulsion. People were recording long before I showed up. People were saving proof.

The Fantasy

IT'S MAY AND I FANTASIZE ABOUT THESE BOYS NOW.

I'm not sure when exactly they began to intrude on my thoughts, but now they are with me as I fall asleep, more docile than in all my waking hours with them. Mine is a complacent interest, not a desire to know everything about them, but a strange satisfaction in seeing them regularly, in watching them dress for and then perform the actions that they're paid to perform. I just think of them. The way they sit, lounged and primed at the same time. The things they find funny I now laugh at, too. Last night, late, when I was finally home in bed, my girlfriend asked me what I was giggling about so loud as she tried to fall asleep. I spoke in torrents about something one guy said at the card table, about how everyone laughed at this other guy whom he said it to, about how anything can be a competition, about the games guys can play with their dicks and wet towels. She looked at me like I was an alien. And I tried again, with a jock's certainty of perspective, sure that there was no way for macho minor cruelty not to be hilarious.

In the stands, we talk about the players as if they're our friends, especially us men who played before we watched, who still clutch instinctively at things that are round and pantomime pitching motions in the bathroom mirror. One of the most surprising aspects of the Baseball Family is its feminine makeup, and maybe that's because there is something so uncomplicated about female fandom. Betty is a grandmotherly fan. So are Cindy and Julie, fluttering the day's program in front of their faces to cool down, wanting, above all, to make sure that these boys are okay. Tammy and Joyce and Deb are women who once winked at ballplayers, made them ache. Now they carry those memories but root with a grizzled, experienced kindness. It is pointless for women to feel in competition with those out on the field, to imagine themselves performing better in those same uniforms, because the premise of baseball will not allow it. Women watch, never play. Women support; sometimes they love. Women, not even visiting mothers or wives covered in newly bought gold, are allowed to be a part of what is worshipped.

But for the male sports fan, our love or hate, any interest at all, registers on a subconscious spectrum of being lesser than. These boys, many not yet fully grown, none of their own ambitions fully realized, still are what we wanted to be when we grew up. Their bodies are what ours could have been. What we lie and say they once were. We eat boneless buffalo chicken tenders and double cheeseburgers and peanuts, and we describe games we once played. We talk knowingly about the boys who still do until each is ever present. Some of us collect their cards. Some tell stories that are exaggerated even when the event in question hasn't had a moment to mature, for the reality to be forgotten in any way. We all wave, call to them, and then swell when they answer. Yesterday I watched one grown man sketch Nick Franklin on an old graph-paper notebook, using the squares to help get the perfect proportions of a body swinging. Then he ripped the sheet out and shyly presented Nick with his penciled, scowling, formidable image.

There are white pelicans in the air today, circling in loose formation over the field, dipping out of sight, down into the Mississippi, and rising again. They migrate along the river, glide through here in a synchronized beauty for a couple of weeks each spring. The migration had slowed, nearly stopped for a while due to river pollution, but environmental efforts brought them back. The birds showed again in full force a few years ago, and their pale shine seems even brighter now, re-earned. They cast elegant, wobbling shadows over the outfield.

The players move through the door in left field, trotting under the wing shadows, their home whites a stark contrast to every other color except for the bodies of the birds. They match each other against the cement-colored sky, the dark, wet grass, the faded wood of the center-field fence. All of us in the seats, watching in our denim, our red or blue or dulled black shirts.

The players sign autographs along the third-base line. I watch children's hands, stubby and eager, reaching for Nick Franklin's shirtsleeves to feel the coarseness between their fingertips, marvel at the thick fibers given to real pros. It's amazing how quickly we can edit what we see in the tangle of what is in front of us. Nick invites that. It's as though, in a few seconds, I've made a frame out of my fingers and held that make-shift lens to the scene, cropping in the ten or twelve closest kids, their giddiness, their reach, keeping Nick and the other players at enough of a distance so that I can't see the poor fit of recycled uniforms and how they hang off a narrow player's shoulders or clump in unflattering ruffles around a big guy's middle. Making sure Nick is centered, backlit somehow. I allow myself to think absurd words. I think of *majesty*, of *grace*. I think in sweeping circles of the significance in each gesture he makes, as though there is a normal, drab, human way to reach out and pat a child on his head, and then there's the way he does it, sinuous arms unfurling, everything so easy.

"Hoo," Tim says, an unintentional exhalation in response to this scene that he has been at the fringes of so many times.

Matt, the mailman, says, "Yep," in answer to "Hoo."

Derek makes a guttural noise, and Ryan, too, the youngest and new-est of the Baseball Family. He wasn't there for the glory days. He does not remember a better team or town. But he shows an interest in the legends, and that is enough for inclusion now that there is a noticeable absence of adults under fifty at the stadium. Ryan is a thin, shy boy who has dedicated himself to lifting weights and wearing tight shirts, to finding the loudest man in a crowd, standing next to him, and repeating everything he yells.

"Gave Nick a ride home last night," Ryan volunteers now with attempted nonchalance. "Played video games. I beat him in hockey. It's not that he's bad at it, because he's good. It's just that I am so fucking killer at hockey video games."

His gaze holds on Nick as he talks. Nick, who isn't much bigger than he is, who is nearly three years his junior. I wonder if I appear as Ryan does when I look at Nick, his head tilted, mouth a little open, body leaning forward into the air. Ryan looks like old childhood pictures that my father saved, me looking up at my brother, squinting at the sun and the magnitude of him, loving but not fully understanding. The adula-tion you only expect from one too young to know any better. Yet here it is. And somehow it's Ryan who can walk out of gas stations holding a twelve-pack of Bud Light above his head like a trophy, while Nick sits in the rental car waiting, hoping nobody comes out to check his ID and find that he is just a boy far from home, but that fact doesn't change this gaze.

Ryan nods at Nick as he gets close and says, "Nick, Nick, Nick."

Nick leads off the game.

He steps in to bat lefty. He is not naturally left-handed, but he hits from both sides and is better now from the left. When he was old enough, twelve or so, his father thought it was good to flip him into the opposite of the way he'd always been and make him hit that way. Nick swung looking into a mirror, his father standing just behind him, over and over, until swinging lefty wasn't just a stiff copy but its own movement, one smoother and stronger than the original. He takes his time in the batter's box. He runs his cleats over the dirt, tills it, claims it as his own. He places his back foot, his left, just inside the chalk line of the batter's box and twists until he's dug in. Then he lets his weight bob down on his back leg. He looks almost serene.

We watch him wave his bat. He starts slowly, little loops made with hands and wrists that have been described on blogs and scouting sites as a trigger, a blast, a whip crack. The circles move faster and tighter as the pitcher steps back and begins to wind up. When the pitcher lifts his leg, Nick's bottom half moves, a glide of his weight onto his back leg until he is coiled and there is nowhere for his body to go except forward, at the ball. We watch him as he unloads his body, sliding his right leg up until he is stretched broad and then launching, violent and smooth, a rotation of his hips followed by the sudden trigger or blast or whip crack of his wrists.

Baseball, and this is why we nonparticipants here get to feel so participatory, is a game that allows ample time for reflection and appreciation. Each movement isn't followed by a quick, dangerous response. The moment stands. The mover, the idol, holds his pose, and we can hold him in still life. Nick follows the ball into the sky, sees it hang for a moment at its apex and then come crashing down over the last row of seats in right field, out of sight because it's out of the stadium. There is a surprisingly muffled popping sound as the ball hits the concrete of the edge of the parking lot that we can't see. There is a minor explosion in the bleachers. Standing, clapping. Tim gives out some hugs.

From the PA booth, Brad, who will assert confidently to anyone that Nick is a good kid, the right kind of kid, announces, "*Home run number seven for Nick Franklin!*"

"Did you *see* that?" Derek says.

"I saw it the whole way," Ryan says. "I *never* lost sight of it."

Tim starts a *Here we go, LumberKings, here we go* chant.

Nick rounds the bases slowly, looking down, not letting himself show a smile that would reveal him to be a giddy boy, one who just hit a ball maybe farther than he ever had, one who will text his father about it in all capital letters in the locker room and then pull out the marble notebook that he keeps with him always, making a notation of this exploit before sliding it back into his bag and walking to the showers. Tamargo, coaching third, is waiting with his hand up for a high five. They nod at each other, and Tamargo gives him a shove on the back, as if claiming his role in this moment. I feel my body rise and lean forward with the others as Nick walks back toward the dugout and toward us sitting above it. Hank Contreras meets him at the top of the dugout steps, whispers something in his ear. Hank is fast becoming like Nick's older brother, but without the competition that strains familial bonds. Nick smiles finally. He turns away from all of our voices—*Nick, Nick*—and looks back at the path that his home run has just traveled, eyes pointed past everything.

The Roadkill Crew doesn't really exist anymore, but it feels as if it does, sitting next to Tim. The Roadkill Crew was the Baseball Family before they started aging and then dying, when they had the time and the energy to drive to away games, attaching themselves to the team. I have, quite happily, become a sort of story receptacle. It helps that the structure of the stadium is still in place, still exactly the same, so sentences can begin with, *I was over there, right there, see where that guy in the red shirt is?* Now, and during every game, Tim makes a second story line, spoken over the image of Nick, as though the two were related—this perfect boy in front of us and all the games that Tim and his friends drove to decades ago.

Tim speaks to me in "*we.*" In fact, I have never met a man less concerned with the "*I.*" In his stories, he is always with somebody or many somebodies, often not named, just there. Every exploit is shared. Tim has never married. He lives in a one-bedroom house a few blocks from the stadium. He walks to games alone, then walks home alone. He makes venison chili in a big Crock-Pot, eats a little, saves the rest for days. He falls asleep in a single bed. These are things that I know but cannot picture.

They drove twenty thousand miles in a summer, easy. And that's not including the trips they made down to Arizona for spring training, never stopping through Missouri and then Kansas and then Oklahoma and then Texas and then New Mexico, speeding through the desert and watching the sun rise over the cacti that stood waving in warning or welcome. Tim has never ridden an airplane, has never seen a reason to. He has absorbed every mile that he has traveled away from Clinton, and then he has retraced them all. The Roadkill name isn't just a joke. More than a few possums were sacrificed for their pilgrimages over the years, left dying with his tire treads in them, tokens of his travels until finally their corpses dissolved in the rain.

Tim calls out to Nick when the half inning is over and he takes the field.

"We love you, bud," he says.

There's that "*we.*" And it's a little different, I think, from the most common uses of the word when screamed by a sports fan. At most stadiums, in most bars, you hear *We did it!* Tim takes no credit. He doesn't include himself in the perspective of the doers, wouldn't presume to. His "*we,*" and, sitting next to him, his bare arm around my shoulders, I am included in it, claims only to love.

Nick Franklin doesn't turn around to Tim's voice. He gets to where he needs to go and stops on the edge of the infield to adjust the brim of his hat. He's not being rude; I don't mean to suggest that. Imagine if he did stop and turn and wave. Imagine, good God, if he did what most people in most relationships do: Awww, I love you guys, too. How the stadium would freeze, all nine hundred people scattered about the front rows. He is not supposed to gush. He is not supposed to feel the way we feel. Sometimes I think he's not supposed to feel at all, a strange demand for a teenage boy.

Tim goes back to the stories, a jumble of them rolling in on top of one another, conflating time and place and character.

Once, back when Springfield had a team, we showed up with maybe fifty or so Clinton folks. We organized a full-on caravan down I-74. We got to the stadium like a swarm of bees, and it was like there were more of us than there were Springfield fans. After we won, the Clinton players said, *We couldn't have done it without you,* which was pretty nice to hear.

Once, we got drunk with the umps before a game in South Bend. It was a generous strike zone that game.

More than once, we had the boys over for barbecues when they looked lonely.

We rode back alongside the bus after the championship in 1991. We honked the whole way. The players pressed their faces on the windows and smiled.

It is easy to reduce Tim's "*we,*" easy to poke fun at the very use of the word. I feel myself pushing away from it when not unavoidably in his proximity. Players see me in the stands next to Tim, ask me later if I'm a part of that ever-present cadre of rooters, and I feel myself distancing, avoiding the reality that when I'm in the clubhouse, surrounded by individuals consumed with competitive excellence, I long to see them all from Tim's perspective again. I know how Tim seems to the players, and sometimes to me, and maybe sometimes to himself. He is a man who is attached to nothing—no job that means more than a paycheck, no family that wasn't the family of his childhood, no voiced desire for wealth or accolades, for any fantasy. His craft, like his fraternity, is his appreciation of things.

The arguments are common enough.

Maybe religion was once the opiate of the masses, but now it's sports.

Every sad sack wants a chance to win.

Those who cannot do root.

But that can't be it. You can't reduce a lifetime of devotion to that— those born unremarkable living vicariously through those who are better, a stranger's body serving as everybody else's metaphor for the type of perfection they will never achieve.

The most frighteningly poignant account of fandom I've ever read was *A Fan's Notes,* a novel that was really memoir. But even that narrator, looking out from the depths of alcoholism, from the back room of an insane asylum, devalued his own infatuation.

"It was very simple really," he wrote. "Where I could not, with syntax, give shape to my fantasies, [his jock hero] Gifford could, with his superb timing, his great hands, his uncanny faking, give shape to his."

So the shortcomings of one man's life and art are confirmed, sublimated, ultimately soothed, by the effortless beauty of the art of another's body. Is that really Tim, then? Is that his brand of devotion? Right now, as Nick warms up in the field, flipping the ball up over his shoulder, flexing, spinning, is Tim thinking about the things he cannot do, the things that have made him freeze and never leave Clinton, the way his body is aging into a stranger's, that hole in the plaster of his living room ceiling?

Of course I'm thinking of my father now, and his voice, and all of those yellowed, overdramatic baseball books that he read to me, and the promises within them. I assumed and he hoped that he was reading a reflection of what I would become in protagonists like the Kid from Tomkinsville, the untainted Roy Tucker. The Kid is the attraction, made to be ogled, and that was what I should aspire to. The fans were written of as eager and malleable, nameless. The Kid, the great one, the lead, he looks up and sees them validated or deflated along with him, their own worth hanging on his lanky frame, a rabble that has to be there but not looked at head-on. I am rabble now. Everyone is rabble. And is Nick Franklin, in comparison, a born protagonist, or do I just need one, and he's an easy fit?

There have been seventy-three bests in this town. Since 1937, there has been a star in Clinton, the only sure thing. Even in the worst years, when the team was in last place, one boy out of twenty-five presented something a little more hopeful than those around him. The best hitter in 1991, the year of all the giddy stories, when the Roadkill Crew traveled to every game and watched the team win its last championship, was Ricky Ward. His career ended in AA in 1994. He's the hitting coach on a rookie ball team in Oregon now and still part of Tim's "*we,*" when Tim chooses to remember him.

I don't care about Ricky Ward when Tim describes him. A solid kid.

A tough kid. Didn't come from anything fancy, so everybody here could relate to him. Swung like he was pissed off at something. Great, fine, that doesn't mean anything to me, no face to it, no surprises. And maybe in five years, certainly in twenty, nobody will care about Nick Franklin. So what does that say about Tim, about Betty, about Tammy, and all the lost or not-so-lost people whose lives revolve around each new season? They are the ones who look at somebody hard enough until a player becomes what they need him to be. They make the fantasy.

For nearly a month, I vacated the batting cage during Nick's personal practice time, adhering to an unspoken rule. There's something about his eyes when he doesn't want you there. Nothing cruel or aggressive, but worse, disinterested. Bored by you. You are slowing him down, standing there being boring.

When I finally joined him, he didn't look at me. He took a swing at the tee he'd set up, watched the ball push through the mesh at the back of the cage, watched it hit the cinder-block wall, watched the red laces fray and spin off it like a blood spurt. He leaned his weight on his bat, glanced finally in my direction but over me. He smiled.

"So," he said. "You came for a look."

It wasn't a question. And he was right.

He kept on hitting until his bucket was empty. He spoke to himself in whispers after each swing, a common habit of his, reanimating the words that his father had spoken to him throughout Nick's whole, short lifetime. A staccato code.

When he finished, he was happy with the day's output. He felt like talking, and I was there. He told me that this place—the field and the town, too—was like high school, which was a good thing. High school was fun. And here it was like being in the hallways, leaning against a locker with your girlfriend, not really knowing the people around you, but knowing who was who, kind of, recognizing faces as they recognized you. It has always been this way. Nick Franklin has never not had something to do. If people wanted to look in at him, they could. But how could he be expected to look back?

He went silent for a moment, and it was my cue to do the same. I wanted to ask him how somebody who made himself so sought after could want so much to be alone. But that would remind him that there was company, and he would turn off, giving one-word answers behind plastic smiles until I left and no longer felt special through proximity. I have, after all, watched his face during team batting practice, with his coaches in his ear, doing the jobs for which they have nearly a century of combined experience, pretending that they don't notice how little this kid listens and how little that lack of listening affects his performance. He nods just to mark the beginning and the end of their voices, the point at which he can return to himself. Then they stand and watch him swing, listen to the sound of the ball on his bat. They make eyes at each other, each planning the story he will be telling soon, that of a skinny kid whom they helped make, just as I will tell people that we became fast friends, that sometimes I put my hand on his shoulder and sometimes he put his on mine. Nick is right. This is high school. And he is that girl that you love forever because she won't remember your name.

I was numb-assed and daydreaming about high-school embarrassments on my overturned bucket when Nick attacked. He left the cage, tossed his bat aside, saw me open and vulnerable. He sprang. He snaked his right arm around my shoulder blades and pushed into my chest with his left. He tipped me back, as if we were dancing and I were the woman. I felt the coarse lines of muscle that ran across his arms, so much of it in such a wiry frame, but probably not as much as I let myself feel. I looked up at him, saw no strain in his face, just a slight smile as he looked past me at the floor.

He held me there.

I heard my breathing, loud and labored compared with his.

"What would you do," he said, "if I felt like dropping you?"

It wasn't a taunting tone of voice, or angry in any way, just flat.

"For real," he said. "What would you do?"

I would do nothing to him. I wouldn't know where to begin.

And I said it. "Nothing," I said, and I heard my voice catch on the spit that had pooled in the back of my throat.

"True," he said.

He hauled me up and then bounced away from me, hands in the air, bobbing from one foot to the other, simulating the roar of a crowd that would have cheered at such a mismatch.

When he sat back down across from me, he actually looked at my face for a moment, into my eyes. I thought he might have been looking for a reaction, for anger. He is suspicious of all the people who watch him. People are fake sometimes, he has told me. People want something. People like to muddle and distract you—maybe it's just their own weakness, maybe it's on purpose. Like sabotage.

This moment was a test that I was failing. Or maybe not. Maybe I was acing the test with my inaction, with how limp I felt, even though I knew my body was rigid with giddy fear. I would not push back. I would not say anything to upset Nick Franklin, the way nobody said things to upset him, and at least I wasn't pretending to be somebody who could affect him the way he could affect me.

He offered me fifteen more minutes of his concentrated time.

"Thank you," I said.

"Bro," he said, genuinely tender. "Don't worry about it. I got you."

He sat up straight and still. I kept looking.

Sociologists and psychologists write often about the phenomenon of fandom, trying to define the specific makeup of sports fans.

Sports fans are:

"The emotionally committed consumers of sports events."

Or:

"Enthusiastic devotees of some particular sports consumptive object."

Or, more specifically:

"[Those who] know about techniques, guidelines and rules associated with the sport they follow; many are walking compendiums of the current status of particular players and teams. Wild applause, cheers, catcalls and groans seem reasonable manifestations of effective involvement."

So the motivation has been acknowledged as powerful and has been tied to commerce. The fan is, of course, the loyal customer, even if some of the wares are out of his price range. And fandom is spoken of as separate from spectatorship. A spectator is anyone who watches, and a fan is more. A spectator retains the dignity of detachment, while the fan is somehow dependent. The fan is participating, and noisily. The fan is searching, in someone else's play, for so many things. Relaxation and also passion. Self-esteem and also companionship. Emotional release and emotional content. Every goal word that I have ever spoken doubt-fully to a shrink distilled into watching.

But to be here every day reveals peculiar and diverse subsets of devotion, beyond buzzwords. In Clinton, in all of minor-league base-ball, every reward is less, so distinctions become more obvious. You are consuming what fewer people clamor to consume, consuming a product that often does not turn a profit. Yet there is still greater desire to be a part of something that shouldn't be desirable. And there are enough spaces in sparse crowds to distinguish the look on one man's face, enough intimacy to see the way individual fans react when a player is close enough to touch.

Do they lean in slowly from the front row of the stands? Do they snatch at hands or jerseys? Are they unable to move at all?

I look around here and I recognize the category of fan that I fall into, the way I was taught to by my father, not a man who hung out with other sports fans, a man who kept his obsessions quiet, a family trait. We, the overeducated and overindulged, are defensive fans. We are hyperaware of the absurdity of our devotion in every moment except those spent enthralled with the action. We find long, defensible, meta-phorical reasons for the love we feel for strangers, the allegiance we feel to a uniform we'll never wear. I see myself, watching the men who sit on the fringes of the Baseball Family, who come to every game, who betray care on their faces but who never yell or plead, who make quick jokes in disappointing moments that lay heavy over the stands before hopping up for another beer.

Guys like Derek and Matt and Ryan, they are more of the competitive fan. They root to win. They are focused in their watching, as unrelent-ing as the players are when they wrestle each other to the ground in the locker room, holding until one guy has to give in. They will yell for the players, but also *at* them. As though they have some power here, and not just the power to make a star feel loved, but the power to affect the outcome on the field. The power to improve things. *Dive*, they will say, as though Danny Carroll out in center will go, *Ah, that's what I forgot to do*. Sometimes they will not discuss the players at all and instead mono-logue about themselves over the game—a triumph in bar-league soft-ball or a long-time-coming "fuck off" to the boss made greater when spoken of in the context of another's athletic majesty.

There will always be more types to find, further examples of how much a fan can care. Next March, when I follow Nick and the others to Arizona for spring training, I will stand for a week by the fence near the practice fields where 165 players compete all morning to keep their jobs. I will stand with other fans who made the trip to suburban Phoenix for some puzzling, burning reason. There will be a Japanese family who purchased plane tickets only to wait in the parking lot outside the clubhouse for Ichiro Suzuki, sitting on heated asphalt for two hours until he drives by with just a slight nod through tinted windows. They will take pictures of his back license plate and hold their camera up as a prize. I will think, *why,* and then I will see Nick Franklin appear, will sprint toward his Escalade with the monogrammed leather cushion interior, hoping that he might just turn.

The LumberKings are playing Cedar Rapids today, and Cedar Rapids features a boy named Mike Trout who is Nick Franklin's age and Nick Franklin's size and got drafted even higher than Nick Franklin with an even better signing bonus. The fat men with bulging binders full of baseball cards crowded by the visitors' dugout after the national anthem to get his signature. Nick would never say out loud that this displeases him, but it does.

Before the game, he talked about Team USA, the tryouts in Jupiter, Florida, how only twenty-five high schoolers from the whole country made it, one of them being Nick Franklin and none of them being Mike Trout.

"Yeah, I kind of know him," Nick said, as though he were speaking about some obscure annotation from his past, not a frightening combination of speed and power mentioned on every baseball blog in America, featured, text and picture, in this month's *Baseball America* currently lying in Nick's locker. "I saw him, and I was like, yeah, he's one of those guys that didn't make Team USA."

Everybody here wants Nick to be the better one. It is important that he is better, recognized as such. He is Clinton's best, and Clinton's best should be *the* best. He has, since first displaying his gifts in April, been a snug fit into the role that every town must fill, that best reflection of us, no matter if he wasn't *us* two months ago. Mike Trout hit his own homer this game, and it was followed by an immediate consensus that the wind was blowing out to right field and the ball only just dipped over the wall anyway, a lazy line drive that happened to get lucky. He must be beloved in Cedar Rapids, known and cheered by more than Clinton can muster because there are 125,000 people there and even after the massive, tragic flood of 2008 the population has grown and continues to, not like Clinton. Young, white-collar professionals and University of Iowa law students cheer for Mike Trout. Somehow the arrogance of his home run trot falls in line with the arrogance of his temporary home.

But Trout is too good for that place and this level, anyway. Everyone knows it. Cedar Rapids has a new stadium with a Jacuzzi in left field and a scoreboard that runs special graphics dedicated only to Trout, comparing him favorably to Superman. Still, you can dress it up all you want—Low-A is Low-A, Cedar Rapids is Cedar Rapids, and he'll be gone before the hottest days of summer. Two months from now, after his all-star selection, he'll be playing in Rancho Cucamonga and then Arkansas. His name will be spoken of by major-league analysts, his face on TV, not a pixilated mini-Jumbotron. People from all over the country who do not care about Nick Franklin, do not care about Iowa, will ask me, *Did you ever get to see Mike Trout up close?*

In the stands today, there is already speculation about the impending loss of Nick Franklin. The best thing, I'm told, from a low-level minor-league standpoint, is a boring beginning and a good ending. If a player's value is quiet enough to only register here, he might stick around. He can be appreciated in this town, hidden. If he starts out terribly, well, then he's probably back to rookie ball or he's cut, and good riddance, really, it's not as if he had endeared himself. But if he's an instant star, pops up all over the Internet next to captions saying, *look out for this kid*, next to a picture where you know you're just a few feet out of frame in the stands, then you probably will never see him again.

"We're fucked if he leaves," Derek says, loud enough, I imagine, for Nick's teammates at the top step of the dugout to hear. "That would just fuck us."

But people aren't meant to stay here. Nick Franklin wouldn't be the first to go. And next year, a shortstop will be drafted in the second round, and another teenager will light it up in the Venezuelan Summer

League, each waiting to star in Clinton, but we do not know that now. And even if we can assume its probability, we still ignore it. Nick Franklin is irreplaceable.

"He's young," Tim says, hopeful always.

"Yep," says Matt.

"Sometimes with a young guy they want to keep him around, they don't want to rush things," Tim says, dropping the *we* when referring to those with decision-making power. "I mean, what's the rush?"

"If I was them, I'd let him stay," Matt says. "A boy's got to learn how to succeed. This place is good for him."

It is a quality of optimism that I have never seen before coming to this town, one that is repeated in the stands every day. It is warm, womblike. It makes me feel a deep, developed, familial care for things that are new to me. Nothing ever really ends here. Nothing will. Or at least it doesn't feel ridiculous to think that, even though Ryan and I stand out, in our twenties at the game when most of the men who watch every day have done so for longer than we've been alive and the fans who are talked about as best, the exemplars of loyalty, are dead.

Nick is so young. He looks like that boy from back then who looked like that boy from back then who looked like that boy from back then.

The pelicans have returned, circling, and I point up at a flock of them that has decided to hover over the field. They look so different from the crows that usually dominate. They look different from the vultures, too, that stain the sky, that make you want to look away. The vultures come for the dead because Clinton County has suspended carcass removal due to the cost. They hover over bloody heaps of roadkill, smaller each day, eaten by maggots until they are nothing but pulp that can wash away in the rain. The pelicans are clean. Their bodies are a pure white, slicked with water and shining. Only the tips of their wings are inkblack, and when the sun is behind them, the ends of the black feathers look like fingers waving down at us.

Jason, another fan who loves Nick, walks over with his video camera, looking up, zooming in, watching the pelicans drift and then come back, as though adhering to the dimensions of the stadium. Maybe he'll put this on his personal YouTube page, documenting everything noteworthy that happens in Clinton and its surrounding rural sprawl, next to the video of an apartment fire, the thick black smoke climbing,

Jason's voice going "Whoa, whoa" in the background. And next to a two-minute silent close-up of a lime-green Lamborghini parked in the driveway of a rich doctor from across the river. Today's baseball exploits will be up soon, too, Nick's home run with an epic, bass-heavy sound track behind it.

When Tim describes 1991, the Roadkill Crew, and the expanse of baseball affection they created, I like to picture thousands of different faces, united, inspired by a collective victory, the most benign of war films. But 1991 came on the heels of Reagan, and things didn't trickle down to this place, and so began the first decade when the population had dropped under thirty thousand. The first time the census showed Clinton shrinking since when the lumber ran out. Tim doesn't have to enumerate all the details that I know, but they are encapsulated in his tone. The impending loss of the last train car shops. The loss of Allied Steel, as towns with multiple flourishing factories became an increasing rarity. And worst, the loss of most of the town's unions when the grain millers' strike was broken, organized laborers forced to move or go silent, an irreversible change to the feeling of his home. And suddenly it was neighbors and friends and fans gone. Clinton hasn't gained it back since.

What does Nick Franklin have to do with all that? As little as possible; that's what is so wonderful. He comes from a place of sun and ruthless optimism, suburban Orlando. He was born in 1991, destined to make that year a significant beginning. The tattoo across his back says so. He doesn't have a history. Just nights after school in the batting cages, swinging until his hands blistered, running sprints until his father told him he could stop. The stories that he tells me smiling and then looks at me puzzled when I have a worried expression.

Homework can wait until your baseball is done.

No rest for the best, just nighttime practice when no one else is awake.

And nobody saw those nights, the making of a millionaire child. That's a good thing. Nick's exploits can still look easy, preordained. In Clinton, as long as the players are here, they can come from nowhere if you want them to, they can be only a future, and that future can be anything.

Hours later, it's the eighth inning and I'm sleepy. Since Nick and Mike Trout exploded early, the way everybody anticipated they would, both teams have looked confused and slow, unremarkable at the plate. Cedar Rapids is up 3–2, and already this inning Steve Baron came up, swung late and awkwardly at a high fastball, and hit a pop-up that didn't even clear the infield. Gabriel Noriega was next, the middle infielder who should be Nick's greatest competition, but he is still more boy than man, with a concave body and a frightened face. His bat looked too big for him, and he swung as if he regretted the decision the moment he hoisted the wood off his shoulders. A weak grounder to first. Now it's Nick again.

Nick takes a curveball low and swings over another one, bringing the count to 1-1. Then the pitcher makes a timid mistake and leaves a slider over the inside part of the plate. Nick gives a vicious uppercut of a swing and releases a grunt as bat hits ball. This second home run doesn't travel as far as the first, but it rises higher. He watches until it looks as though it's as high as the pelicans, and then it's gone and he trots again, unsurprised, while we rise again for him and Brad screams even louder into his mic.

"Are you ever worried?" I forced myself to ask Nick in my allotted fifteen minutes. "Do you ever think that maybe things will get different, get really hard, something like that?"

I had been trying to think of a better way to phrase that, not just, "What happens if you fuck up?" Or, "Failure, failure, what about when you fail?" So much of the minors is about things fading until they end, so much of the game is about missing, but those inevitabilities aren't spoken of here, certainly not with him.

He didn't pause before saying no.

The answer itself wasn't any shock. All his teammates would have said something similarly stilted and rehearsed, the kind of irritating optimism that athletes are taught. Danny has said similar things to me, and Sams, and even Hank, who never plays. But there is nothing sure in their eyes when they say it, almost guilt in Danny's case, as though caught in a lie.

Nick held a bat as we spoke, one of the many that rest bundled in his locker. He wasn't lying. I wasn't sure how to respond, so I stuttered for a moment and waited for him to fill the silence.

"Have *you* ever, like, I don't know, failed at anything?" he asked me. He likes to redirect questions, and I find that quality charming, proof of his interest.

"Well, yeah," I said. "Yes. Of course. I mean, that's what happens."

He looked past me and shook his head.

"Man," he said. "I don't know. That must suck."

I shrugged. Then sat still. He continued.

"It's like, I see some of these guys on the team and it's like, damn, time is passing and they aren't going anywhere. That would scare me. Do you think they're scared?"

Of course they are. Baseball is terrifying. So is turning a year older than you were. Everything is terrifying.

"Probably."

"Some people think that I'm cocky or whatever," he said. "But I'm not. It's just, I've never really failed. Why am I supposed to think that can happen when it never does?"

He gave a smile, a small one, a bit impish, but then his face was serious again.

He is, up close, ordinary. He is listed at 175 pounds, and that's generous. He is just shy of six feet one inch. There are things that he does poorly. The double-play throw. Choosing his spots when he steals bases. He swings too hard often, and so often he misses. These things are all a part of his reality, and I know that, everybody does, everybody has seen evidence of Nick's flaws over the course of each game, but they don't resonate. They are talked over and forgotten when he does something that shines because when he shines it is so much, it carries so far, and everything about him is a horizon line. Nick Franklin is all hyperbole.

His teammates, guys like Sams and Danny and Hank, they are fun to hope for, but still you're aware of the act of hoping, aware of waiting to clap your hands when an underdog wins. They've been seen before by these fans, have returned to be seen again. They are grounded in the probability of fading away. They will cease to matter just as everything eventually does.

"Is it cool to be the favorite here?" I asked him. "To have people, you know, love you like that?"

He shrugged.

I wanted to sit even closer to him. I wanted to feel knee on knee. It wasn't about how he would never fail. It wasn't that he was the best. That's not the appeal. He will fail in some way, probably. Definitely. He will never live up to the inflated expectations that have been placed on him. But he doesn't know any of that yet. That's what we see when we watch him. Somebody who doesn't know that things get worse.

The game seems paused after Nick's second home run. The score stays the same, 3–3, past the ninth, into the tenth, and there is nothing worth watching that happens when he is not at the plate. Then, in the bottom of the tenth, there he is, up on the top step of the dugout, helmet on, bat in hand, waiting. Steve Baron and Gabriel Noriega actually manage hits, and with two outs there are men on base for Nick to knock in to win the game.

"He must be nervous," I say.

"I would be," Tim says.

"Kid like that, never nervous," Matt says with finality.

All of our bodies are tensed. I feel the extra weight of my own torso, the low numb in my legs from sitting for so many hours, standing only to get more food. Matt, who was an athlete in the army in the 1980s, something that he announces freely and often, rests his dimpled hands on his knees, covering the scars of a double surgery that was performed so that he might be able to walk into his fifties. Tim fidgets with his tank top from the 1991 championship season when he looked more like a peer to the players. The shirt is getting too small and he shouldn't wear tank tops anymore.

Nick doesn't look nervous, that's true. But there is the unspoken reality that not one of us has any idea what a boy like Nick Franklin is thinking in a moment like this. As he scrapes at the dirt with his cleats, the only certainty we can muster is that this is *big*, this moment, and that he is right for it.

Nick falls behind, fouling off a fastball with an eager swing and then taking a breaking ball for a called strike. He lets one go by in the dirt. The stadium is silent, rapt. We look only at the field, not at the empty seats around us.

Before the next pitch, I see Nick shuffle forward in the batter's box, putting himself inches closer to the pitcher, like he has figured something out. I tap Tim on the shoulder and hear the proud, knowing tone in my voice when I say, "Look, he's moving up," like I've figured something out.

"Sure, yeah," Tim says.

The pitch is a changeup, slow and dipping down. Nick waits, balanced—there had been no doubt in his mind what was coming. Late, almost too late, it seems, he flicks his wrists in a blur—that trigger, that blast, that whip crack—and the ball carries. Trout is after it in center field, and we watch him with fear and fury, able to work this moment into a narrative of two men facing off for the role of the day's champion, though Nick just swung as hard as he could, though Trout is just doing his job chasing down a fly ball.

We try to gauge the angle of Trout's run and the ball, see a second into the future to know if they'll meet. But Trout slows up as he nears the wall and just watches it. He's not going to get there. The ball skips away and Steve Baron scores easily. The game is finally over. This long, vital, unimportant contest has been decided. The LumberKings have moved to .500, still squarely in fourth place in the Western Division of the Midwest League. Everybody on the field has stopped running except for Nick, who trots into second base and plants both feet on it, satisfied, momentarily serene before turning and facing his dugout.

It is a feeble sound we make, those of us clapping hard. Our cheers echo off the mainly empty metal benches, each of us trying to be the loudest. The other LumberKings pour out of the dugout and run toward him. Danny is in front with big eyes and coltish legs stomping, willing himself to be happy for a teammate who is celebrated enough, who lives life with the kind of constant praise that Danny used to know. Nick faces them all with his head cocked, interested, maybe even happy. He doesn't move to rush into their arms. He stands, shoulders squared, and waits for them. They jump at him, slap him on his head and his back and his ass. He weathers it all and finally trots away, lets them follow him, still cheering.

Nick is alone in the tangle of bodies as they walk back to the dugout, glancing up at the fans, the ones he sees every day. The other players are still reaching out to touch him, still yelling in his ear, but he is something entirely apart, something that stands out to be preserved, beautiful and so young, moving past one conquest toward another, of course another. And then, so soon, he's trotting back to the clubhouse before hands can reach at him for a signature, only his back visible, until even that disappears. I look at the sky, and the pelicans are gone.

1 2 3 4 **5** 6 7 8 9

The Pzazz!

THE PZAZZ! FunCity is big and it is gaudy. You can't see it at first when you leave the Burlington Bees' field, but then you go past the Taco Bell parking lot, and boom: a city of fun. I like the cursive lettering on the sign, packed with z's. Even the fake word is remarkable, a collection of characters that shouldn't be together. It makes me think of Phil Rizzuto, the former Yankee shortstop and announcer, because as a boy I'd see his name written in the paper and I'd think it was a typo, z's pushed together like that. I looked up his minor-league career the other day. I've been doing that lately, trying to see who came through Clinton, Iowa, immersing myself in the improbability of their onetime presence in the town. Phil Rizzuto never played in Iowa. His first stop was with the Bassett Furnituremakers in Virginia, one of those Depression-era teams that didn't even make it to the war before folding.

They were Furnituremakers when Bassett was a center of furniture production. Now Bassett is not a center of anything, and there is no team, a sad fact, but more logical than a baseball rebirth as the FurnitureKings.

I texted my father: *Did you know Phil Rizzuto played for the Bassett Furnituremakers?*

The LumberKings are still stuck in fourth place, seemingly unable to hit, and that makes everything temporarily heavy—their shoulders, their street clothes as they dress after the game, their giant headphones as they try to slouch past Joyce's attempted encouragement, notebook out, pen out, *Great job!* In the clubhouse, Kalian Sams is silent next to Hank Contreras, who is also silent, though not as simmering mad as his friend. Sams plays every game and lately has struggled through most of them, watching his spot in the order dwindle from cleanup to fifth to sixth to eighth. Hank has only played in three games so far this season, so a loss or a poor team performance is something different for him. *He* has lost nothing. He didn't fail to do his job well, because he wasn't allowed to do his job.

I did expect the post-loss malaise to last longer. I think everyone does who isn't on the team. When we in the stands say, "That was a hard one," or "They won't forget that one anytime soon," we mean us. We mean that we will relive the slow ache of a game where the people we want to win don't, the injustice of it all. And it is comforting to think that a loss that is significant to the spectators must be way more significant to the actual players. If they don't care, why would we?

But for the players tonight, there is the Pzazz! There is a city of fun. And what they will tell me, but never the local, loyal fans, is that they look forward to road trips every night they are "home" in Clinton. I have driven Sams and Hank down Camanche Avenue after a home loss, feigning gags as we bounced alongside the factory, stopping at the house where they rent rooms, the landlord barging in to say they're like her sons and she tries to be good to them, so why don't they do a little more to drum up business for her restaurant? I have sat on the couch with Hank and Sams and watched major-league highlights, more enthralled than they want to be. I have asked, "What's your guys' record now?" and they have not once remembered.

There is a huge pool at the Pzazz! with a triple waterslide and five-hundred-gallon dump buckets and a lazy river. The players don't go there, because it's for kids, which they most certainly are not, but it's still nice that it exists. There are bumper cars, too, and laser tag and mini-golf. A whole arcade. The casino is the biggest draw, though, larger and more glittering than the Wild Rose in Clinton, where Joyce works. A combo sushi restaurant and steak house is adjacent, and a family-style place and a sports bar, all offshoots of the gambling nucleus. I told the LumberKings' manager, John Tamargo, that I'd buy him a drink after the game so that we could talk. He nodded and gave a smile that frightened me.

Now he limps through the Boogaloo Cafe, and looks important. The blended polyester of the polo shirts that only baseball coaches and golf pros seem to wear does well at night in bars. It catches sparse orange light and reflects it, not too much, not shiny like a woman in a dance club, but still more than the fathers in cotton T-shirts on family vacation, more than the middling businessmen in their dull blues and grays. His Rolex is freshly shined, as is his tanned bald head, as is his championship ring, seventeen years old and impeccable.

He sits down across from me, and the waitress, who is very young and has an inexplicably popular skunkish, half-blond, half-black, hairstyle, asks him what he'd like. He calls her sweetie and looks at her with hunger. I think she'll mind, but she doesn't seem to.

He says, "Johnnie Walker Black," and looks at me to see if I will say no, not on my tab. I say nothing and watch my fingers rip up my cocktail napkin.

"Double," he says. "Double of Johnnie Walker Black."

He smiles and runs the tip of his index finger over his championship ring.

John Tamargo is comfortable in this place. Not just the Boogaloo Cafe, its snaking row of flat screens and wax-shined fake-mahogany tables, its staff of eighteen-year-olds and their hopeful, excessive makeup, but any equivalent of it, the kind of place that is in every mid-level hotel in every town. Now they all seem to be attached to casinos. There are hundreds of casinos in the corn states, a casino for any town where the local industry was dwindling, that was promised a gleaming lure and a fresh start. It seems as if every town with a minor-league team also has a casino, and he's been in them all, or if he hasn't been in them *all*, it still feels like it because who can remember which one is which?

"Nice place," he says and takes his first sip of Johnnie Walker Black.

"Oh yeah, definitely," I say.

"You hungry?" he says.

"Nah, I'm—"

"You should eat. You should have some sliders." And then, to the waitress: "We're gonna have some sliders."

Everybody from John Tamargo's world is scattered throughout this restaurant. There are fans who recognize him and smile because he hopped up out of the dugout today to scream at the umpires about some calls. He watches them notice him. The umpires themselves are at the bar holding sweating beers and watching highlights. He trades rueful grins with them. They raise their bottles in our direction. He humors them outwardly and mutters, "Fucking idiots." BJ, the trainer, is at the bar, too, talking fast as he always does, making dirty jokes that never seem quite right coming from him. And, of course, his players are dotted around the restaurant. They tear into burgers and talk quietly. They look up, see Tamargo, then look away. He points at Sams and Hank, sitting together. Hank holds up his beer and gives a short toast to his boss. Tamargo likes the boldness of the gesture. He raises his eyebrows like he should be mad at such open post-game unwinding, but he will let it slide this time.

John Tamargo is performing for me now, the role of hard-ass manager, exuding wizened charm. He externalizes what could have been internal monologue when he spots a collarless shirt at one of the tables full of his players. He looks over my shoulder and says, "Is that . . . ?" as though the ending words to his question could be catastrophic. "Is that little shit not wearing a . . . ?"

He pops up and goes to stand over a relief pitcher, leaning in his ear, thick fingers jabbing at his black cotton T-shirt. The boy stands, six feet four and broad, a different breed, almost, from his manager. He nods in penance and trots toward the elevators to change. His teammates laugh. Tamargo lets his finger point around the room at all of them, making sure that everyone has seen this, and then comes back over to me.

"I like when things are done the *right* way," he says. "Wear a nice shirt. Look like a goddamn professional."

I am not the only one who loves this display, though perhaps I'm the most obvious about it. I can feel the grin on the corners of my lips, my face warm, and how babyish and red I must look. But the umpires, too, clearly the kind of men who love both baseball hierarchy and rules in general or they would have found a different, less abused profession, clink their bottles at the bar in celebration of the defense of righteousness and dress shirts. BJ is overjoyed both by what has just transpired and by the fact that he is a colleague of sorts with everyone involved. Even the waitresses smile. And the few suited traveling salesmen here tonight, drunk and paunchy, lean into one another and begin talking excitedly, and I know, just know, as someone who would be doing the exact same thing, that these conversations are about high school coaches who were real ballbusters, and remember when men were men?

John Tamargo is being everything we want him to be.

He asks me if I want to try the Johnnie Walker Black that I'm paying for.

"Go on," he says. "This is the good stuff."

"Go on," he says again, so I take the glass.

He gives an expectant smile, a kindly one, I think, happy to be introducing me to something better than what I've known. I sip and I notice how sharp, how white his teeth are. I swallow quick and avoid a cough.

"Good," I say.

"You gotta drink the right stuff," he says, and I nod. We are dancing now, lilting through our interactions. He is old and salty and tired in the exact way that I envisioned the older men in the books my father read to me, his voice hardening when speaking their dialogue. I'm soft and still unformed, letting him mold me for the moment, letting him impose on me. That is his job anyway, to be hard, to impose, to be the expert in the one kind of life he has devoted himself to knowing.

John Tamargo has been a lot of places. He tells me about some of them tonight, and I don't tell him that I already know the basics of where he's traveled. You can trace his life online at Baseball Reference or the Baseball Cube or any of the other Web sites set up by indefatigable amateurs to chronicle every movement of every man who ever played the game.

His professional life, the bulk of it at least, begins with his release from the Montreal Expos. His playing résumé is short. Before his time with the Expos, there was a rise through the minors and then four years in major-league cities like St. Louis and San Francisco. There was a .242 lifetime major-league average, 244 at bats that were recorded, that nobody can take away.

And then: "April 1, 1981: Released" is all it says.

There must have been a moment then, in April 1981, when he cried. There must have been a moment of upheaval, of the nausea that I can't imagine not having, one of seismic uncertainty, of the thought of his choices being made invalid. He must have considered selling cars or real estate, going back to school. He must have considered things not baseball. I ask him and he says no, and maybe that's a lie, but it doesn't matter, because there is the rest of his life on the Internet, organized by season. Miami, 1982. Then Columbia, South Carolina, 1983. Then Lynchburg. Then some unspecified town on the Gulf Coast. Then Tallahassee. Then Binghamton. Then Kissimmee. Then Houston. Then New Orleans. Then Brevard County and Durham and Everett. Then Clinton. He was a bench coach in some places, a hitting coach, too, and finally a manager.

He's won a lot of games, over eight hundred, he knows that much. He's lost over eight hundred as well. He is nearing the minor-league record for both. In a life of trying to win, trying not to lose, he has just about broken even. He could start over now, say that nothing from before counts, and it would be the same. When I Google him and his stats pop up, sometimes there are little annotations written about his life by the nerdiest, most diligent of baseball fans. They always begin with something like "John Tamargo: you may remember from his few years as Gary Carter's backup." And people leave comments to say, oh yeah, they do remember that.

The only reason I started talking to Hank Contreras was because he lived with Kalian Sams. When Kalian Sams started the season with the best-hitting two weeks of his life, competing briefly with Nick Franklin for idol status, I tried to be where he was as much as possible. I waited for the right to give Sams a ride home, and when he looked around for something better, saw nothing, pursed his lips, called shotgun, and folded all six feet two inches and 248 pounds of him into the passenger seat of my hatchback, Hank slipped in behind me.

He introduced himself, and I pretended that I knew him, that I'd seen him play or at least found his name in the program each night. He didn't believe me.

"We don't know where to put you" is what Pedro Grifol, the Mariners' minor-league director had told him in Arizona as spring training ended and everybody else had found out where they were going to be.

"We don't want to cut you," he said. "You don't deserve that."

Hank waited.

"We want to give you a shot, but, I mean, where?"

Hank waited some more.

Pedro sent him to Clinton, saying that he wasn't a man to mince words, so Hank should know that he wouldn't play. Pedro said they all liked Hank, they thought he was a fine ballplayer, more important, a good man. The other players, those starting above him, could learn a thing or two from him, especially the newly naturalizing Dominicans and Venezuelans who need extra bilingual care.

Hank bore this quietly, said thanks.

Every time we speak, I try to think of some way to ask without it being cruel: Why? Why be here? Why keep playing when nobody has even taken the time to throw you that kindly lie: you've got as good a shot as the next guy? I look over his manager's shoulder now at Hank, drinking his beer, saying something that makes Sams scrunch his enormous face, purse his lips, and go, "Man, shut up." He doesn't swagger or yell or stare past you like some others. He is shorter than I am by two or three inches, a square frame that would be formidable in any other context but among his teammates reads as squat and ordinary. Even his ethnic otherness is muted. The black players are like celebrities here in the Pzazz! and certainly in Clinton, visitors from another world, for sure. And the Dominicans and Venezuelans, too, are so distinctly different, tall mestizo aliens with diamond earrings and confused faces when English is spoken fast. Hank is Mexican, with a tan Aztec face. Everybody has seen a Mexican. And when Betty leans over the railing and says "¡Hola!" he responds with an unaccented "Hi, ma'am, how are you?" and puzzled looks ripple up the bleachers.

"Did you know that Mickey Mantle was five eleven," my father used to tell me. "Just like I am."

I would say no *way,* and he would say yes, maybe even five ten, not a steroided bicep or a cobblestone ab muscle on him. My father would stand over the coffee table, put his chubby fists on his hips, and hold the pose.

"This is how Mickey looked," he would say.

I sat with my fingers digging into the unformed rolls of my sides, picturing a black-and-white Mickey Mantle head on my father's familiar body, back to his own, then back to Mickey's, like a lenticular poster that shows something different depending on the angle you approach it from. That is the way fathers teach baseball to their sons. The democracy of the game. The idea that what makes someone exceptional comes from an unquantifiable force *within* them. There are no absolutes in the game beyond will, and that is the appeal that Hank Contreras draws upon, for me, certainly, as I watch him chew his burger. The fans in Clinton can see him squatting in the bullpen every day, mask on, dirty and underappreciated the way real people are, yet still a player, his uniform that same heavy white fabric that only professional uniforms are made out of.

Hank and Sams finish their dinners and run out of things to say. They stand up together. They smooth the fronts of their required polo shirts, look down, and admire the way the fabric clings to their torsos, Sams especially, but Hank, too, because he worked to lose twenty pounds in the off-season and the team noticed, they told him so. Hank gives a quick salute to Tamargo, who laughs and reciprocates.

"You going to the casino?" he calls out.

It is a joke, I think, because he knows these two and they're not exactly the big spenders of the team. They can't afford to be. Some of the players have already been in the casino for hours, along with Dwight, the cowboy pitching coach who beelines to any place where you're still allowed to smoke indoors, everyone blinking in the fluorescent, windowless cavern, the baseballers towering above the old ladies and obese men on motorized scooters who dominate the slot machines, forgoing the levers to just push the red button and watch the pictures spin. Some players read how-to-win-at-blackjack books on bus rides. They dip into their bonuses to throw down hundreds and sometimes come away with thousands, the toast of the locker room until something more interesting happens. Hank's bonus was in the thousand-dollar range, a good night's winnings for his bolder and richer teammates, signed over on the spot when he didn't yet have an agent.

Tamargo points to Hank's back as he follows Sams out of the Boogaloo, maybe to swing by the door of the casino, just to peek in over the velvet rope before bed.

"That's a *man*," he tells me, nodding as though I should make note of this on a bar napkin, put it in my wallet as a reminder of what to aspire to. As though that commendation for living correctly, for being the kind of person people automatically like, could be enough.

. . .

The casinos are supposed to cater to the tourists. There are seventeen casinos in Iowa, so there must be seventeen casinos' worth of people flooding this flat and landlocked rectangle for their yearly vacations, ready to pour money into the state in return for the endless excitement supplied through hands of digital three-card poker. It is easy to wonder in Burlington and in Clinton: Where exactly are all the tourists? This snarky tone is easy, too, especially for me, someone who lives outside a casino town. I know Joyce noticed it when I spoke to her about her job as a blackjack dealer, and she said adamantly, "I work for good people. I work for people who give back."

But that is always the question in a relationship, always what is at stake. How much is being given back by the entity that is huge, that controls everything and will always win? How much does it mean that the Wild Rose gave a few grand, or one man's losing streak, to the Clinton Red Cross? That's not fair. I've been told that the Wild Rose has given back a million dollars in one way or another to Clinton. It's helping fund the Sawmill Museum, an homage to the greatest part of Clinton's history, and that must mean something.

There are pictures around the Pzazz! FunCity of the usual things, a blond woman with red lips in a low-cut sweater, throwing gold coins over her head after an apparently easy slot win. That blond, red-lipped, cleavaged woman took something back from the casino, we are told. She won. We could, too, after our meal. There are so many places we could win. The Pzazz! and its Catfish Bend Casino may be billed as utterly unique, but there is another Catfish Bend in Fort Madison. And Jumer's of Quad Cities, "Vegas without the airfare" in the local TV ads, is just like the other ones that the Delaware North Companies own in Arkansas and Arizona and New York and Florida and Oklahoma. And Joyce's Wild Rose is not the only Wild Rose that has grown in Iowa, a fertile ground for such plants, what with the tax breaks extended to welcome them.

John Tamargo will gamble tonight, I know that as we talk. Why not? He will light his cigar and stand over the craps table, trying not to think of an offense that can't seem to score more than two runs in a game, a season in which wins don't come in pairs, let alone groups.

He and his players and Dwight will be those tourists whom the casino attracts. But they will likely be the only out-of-town big fish, no matter how questionable their bigness. These Iowa casinos aren't really made to be flooded with visitors. That's not where they make their money. The majority of the clientele in a casino like this one will drive home tonight and then back the next day, not here for an occasion, but to feed a compulsion, drawn to this biggest, shiniest neighbor that offers a chance for immediate and repeatable victory. Joyce is working at the Wild Rose tonight, dealing blackjack to the same people whom she has dealt blackjack to for nearly as long as Hank Contreras has been alive. That's the only reason she didn't make the two-hour trip to Burlington tonight. She will be busy until 2:00 a.m., until the last of her neighbors is told to leave.

John Tamargo has ordered another double Johnnie Walker Black, and when the waitress asked for payment, he pointed at me. He is happy that I will pay and that I will listen. He is happy that I am scared of him, the kind of fear that makes me want to stay, not leave.

We talk about his players, but he will not say which ones we're talking about by name. We discuss types, and it feels appropriate because it's so easy to see the players that way, all the same from a distance, no name above the numbers on their jerseys, defined by how much playing time they get and what happens in those innings.

The ones who are supposed to be succeeding are doing what they're supposed to do. That means that Nick Franklin is off to a hot start. The organization is pleased.

Some of these guys need to learn that life ain't a goddamn handout, but that's all right, they'll learn, everybody does, they'll be just fine. That means he doesn't like players who complain because he feels that, in his day, complaining did not exist.

And then, as nonchalant as all the previous statements, Some of these guys, most of these guys, will never make it past here. Talent is talent. You can't tell them that; it's something that they've got to realize on their own.

We are silent together after that one.

He pushes ice with his straw and says, finally, "Good whiskey."

I think of the sign in the hallway with the winner on it, her red lips and cleavage freckles.

"That's kind of sad, isn't it?" I say.

And those words linger as well, embarrassing me the moment I release them. They are soft words, and also pointless. What does sadness have to do with the reality of things? Tamargo keeps his eyes on the ice and the straw.

"What?" he says. "Oh yeah. Yes, it's sad, I guess. Yes."

His brow is furrowed, reliving tonight's game still, first thoughtful and then increasingly upset. He leans forward toward me.

"Listen, when I was twenty-one, I didn't give a shit, because I knew I was good," he says. "That's the way it's got to be. You see a guy who doesn't believe he's the best fucking hitter in the building, well, then he isn't going to be shit. I don't have to tell you the names. You see these guys. You see the ones who are the real deal, they know it. They wake up every day and look in the mirror and say, 'I'm the shit.' I was the shit and I knew it, so I made it."

It is the longest, loudest burst of speech he has given me since I met him, and he leans back against the sticky plastic of the booth, smiling, remembering. His fists are balled on the table, and his ring, engraved with the record of a championship won miles and decades away from here, absorbs all the dim light. He is describing a version of himself that was more than half a life ago but is still vivid, when he tore through A-ball after being a sixth-round pick and ended his second year in the minors in AA, his third in AAA, the exact sequential order that life is supposed to take for the guys who progress the right way. And why should he be soft and sympathetic toward his players who are stuck in A-ball because they can't adjust, who mope around hoping for things to change, muttering that they're getting cheated, when if they were man enough, they would have just done what they had to do the way he did? Most of the time, he *is* sympathetic. He is good to them on the field, in the clubhouse, when they sulk after games like the kids they are. It is a frustrating job.

"When I played, if you didn't move up, you were gone," he says. "You couldn't hit a pitch, shit, you better learn how."

And then, just as fast as he inflated, he returns to a soft grumble, to fat, liver-spotted hands unclenched and resting on a table that keeps pissing him off because it still hasn't been wiped down and how fucking hard is it to wipe a table if that's your job?

"Look, I was a 4A player," he says.

"They had Quadruple-A ball then?" I ask and realize, as soon as the words are out, what he means. He looks at me, and I notice for the first time that his eyes are a pale green, beautiful in an entirely unexpected way.

"No," he says quietly. "There never was a 4A, just 4A players. Four-A talent isn't enough. You're good enough to get there, and then you look around and notice that you ain't near good enough to stay. That's 4A. The point is you gotta realize what you are."

Quiet again. His straw and his ice again. My breathing.

"Some of these guys," he continues, gesturing at the booths around us, now almost entirely empty of players because the players hardly ever drink as often or as long as their coaches do. "Some of these guys, you know that they realize who they are. They're just waiting around for someone to tell them. And so soon someone will."

It's not as if this should be a surprise, this type of man or these words. There is loss to it all, a sensibility that makes for a stoic symphony, a man coming to terms with limits. The way I learned it and imagined it, there was some lovely honor to the solidarity of men pushing themselves as far as they could go, knowing it wasn't far enough, but leaving some mark with the effort. And now, again, I am back in my father's John R. Tunis books, *The Kid from Tomkinsville*, Dave the catcher in that book, old and stooped and smart and persevering and resigned. How do I remember that all so well? And one scene in particular: the young protagonist, the Kid, who has just won the pennant for his team, refusing to smile, refusing to celebrate, watching Dave, the old one, pulling off his jersey for the last time because things have finally run out for him. I remember that the shirt is wet and worn. I remember that Tunis wrote of the lines on his face, and I thought of a knife carving into stone and I wanted to be stone. I remember that the sentence beginning the next chapter was something like "The Kid missed him so bad." *So bad.* And my father's body next to mine as he read, the certainty of it being there, the words coming from his mouth that meant that things resonate even after they end.

But across the table from John Tamargo, who is real, even though he is all those tropes, grizzled and weary, a catcher, all I can do is wonder why he is here, fifty-eight years old and increasingly drunk at the

Pzazz! FunCity, making less a year, probably, than the manager of the Boogaloo Cafe and talking to me over a still-unwiped table, the waitress coming over to say that her shift is ending, if we want to keep it up, we need to sit at the bar.

He has a wife at home, he tells me. She is the same woman who married him when they were nineteen and bore him his first child when they were twenty-one and he was on the road someplace a lot like Burlington, Iowa. They have never been together for more than six months out of a year, and that is the only way they know how to love each other, the way their children were raised. John Tamargo Sr. begat John Tamargo Jr. this way, and John Tamargo Jr. made it to AAA and stalled out, never got the four home runs that his father did in major-league ballparks. He is coaching in the Midwest League now, too, and in a couple of months he'll be made interim manager of the Lansing Lugnuts, and he will lead his team to a win against his father, and a human interest article will run on MiLB.com calling John Tamargo Sr. a proud papa and quoting him saying that his son has been around baseball his whole life, knows nothing else. That he could make a pretty good manager someday.

John Tamargo Sr. is not done with this night, so I follow him to the bar. The Boogaloo Cafe is almost empty. Two blond men who look like brothers are laughing and shoving each other at one end of the bar. They are the only people here, aside from Phil Plantier, a former rising star with the Red Sox and, thus, one of the first athletes I remember having the power to make me, a five-year-old Yankees fan, hate him. The sight of him leaves me feeling starstruck and far drunker than I'd previously been. His major-league career ended quickly. He's a roving hitting instructor with the Mariners now, staying a few weeks in each minor-league town. He is spitting tobacco into an empty Corona bottle, trickles of brownish-green spit settling in his chapped lips. I don't want to see that.

Tamargo extends his hand to Plantier's still-formidable right shoulder and presents him to me with pride.

"*This,*" he says, "is my friend Phil Plantier. Hundred home runs in the bigs."

"Ninety-one," Phil Plantier says and spits.

. . .

The maddening thing with Hank is that it's impossible to say that his talent has run out or that he played himself out of the lineup. When he plays, he hits. And when he runs the bases, he is slow but determined, always getting dirty in that way that baseball celebrates above all else, always clapping his callused hands together when he stands on base and yelling, "*Sí, sí, sí*," so that his teammates, the fans who hardly recognize him, and even Tamargo on the bench smile. None of that matters.

He is lauded for being workmanlike, uncomplicated on the field. He plays according to the blunt maxims that Tamargo has been preaching all year. On a whiteboard, near the entrance to the locker room, is written, "JT's words of wisdom." The wisdom hasn't changed since the first game, because it's not being listened to.

"It ain't that complicated," the board still says. "See a fastball and swing the fucking bat."

Many fastballs have been seen, and many bats have been infuriatingly inert, to the point where even the drunkest, most casual of LumberKings fans have begun to make the connection that when a ball is pitched straight and fast and hits the catcher's mitt for a called strike, chances are Tamargo, in plain sight coaching third, will roll his eyes, slam his palms together, and mutter obscenities while waddling circles on the grass like some enraged, hypermasculine Charlie Chaplin. And then Hank, in the three games so far that he's played, gets up and hacks at the first pitch he sees, a vicious, flat line drive swing. And when he gets a hit, it's nice, it's extra. It's a surprise, even though it shouldn't be.

Potential is a seductive thing, and in the minors it can seem like the only thing. All of this here is geared toward the future. The present only matters in what it can promise for other teams, other places, and there are reminders of that fact that every fan wants to ignore, written into each game's lineup. James Jones, the fourth-round-pick outfielder who likes to put on a fifty-pound weighted vest before doing pull-ups, can be hitting .213, but when he connects, oh, man, everyone sees what *could* be. This dynamic is even more obvious with Steve Baron, that near millionaire. His team-worst batting average is inconsequential compared with his young, fast-twitching body that hasn't even filled out yet. In batting practice, Baron will be frustrated for rounds until one ball leaves his bat the right way, a smooth, rising line drive that somehow crashes off the right-field wall when it looked as if he didn't even swing that hard, and the coaches will all glance at each other, eyebrows up, thinking ahead.

I leaned on the batting cage and watched Hank take his swings before today's game. For him, it *was* the game; these would be his only swings of the day. Hank kept his knees slightly bent, bat slightly raised, ready. He produced grounders that hissed over third, low line drives that two-hopped the wall in left. I found myself clapping my hands together when he hit what might have been a double in a game that mattered, happy to see it and then instantly embarrassed about such a show of favoritism, such a reminder to all that I was there. But I wasn't the only one. His teammates called out to him. "*Vamos, Hanky*" from the Venezuelans, "Hanky Panky" from the Americans. Terry Pollreisz, the hitting coach who is the gentlest, most paternal of the staff, entered his own "Attaboy, Hankster" to the chorus.

He is the one who's easiest to root for, maybe because the expectations are low or because he isn't a threat to the careers that his teammates feel promised. Watching his swing, his good but not seismic line drives, I let myself fall into absurd thoughts about how, with a little more hard work, I could totally have been a pro ballplayer. Which is so insulting and delusional. There is no room for personal fantasy when I see a ball leap off Nick Franklin's bat and clear the high wooden wall in center by fifteen feet.

"Coming out," Hank said before his last swing of the day. He got an easy pitch and he swung up, unloading on the ball. The field erupted in "Ooooohs," which always happens when a hitter really tags one, as though everyone were worried about the abuse that poor ball just took. Mine and Hank's and thirty-odd other heads followed the ball, arcing high toward scattered clouds, its stitches still barely visible. Hank took a couple of steps down the first-base line and craned his neck forward as if that could have some effect.

The ball hit off the bottom of the fence in left center, rolled for a moment, and stopped. Tamargo called out, "Little man hit it," one of his standard punch lines any time a player comes up just short of a home run, but the words felt more loaded right then. Everyone still laughed.

· · ·

Phil Plantier is displeased, sitting at the bar of the Boogaloo Cafe, and his ire returns Tamargo to the mood he'd been in immediately after today's loss.

"I'm so goddamn frustrated," Plantier says. "It's so goddamn pathetic."

"Well, shit," Tamargo says.

They both swig whiskey.

My drunkenness becomes acute and unavoidable when balancing on a bar stool and remembering Phil Plantier's name at the same time proves difficult.

"Mr. Liambeer," I say and then realize that Bill Laimbeer is a former Detroit Piston's basketball player and is not anywhere near Pzazz! Fun-City tonight. "I mean, Mr. Plantier. What's frustrating?"

"Who the fuck is this?" Plantier says, and Tamargo tells him again. It doesn't improve his mood. He glares at me and spits again.

"What's frustrating?" he says. "We go find and overpay these children who can't put the bat on the ball. That's fucking frustrating."

He looks past me to Tamargo and continues. "I mean, you see it every fucking day with this guy. How do you deal with it? You tell him, 'Hey, maybe don't watch the first two pitches and then swing as hard as you can at a fucking curveball you can't hit.' He doesn't listen. It's not that hard."

He's talking about Sams, whose series of ugly swinging strikeouts was perhaps the most entertaining part of tonight's game.

"Are you talking about Sams?" I ask.

"Mind your own fucking business," Plantier says, and then, "What the fuck do you think?"

He and Tamargo fall into a conversation that feels so worn, so common for them that it's almost rehearsed. I imagine it repeated, honed in a lot of bars like this one, drunken agreement, commiseration, Plantier glowering, nasty yet proud, at the strangers who stare at him because they know they've seen him somewhere but they're not sure where. These two men have seen so much of the same thing. They are both still here. They don't know how to do anything else, really, how to be any other kind of person. Tamargo will freely admit that with a mixture of pride and wistfulness. It is so obvious. What would their conversation be other than what is wrong with this modern game, these players who are not them, whose careers they now have to serve? They remember themselves suffering more, playing harder and better, *earning* it, unlike how these boys under their care never have to.

"It's ridiculous the way it is now," Plantier says, like a parent at a PTA meeting. "We go to these countries, we watch these motherfuckers hit one good ball and watch them run fast, and, boom, we give them a million fucking American dollars."

Tamargo is quiet. He half nods and drinks. He is the son of Cuban immigrants, and both his childhood in Tampa and his life as a ballplayer were bilingual. He is acutely aware that after all his years playing, his major-league career and half century of baseball knowledge, his best professional asset is the fact that his Spanish is fluent and he can tell a Dominican prospect how to shorten his swing without translation. He is kind to foreign players, more than any old-guard guy I've come across. Sometimes I hear him make quiet jokes in Spanish that only they can laugh at, small intimacies that are tender and necessary. But he won't argue with Plantier, maybe because the solidarity is nice, maybe because Plantier was a better baseball player than he was and, even all these years later, that is the most important thing.

The bartender is a young woman with blue eyes and a small mouth whose work shirt is too tight and was probably given to her that way intentionally. She watches us because there's nobody else to watch. The baseball men call her sweetheart and ask her how old she is. They tell her she's too slow when she brings things. I wonder if she knows they're baseball men just by the confidence, the watches, the rings. How many Midwest League vets have been to the Boogaloo Cafe this season, staring at her body and telling her everything that she's doing wrong?

"JT, how old were you when you made the bigs?" Plantier asks.

"Twenty-two," Tamargo says. "And I was a catcher, remember. We take a little while. We've got a lot of things to learn."

"I was nineteen," Plantier says. "Some of these guys here are twenty-three, twenty-four, and they can't hit A-ball pitching?"

"It's true," Tamargo says.

"I got a seventeen-year-old son who could track that eighty-seven-mile-an-hour heater the guy had tonight, and our professional players can't," Plantier says and spits. "These aren't men. You can't call these men. These are fucking pussies."

This is the kind of conversation I always fantasized about hearing, even taking part in, though I could never figure out how. Voices hoarse from a lifetime of cigars and yelling commands, guys who've been around long enough to pine for better, purer days. But these aren't wistful words; they are biting and spoken too easily. In Plantier's nostalgia, there is an equal dose of xenophobia, so I focus my gaze on my fingers ripping apart yet another Budweiser label and try not to make an expression that suggests that I don't want to be around the great Phil Plantier anymore, that I'm shocked that he wouldn't care how loud or to whom he said these things, as though he's not saying anything wrong, as though nobody could think to disagree.

Once, in the late 1980s and early 1990s, Phil Plantier was Kalian Sams, the white American version. The better version, too. He was a big swinger who struck out too much, but in the major leagues, not in fucking Iowa. He was worth more. It seems so important to him that I know that, even though everyone already knows. I remember his batting stance, crouched so low he could touch the dirt with his fingers, how especially menacing a player he always seemed because of the torque of such a big body pressed in on itself, waiting to explode. But he is coaching Kalian Sams because he got injured and then he got old and nobody would pay him to play anymore. And, like almost everybody coaching these players, he didn't plan to spend his life developing others' talents while forgetting his own.

Phil Plantier probably has no idea who Hank Contreras is. He is paid to make the big investments pan out. He rages in bars about the likes of Sams and the infielders Gabriel Noriega and Mario Martinez because the team went to Venezuela and, in Sams's case, all the way to Holland and paid them market value. So every time Noriega grounds weakly to second because that body he was paid $800,000 for at sixteen hasn't filled out by nineteen the way people thought it would, those failures are both Plantier's job to fix and a slap in his underpaid American face. Hank fits into Plantier's general scorn, twenty-four, still here in Clinton, on this mediocre team, but he has done nothing to disappoint. He has done nothing.

"When I was in the minors, I knew I'd make it," Plantier says and finishes his drink. "Everybody knew I would. That was it. This team. You look around and see maybe one guy who has a shot to make it in the bigs. And we're still paying all these other pussies the bonuses."

Tamargo changes the subject to something happy, to the happiest thing.

"Man, you had a *swing*," he says.

"I had a fucking swing," Plantier agrees, and then he is finally silent for a moment. I see him stretching his fingers to their full length on the bar in front of him, as though preparing to do something.

"Tamargo," he says finally. "I'm gonna take a piss. Then, casino."

The Catfish Bend Casino at the heart of the Pzazz! FunCity is still bright as everything around it closes. I follow them over, but I don't go in, content to stand at the entrance and squint into the lights, listen to the babble of programmed video poker chatter. Tamargo surveys the room and lights a cigar. He sees some of his players and points at them in mock threat. He sees Dwight, his pitching coach, cowboy hat on, sucking down a cigarette at the blackjack table, looking as if he can't be real. He smiles.

His team is 21-20, almost as if the season never existed, the same way nearly three decades' worth of managing has been. He is in the Pzazz! FunCity, and some of the dealers are looking at the shine of his ring. Hank Contreras is upstairs, probably sleeping. In a week and a half, he will play again, go 1-4, but hit the ball hard each time. I will wonder if those four swings were worth it.

I have no money to gamble with, and I leave, begging that young bartender in her too-tight shirt for coffee in a to-go cup as she wipes down her station. I sip and try to sober up in the front seat of my hatchback, parked next to the team bus, the only evidence of the visitors who should theoretically flock to the Pzazz!, its never-ending expanse of fun bigger than everything else in this town other than the ammunitions factory. Gamblers make their way to their cars, all with Iowa plates like mine, most from this county. One woman is on a cell phone hollering, "I won, I won," and some other people are glaring in her direction because tonight it wasn't them. But they will be back tomorrow and their time will come and they will win.

The Collector

HOW MANY PEOPLE COME to a Class A minor-league baseball game? Say it averages out to a thousand. Multiply that by the hundred-plus games a year that Joyce attends at least for a few innings before she has to go to the casino, most at home in Clinton, some on the road at stadiums dotted around four landlocked states. Multiply that by fifteen, twenty years. And how many players? Twenty-five on a team at any given time, the rosters always shuffling, new bodies in old uniforms. The exact sum doesn't matter. The point is its huge, and that Joyce has seen all these people. She tries to greet them all, give them something, take something from them. She cannot be ignored. If you leave a Clinton LumberKings game early and you turn on 1390 KCLN, you will hear her if you know to listen, a little louder than the rest of the ambient noise, her hollered encouragement as much a part of the nightly soundscape as the bat crack and the commercial for the Clinton County Landfill.

Sometimes, I admit, I slouch in my chair when she yells, letting my shoulder blades dip below the top of stiff, plastic seats, bringing my hat brim to an exclusionary, acute angle, hiding my eyes and my nose, everything but my chin. No matter how many games I spend next to Joyce, I can't quite shake the self-consciousness I feel when half the stadium hears her and turns to look in our direction. But she, at least, doesn't seem to judge me for that. She responds not to action or inaction but to care. If you show up, then you care, and if you care, then it is unquestionable that you deserve to belong.

Joyce likes to wait until the rest of the crowd is silent before she yells—why waste needed energy on a cheer that will get swallowed up in a collective roar? And she yells phrases meant to be distinct. To Vinnie Catricala, the LumberKings' power-hitting left fielder, she yells, "Go,

Cat, go!" a reference to the nickname bestowed upon him by his team-mates *and* a rockabilly song released thirty-three years before his birth. He always hears her, looks over amused or terrified or angry, depending on the kind of game he's been having. But he always looks. And Joyce waves, and I slide down in my chair. The same goes for Tim "Timber" Morris and Mario "Go, Go, Mario" Martinez and, of course, Nick "Nick Franklin, You're *Hot*" Franklin.

Often, we are the only Clinton representatives to make the trip to away games, and so, Joyce says, it is up to us to make the rival fans remember. I pull my little blue Ford in to the lot in Burlington or Cedar Rapids or Davenport or Peoria or Appleton, and Joyce is there before me, always, smoking a Pall Mall, drinking a cherry Pepsi sheathed in a Louie the LumberKing cozy, smiling as she watches my air-conditioning fluid puddle on the hot asphalt beneath the car. She waves.

She's in her early fifties now, with long, graying hair and thin-rimmed glasses. Her face is round and her body compact, and she shouldn't be particularly noticeable. I wonder if she knows that. I wonder if she used to be the kind of toned, achingly hot groupie who made summer feel worthwhile. I squirm as I think it, because it is wrong to think. She doesn't have to have been a sexy stereotype to be allowed a personality here. But sometimes I hope that she was and imagine such a former version, because maybe a lineage of attention would give a clear reason to be at the games, calling out.

Rival fans shuffle past us through the gates. She grins and says, "We're coming for you." They squint, see her outline in the sun, denim skirt, oversized Louie the LumberKing T-shirt, Pall Malls, cherry Pepsi, and they recognize her. "Oh, it's *you*," they say, but they say it grinning. She jerks her thumb in their direction as they move away. "You see," she says, "they know." I nod.

She told me once about the strike that started in 1979, back when Archer Daniels Midland hadn't yet bought the corn syrup and ethanol plant and it was still Clinton Corn, back when the town's population hovered around thirty-five thousand. Joyce's people came to Clinton for work. Her grandfather and his brothers were Clinton factory laborers, and then her father and her uncles stayed on at the same factory. They came home smelling like something edible but not something you'd want to eat. And Joyce didn't like the way their hands looked, gnarled. "We are farmers here, basically," she told me. "Everybody farms something. It's just a matter of who you're farming for."

But that is a reaching, romantic way to put it. Because manufacturing isn't farming. Of course it isn't. Yes, the Clinton factory reaps Iowa's farm crops. Yes, I've seen the trucks full of thousands of acres' worth of harvested corn lining up to sell their wares. And, yes, I see the trains always rumbling out, sending that once-raw Iowa produce to the world. But it's not easy to think of individual farmers in that equation. Because even the farms that supply the mammoth appetite of ADM are, themselves, mammoth. Sometimes fans talk to me about the family farm that they once had, two hundred acres, self-sufficient. The ones who still farm do so on the side and only because it feels part of how they know themselves. They work full-time at factories to make the farming possible. Families like Joyce's came to work, never to own.

The strike seemed inconsequential until it resurfaced in so many of our conversations—the year the town became something loud and then quieted into a hush that hasn't ended. Joyce's family had lived just blocks from the factory in the neighborhood where most of the old Irish families had always lived and worked, then moved to a little nicer part of town. Everything was familiar, and then it wasn't. She could walk over and see the factory and the throngs, hundreds of men identical from a distance in jeans and boots and stained T-shirts, holding signs. She could see other men get out of trucks with out-of-state license plates and push through the picket line to take up new jobs. There were hundreds of workers coming, replacing nearly a thousand who had seemingly always been there but were soon to be squeezed out. She couldn't make out her father. Rocks were thrown; the police came. A few people got the shit beaten out of them, but it was hard to tell by whom. There were gunshots once, ringing out from somewhere in the middle of it all. The smoke rose above the scene, always, never a day when production was stalled.

That was thirty years ago, but it seems as if history stopped then. Or, rather, it seems as if the way things had been, were supposed to be, stopped. It was the beginning of what is now.

Joyce sings the harmony during the national anthem because everyone else sings the melody. That's how I noticed her first. A hoarse, lilting voice an octave below the rest.

"Who is that?" I asked Betty. Betty gave a warm smile.

"Oh, singing so loud?" she said. "That's Joyce."

It was April then, still cold, and I saw her breath as she sang. I'd heard about her before, always from men, never anything nice. On that snowy day in February, my first in town, Ted, the general manager, slugged down a Mountain Dew and said that if I was going to get to know the team, there would be some fans I would get to know, too, right ones and not-so-right ones. Joyce was an ever-present face of the not-so-right, a bitch on wheels and a psycho hellcat all in one breath. Joyce will always be around, he told me. Joyce is always wanting *things,* he told me.

I first spoke to her on the benches beyond the left-field fence, and I was wary. It was 4:00 p.m., batting practice, and we were the only people in the stadium not in uniform. She sat with eight or ten freshly gathered balls in a ring on the picnic table in front of her. She held one up for me and displayed a frayed bit of red seam dangling off it. She said Vinnie hit that one so hard that it started to unravel itself. She told me I could touch it if I wanted.

"Do you sell these balls?" I asked her.

I liked that she pursed her lips and wrinkled her forehead and looked full-on offended before saying no.

I'd already become annoyed by the kinds of opportunistic fans who elbowed for position above the dugout and then pretended as if they hadn't. Men, always, with piles of black three-ring binders at the ready and checklists of players' numbers organized into columns of "worth it" and "not worth it." I saw them daily, scurrying to snatch up whatever commerce could be taken from a twenty-year-old's promise, the scavengers of this ecosystem. When a first-round draft pick like Nick "Nick Franklin, You're *Hot*" Franklin walked by, I watched them ask him to sign eight identical cards, all of which would go on eBay. When brown-skinned Latinos in uniform walked by, I heard them call out a wrong name and then, when their target didn't turn around smiling dutifully, mutter about the highfalutin attitude of foreign prospects ruining America's game.

"Most of them are worthless," a fat man in a sweat suit told me once as he closed his binder, referring, I think, to both the cardboard rectangles and the men whose faces adorn them. "But some are worth a dollar, some two, and some can be worth a thousand, so you keep coming back."

No, Joyce shook her head at me. No, that's not the point.

When batting practice was over, the players trotted through the door in the left-field fence and headed down the path to the clubhouse, spikes clacking on concrete. Joyce cut a diagonal line toward them and intercepted Vinnie. She held up the ball with the frayed stitching, proof of his power—*look, look at what you did.*

He signed it in looping, practiced cursive, a huge *V,* a huge *C,* and then little sine waves in the middle. And his number, 43.

"I'll be here every game," Joyce told me after the players were all off-limits inside the clubhouse. "You can come sit with me during batting practice if you like."

She gave me one of the balls she'd picked from the grass, hit by Nick Franklin. A gift. She showed me the smudge of wood grain where the bat had connected, like a fingerprint.

Today, we're in Cedar Rapids, and Joyce is humming along to the pregame music piped from stadium speakers, country songs, all so instructive about how we should be. As she hums, Joyce surveys the players' numbers on the field. Thirty-three is here and 50 and 43 and 46, good, good, the players she likes still filling their assigned jerseys, no surprises, no covert, nighttime van rides to the airport, robbing her of a chance to say good-bye. And 3 is here, Nick Franklin, the best. Thank God.

But where is 14, Brian Moran, her favorite relief pitcher? She enlists my help, and we look together, running the tips of our fingers along the distant backs of the players, until it becomes impossible to ignore that there is no 14 in green and gray.

"I think he's gone, Joyce," I say, and then I regret how flat, how commonplace, I sound.

She finishes her cherry Pepsi with a loud gulp. She begins to nod her head, slowly at first, then progressively faster, building up affirmative steam.

"Good," she says finally, a hard word to get out. "Good. Good. He deserved to move up. He had such a funky delivery. Do you remember?"

Nostalgia has never been so instant. In this type of fandom, providing unrelenting support and the occasional baked good at the starting point in the trajectory of careers, things end fast. Things move by. If you don't grip hard to the moments that happened in front of you, if you can't quantify them, then they're gone. Brian Moran will never come back to Iowa, barring a major career collapse on his end. His promise will propel him forward, maybe into the major leagues, probably not. Either way, he is no longer flesh here. He is already a story to covet and mold.

Do you remember? Do you remember?

In Joyce's notebook, there is the beginning of a draft of a letter that was supposed to be the first in a series. It begins with "Dear Brian." So far, it ends with "I like the Beatles, but I also like ZZ Top. What kind of music do you like?" There was supposed to be more. It was supposed to begin a pen pal relationship in preparation for the day when Brian Moran left, but Brian Moran has already left, and he never wrote down his address. "Facebook me," was the last thing he said to her, called out over his shoulder as he trotted to the clubhouse a few days ago.

No, no, that's not the point.

There used to be a tin shed behind the stadium. If you got up there, you could stand and watch the whole game for free. Joyce and her brother could get there on their own. They could walk from their home in south Clinton, a mile down Second Street, right on Sixth Avenue North, as if blindfolded, stopping at the right moments, subconsciously measuring steps and knowing they were close when they smelled low tide off the river and heard the hollow pop of baseballs burrowing into old leather.

On top of the shed, older boys jostled for position to see the game and then past it, the town, their neighborhood, the factories, the river, Illinois to the east, and the suggestion of all the other states beyond it, laid out next to one another like patches of fresh sod.

Joyce was going to climb up. And she was scared of heights. But even ground-bound, she managed to watch. She stood alone, fingers gripping chain link, peering through a gap to see the players. And she didn't feel closed-in like she usually did, like a bird caught in flypaper in the summertime, so much moving and flapping, losing feathers and going nowhere.

I imagine her there watching, when she tells me about it. I imagine her shrunken down, unwrinkled, seeing the smoke, thinking of her father cleaning the petrified edges of corn syrup tanks with an old broom handle. She smiled when she looked at the field and the men in white uniforms, bleached every night, gleaming like teeth right after you come back from the dentist.

There are two Cedar Rapids Kernels players whom Joyce hasn't yet propositioned for an autograph. They're new to the squad. Two budding stars have been moved up to AA-ball in Arkansas, and these are their replacements. Joyce bolts for the home dugout seven minutes before the game begins. I hold her bag and shuffle behind her, watching her broad, rounded shoulders dip and shimmy through the rows.

When she reaches her destination, she glances back as I try to catch up. Speed is crucial. Some players will look for any pause or slackened body language as an excuse to flee. It seems that after spring training, the thrill of being sought out and cooed at and commodified wears off, and the players grow instantaneously world-weary, so damn tired of these overeager rubes squawking their names. But some stay nice. You can't tell until you meet them. So you have to rush your pens and your keepsakes into their hands just to make sure. Joyce needs a ball.

Finally reaching her, I rummage through her purse, shaped and designed like a baseball, for one of twelve baseballs that have been stored within. We picked them together last week behind the left-field fence, like careful farmers. She reaches out to the young men below her on the field. They are polite ones. They ask her name. "Joyce," she says. "Joyce. Oh, you'll know me soon enough." They smile and they shrug and they sign. "The complete set," she says.

I used to want to be obsessed. Obsession, particularly with something odd or something past, felt like a badge of personhood. It was noble, careful. My brother was obsessed with über-masculine German folktales, so he bought them as instructions for how to be, tried to read them in their native tongue. He was obsessed with music, with listening to things nobody else listened to. So he saved records and mixed tapes, racked in immaculate order, even when everything else began to dissolve. It was pride I felt when, after the funeral, I was the one who laid claim to all his former possessions. But then I ignored his record player until it broke, threw his records and storybooks in a sloppy pile in storage, along with all the other gifts that I never cared for, that I left behind. I did not have it in me to appreciate what all the saved things meant.

Maybe that's why I feel nervous sometimes next to Joyce, yet surprisingly loving other times. I want a mania that feels noble and scholarly, the kind of obsession that comes to those with the capacity to see the importance of what might otherwise seem mundane. A legacy that I want to think I was born into, the way I have always imagined every person with a deeper sensitivity to the world to be.

"It is a pleasant thing to sit here, this rainy afternoon, with the books and the 'collection' close at hand," Adrian Joline wrote in 1902 in *Meditations of an Autograph Collector*. "I have certainly been arranging that collection for ten years, and it is not arranged yet."

I like that he doesn't sound crazy, just precise.

After I first met Joyce that day on the benches beyond left field, I drove home and watched a marathon of *Hoarders,* the reality show about pack rats. I ate a whole bag of pita chips, condescendingly enthralled by the directionless mania on-screen. People, mostly women with missing teeth, wailed at the camera and ran their hands through cracked, caked, arbitrary garbage as if it were tillable earth. Pet carcasses were discovered. Lives that had become forgettable in the accumulation of stuff. This was beyond sensitivity. Look at the freaks. I wondered if this was how I should categorize Joyce, the fierce dedication in her blue eyes, her dead front tooth left unfixed.

But that was before I really watched her, when the misogynistic warnings about her were still fresh in my mind. That was before I saw how little was arbitrary in her actions. How delicately she approached each morsel of memorabilia. There was care to everything, and thought. Like a true collector, I've begun to think, Joyce musters up affection for each saved name and object. Like Joline's books. Like my brother's old Abba records with the chicken-scratch notes still taped on: *Every song is just a little bit flat. That's what makes it work.* It's not so much the keeping as the breathing of significance into the boredom of what is kept.

All these afternoons together and I've begun to study, maybe fetishize, the work involved in assuming the importance of baseballs and signed names, especially in a world that is easily distracted and increasingly digital. I see her swimming upstream. There is always, to the collector, something new to threaten her pursuit.

Bored at his lawyer's desk in Princeton, New Jersey, a century and a thousand miles from this Clinton, Joline wrote: "The type-writing machine is the discourager of autograph enterprise, the grave of artistic collecting, the tomb of ambition." And in this stodgy pride, I see Joyce. She doesn't Facebook Brian Moran or any other ballplayer, the way so many fans do. And she hasn't bought a cell phone or set up an e-mail account just to have the fleeting satisfaction of flippant digital messages from players, saying, "thx for the support, ttyl maybe." That dilutes the care, the craft of possessing a tangible piece of history. Of holding a part of the game until you, still holding tight, have made it resonate.

After the season, Brian Moran and Nick Franklin and some others will stop texting and will drop their public Facebook accounts. Nick will change his number. Joyce alone, clutching discarded equipment and permanent ink, will be the chronicler of their time in Clinton.

Joyce's father was never a noisemaker or a rabble-rouser, whatever you want to call it. And neither were her uncles. Or her brother. Joyce sang at the breakfast table.

Fathers were always around in 1980, during the strike. In Clinton, a town built on an endless cycle of production, the old cliché of a high school degree and then the next day a union card, like all the Springsteen songs I love and half-understand, this was chaos. How demeaning it must have been when the strike continued and fathers stood in the kitchen scrubbing breakfast dishes with stooped heads, their gnarled hands holding Brillo pads and tea saucers.

The impermanence felt so cruel and made Joyce's father and the other men who were around now at two in the afternoon grumble. When did seniority and dedication and patience cease to mean anything? That was a question worth asking. There had been, the union leaders said, a "social contract" by which the company and the workers had peacefully coexisted, with promotion coming from inside the ranks and reasonable benefits going unquestioned. And then it ended, so quick and flat, but to fight it, to be loud, was going nowhere. And by June, nearly a year after the strike began, when the voices of protest grew more panicked, less sure, a memo from the company lay open on the coffee table, blandly stating that temporary strikebreakers, the men whose Tennessee and Missouri plates stood out in every parking lot, were to become "permanent replacement workers."

Joyce thought, I'm never going to work in a factory.

She has brought me her writing today, professionally copied on thick white stock, bound with clear plastic on the front and red plastic on the back. She has had so many muses, two decades' worth of lithe, remarkable young men in white jerseys and green hats. Boys otherwise forgotten. She calls some of her pieces stories and some poems and some letters, but all of them, I think, are odes. The players get a copy if she can find them when she's done. She asks them to sign the original and send it back.

On the field, Erasmo Ramírez strikes out the last batter of the first inning and bounces off the mound back to the dugout.

"Attaboy, *E-mo!*" Joyce yells.

She leans into me.

"Maybe he'll get a story," she says. "E-mo. That's a good name for a story. Who knows. There are so many things that I want to say, you know?"

I wipe nacho grease off my hands and flip through her pages. A story about the tallest umpire in Midwest League history. A story about the LumberKings first, brave batgirl. A tribute in couplets to some superstud named Chad Tracy, who, three years after his star turn in Clinton, still hasn't played a game in the majors. It ends, "And when you make it, like I know you will, all the way to the Show/Perhaps these words will hang in Cooperstown—hey, you never know."

I tap her shoulder and say, "I like this one."

"Hey, yeah," she agrees. "It's good."

She has turned her attention away from the action, focusing on the relief pitchers, a tangle of legs splayed, spitting sunflower seed shells in the bullpen along the left-field fence. Brian Moran would have been third from the end, probably, next to his buddy Cooper. She would have been able to see his smile because he was so tall and he smiled so big. His spot has been filled by a boy from Arizona with a frowning, acne-pocked face.

"Did you know Moran pitched for North Carolina?" she says. "He was the best relief pitcher in all of college. It helps he's a lefty. Did you know it helps you as a pitcher if you're a lefty?"

A man with a strawberry-blond crew cut and his two boys with strawberry-blond crew cuts turn around from the row in front of us to look at Joyce, this rasping, unending monologue of minor-league baseball knowledge. She straightens up and peers down at the boys.

"Do you want an autograph?" she asks. They stare back, blank. Their father stares, angry more than blank. He takes a swig of his beer.

"Do you want an autograph?" she repeats. "I can get you one. You want one?"

The little boy nods, and the bigger one shrugs.

"Why?" the bigger one asks.

"Because then you have it," she says.

She roots into her bag and finds a newly signed baseball. She holds it out, and I stare at its peculiarities, the small things I notice now that I watch games with her. There are gossamer fingerprints in smudges of dirt. And bruises from bats, chalk from baselines.

There are, I think, many things that she wants to tell this strawberry-blond family. *Look. Look at everything that makes this baseball unlike any other one.* And then the name goes on top of it, the swoop of a *G,* how an *S* can become an underline, the way a player will write his Class A number next to his signature as though it will come to define him, as though this arbitrary assignment will be the number that he makes famous in the majors. And then there's the teasing possibility that it might actually work out that way.

The inning is over, and Joyce half leaps from her seat.

"Vinnie!" she calls. "Vinnie! Vinnie! A ball for the kid?"

He flicks one with easy assurance, doesn't watch it into her hands.

She presents it to the boys. The younger one grabs it, and the older one shrugs.

"Keep this," she says.

Joyce became a dealer at the casino boat moored on the Mississippi River in Clinton, right beyond the outfield fence. This was before the Wild Rose outgrew the boat and built an expansive new home on the edge of town. It was in 1991, that year again. The end point of the steepest drop in the steady drop that would continue through the present. It came a full, depressing census report after the strike, when her father lost along with the rest of the union, ducked his head, ceased his protest quietly, and returned to the factory, only to get hurt on the job and have to find new work as a janitor at a coupon warehouse. A decade after the Local 6 Grain Millers were disbanded and 750 people who shouted for what they deserved never got their jobs back, many, like Joyce's brother moving out of state for good. A decade after everything went quiet and the media vans left and the Communist Party stopped sending in supporters, and it became abundantly clear that Angela Davis would not be coming back to town to give another speech.

Nothing significant had happened since. Nothing was gained. Archer Daniels Midland now owned the factory, bought it pretty soon after the labor force was disorganized. The plant still looked the same from the outside, just a little bigger and newer with fewer people working it. All the white wooden houses looked the same, too, the only difference being that more of them had gone empty.

Iowa had just become the first state to pass riverboat gambling legislation in an effort to save its river towns that were losing people and industry. The chance to win brings in those who want to. The Lumber-Kings happened to be winning. Maybe that was a good sign, too.

A dealer's hands are specialized hands. They move in a way other hands can't.

Four decks of cards flowed in a cascading wave with the flick of her wrist and then back. Farmers said, "My God, look at Joyce's hands moving." And the music overhead. And the water below her feet, the tide tugging like the line could just break and she would no longer be moored. And the ballplayers who came in after games, how you could always tell them by their cologne and collared shirts, their rigid posture, boys who never let themselves sink into a couch or forget what day it was. I imagine them smiling at her, saying, "Man, look at those hands." I imagine them signing cocktail napkins before they left.

Once she was going to deal on cruise ships. She drove down to Galveston and began to call it her home for a few months. She woke up every day and saw the gulf expanding in front of her, cleaned ships when they docked, planned to stay working on them when they departed, until her grandmother died and she spent all her money getting back to Iowa. She thought she might go again, to somewhere, but she didn't. She is now the senior-most nonmanagerial employee of the very-landlocked Wild Rose. There is no current underneath her, no chance of floating away.

In the fifth inning, Nick Franklin gets a hold of an inside curveball that didn't curve. He takes his long, exaggerated step and then yanks, his still-growing shoulders helicoptering the bat into the ball, into the air, into the parking lot over the right-field fence.

We stand.

"Nick Franklin, you're *hot!*" Joyce screams.

The strawberry-blond family turns again.

I can tell what the father thinks. That this is some expected case of women in love with baseball. It's the movie image of jock groupies that he saw in *Bull Durham* and that his sons can find in *Summer Catch*: they take the boys home, rub at their sore, naked bodies, cook them something soulful, fuck them and mother them all at once. But there is no permanence in that. Carnal connections are fleeting. Unless of course there is a baby, unintended permanence. It happens. As one fan put it to me, with a smirk, "This is a lily-white town. You see a girl who looks like she was once pretty with a mulatto baby, you sort of know what happened."

No, I want to say on Joyce's behalf. No, that's not the point.

She flips through the program for today's game and finds Nick Franklin's home run total. He's at fifteen already. Eight more and he'll surpass the franchise record. I am often amazed at her memory, and now, as though the fact had been waiting in her mind to leap out, Joyce informs everyone in earshot that the record hasn't been broken since Dick Kenworthy set it in 1961. Kenworthy died in April, in obscurity outside Kansas City—I don't know how she knows.

"Can you imagine, a race for his record the year that he's gone?" Joyce says. "And you and me, right now, we're saying his name, we're remembering him."

"I'm going to write a story," she says. "'Nick and Dick.' Is that a good title? It's going to be about a skinny boy chasing a record that's older than him."

It hasn't cooled off, and I feel sweat molding my thighs to my shorts to my chair. The game seems to halt entirely as young pitchers get wild and look panicked, their managers trudging onto the field to calm them down. And so we sit and melt while they pace around the mound.

"You tired?" Joyce asks me.

"No." I try to sit up. "No. It's just, I want to get home."

"Oh, I never want it to end," she says. "It's the lasting that makes the game."

I stifle a yawn. I feel bad when I yawn around her.

"Did I ever tell you about the rain delay in Burlington?" she asks, after a pause.

Yes.

"No."

"Nine hours. I was the only one stayed."

She tells me about it until the game ends and the LumberKings win. Then we walk as if there's no other place we could be going, down to the exit by the visitors' clubhouse, waiting for them. Joyce readies everything that can be signed and can be written with—blue pen, red pen, notebook, hat, three baseballs, and a Nick Franklin card. He comes out last, as always, because he's the best and he's nineteen, so he likes to test the limits of what the best can get away with. I stand a few paces back and watch their bodies close as Joyce rushes over to him.

"Hi, Nicky," she says.

He smiles. "Hi, Joyce."

"That's cool about Moran, huh?"

"Huh? Oh yeah, cool."

They wait in silence for a while, and I can hear her red pen in his hand, scraping over a plethora of surfaces with nonchalance. I see Joyce bounce back and forth on the balls of her feet.

"You might break the record," she blurts out. "Dick Kenworthy's home run record. Did you know?"

She has her hands clasped in front of her chest, looking up at him.

"I had no idea," he says. "Oh, man. Joyce, you've got the best memory of anyone I've ever met."

They smile for a moment, and then he gets on the bus. Joyce and I walk to our cars to drive home. She puts her inventory back into her bag. She looks happy. The baseball that Nick Franklin signed will be placed prominently in a collection of 850 that sit in plastic cases along the walls of her house, each with a different name on it.

She will drive home alone, singing the harmony to whatever is on the radio. It's an hour and a half back to Clinton, along Highway 30, running her wipers even when it isn't raining because the corn sweats at night and everything is fog. People have said for years, "Joyce, Joyce, it shouldn't be one woman alone in that old car, in the middle of the night. What if you break down or get lost or drift too far?" I like the pride in her face whenever she waves her hand at these people and walks away. It's the same as when some kid laughs at her baseball bag, the weight tugging at her torso. Or when she hears whispers about that kooky, gray-haired lady in the oversized T-shirt wasting her time yelling at every game.

To blend in and make sense is not the point.

"No one will ever be as fond of my pets as I have been," Joline admitted in the conclusion to his manifesto a century ago. "And at no distant day they will be scattered among the bidders."

He held out hope that even as his own attachments with the signatures and letters faded, he would leave a legacy in how he curated them, how he kept what was important. Joyce doesn't expect to leave Clinton anymore. I asked her once what will happen to her collection, all of it, the stories and letters and names. She has a nephew who loves the stadium, she told me, maybe it will go to him. And then maybe to somebody else. It should stay in Clinton. You never know if the team will always be in town. Things leave. And now, as big cities like Dayton snatch up A-ball teams, as Clinton shrinks, the LumberKings are the smallest market in all of full-season minor-league baseball. She says this with pride and also worry.

Maybe her material will serve as a reminder of all that happened here, who played, who watched them.

A few weeks later, I sit in the offices of the Clinton Labor Congress, which used to be its own building, a massive, arched temple, and is now a side room of the local Democratic Party offices, across from a cash-for-gold storefront and a Pizza Hut. The strike was broken in June 1980. By July, with the largest local in town gone, the labor congress couldn't pay upkeep or property tax for their offices. So the collection of eighty-year-old bricks in the heart of downtown, used for the same purpose even longer than the stadium down the street, was sold to a private developer.

A man named Bob is explaining to me that he's one of the few who keeps coming. He is the secretary of the Labor Congress that Joyce's father used to be a part of, like everyone else. There were thirty-five thousand people in this town and 119 local unions. Now there are twenty-six thousand and 4.

"After the strike," he says, "after we lost, people just stopped wanting to make noise for themselves, stopped wanting to hold on to our identity. So we shriveled."

I ask him if he remembers Joyce's father. He shakes his head.

"It's hard to remember," he says. "In this town, I think, it's easy to forget."

Outside the window, the factory funnels smoke up into the low gray clouds, until it looks like the chimneys are creating the sky. Joyce, I know, is at the stadium, perched on the benches in left field, watching batting practice. She isn't looking at the sky. Surrounded by her notebooks and her pens, her baseballs, she's looking at the players limbering up, moving in their newly washed whites, gleaming like they always have.

Next summer, when I travel to Venezuela to trace the lives of players before they showed up in Clinton, she is a lingering presence there, impossible to forget whenever I'm watching baseball. And in Venezuela, I'm always watching baseball in the shadow of a factory, so the connection is even stronger. Polar Beer, Latin America's most popular brewing company, built a thirty-million-dollar sports performance center—a pasture of perfect fields directly adjacent to the enormous steel facility where the beer is made, all off a two-lane rural road. And Firestone tires, a longtime American presence in Venezuela, built a complex in the urban sprawl around Valencia, a few blocks away from where a major-league prospect will be kidnapped for ransom a week after I leave. Everybody congregates under the Firestone sign for games. Fathers scream, agents watch, boys compete.

It starts pouring as I'm watching the most intense all-male softball game I've ever seen. It's the kind of flash thunderstorm that can't be played through, that turns the infield into mud even as the players flee for shelter. Everybody crams into the dugouts. The bleachers and concession stands aren't covered, so fans, family, scouts, those just passing by, we all take refuge with the players. We all stare at the Firestone sign through the rain, listen to the sound of water off the impenetrable metal of the factory. Joyce would love to see this. Joyce would love to be among these people, baseball people all, not one rushing for his car, but waiting it out until the rain stops and the game finishes before morning. All the softball players once imagined they were going to be baseball prospects. Some of them were. Now, probably, none of them are, but they play biweekly and everybody watches.

I don't know how far Joyce would travel for baseball if she could. If she had the money, would she fly to the World Series, or would that be too much, too distant and overwhelming? She is still, after all, afraid of heights. What I do know, shivering, wet, is that when I get back to Iowa, I will drive to Joyce's home and she will be exactly where she was the last time I saw her. She will ask me if I was scared all the way out there, alone. Yes. That's what I'll say. Her eyes will get big. She will be interested but not jealous, not fawning either over where I've been. It's about carving out space. You can run off and try to push to do something wild, to set your exaggerated stories all over the world. But somebody has to stay and remember.

How They Go

WELINGTON DOTEL IS WAITING for me to get the pitching machine right. I'm turning the crank, adjusting angle and velocity, and he is waiting for me because he has to. Welington Dotel wants extra batting practice, and there is no reason for a coach to attend to him because he will not be hitting in the game tonight, nor has he for a week and a half. So when the starters clear out to shine cleats, pine tar bats, flex bodies, and when the coaches leave to groan into their office chairs, pull at their loose skin while they call their wives, I am the only one left.

Months later, I will realize that my appeal was, is, rooted in my complete naïveté, the fact that I could ask him with a smiling, sincere face, "You excited to get back in the lineup?" And he could respond with charming cheer in his gentle rasp, "Oh yeah, I'll be ready." And there wouldn't be any of that awkwardness born when people talk around what they know to be true. So he asks me to be his assistant, and I blush. I think of how I'll describe the details of assistanthood to everyone else in the stands and the way he claps my back with his big, callused right hand, smiling as he dubs me *Amigo,* a title that I hold up to the legacy of Sancho Panza.

He practices his swing now as I crank, humming to himself, barely audible over the industrial ceiling fans. I catch him looking toward the door to the clubhouse. I ask him if he wants to wait for someone else. He says no.

Dotel has had to rush ever since he became a professional baseball player. After all, he was signed at eighteen, quite late for a Dominican. A Venezuelan agent will tell me that the rule of thumb in Latin America is that if someone wasn't signed at sixteen, you have to wonder what the problem was and if it persisted. And signed at sixteen means getting an agent at fourteen, being on his radar before your sophomore year of high school, or what you would have been had you not dropped out, which you probably had by then. Welington Dotel was too thin at sixteen, underdeveloped, not worth it. It was only later that he sprouted, six feet one inch, chiseled, with power on his résumé as well as the speed that had always been there, but an irreversible two years behind his friends.

He is nearing twenty-five now, one of the few players older than I am on the team. He was signed in 2006 in his home state of Baoruco, when I was quitting college baseball with no consequences to the decision other than shame, when Nick Franklin was entering high school and his favorite subject was English and he liked to go waterskiing on the weekends.

Welington looks like a man, more so than any of his teammates, which is odd to say, considering the six-foot-six relief pitchers and bruising power hitters with whom he shares a clubhouse. Their appeal, unlike his, is how unfinished they seem. They have "body projections," as the same agent will describe them to me, worth gambling on. Body projections are what the experts get paid for. A giant already but hardly a beard on him—how much taller can he get? Rail skinny now, but look at those broad shoulders. How much muscle could be hung on that frame? In Latin America, agents and scouts meet parents to see how tall they are, study the hands of prospects, their feet, how wispy and unfinished their peach fuzz is. In the majors, you might see a finished product. Every other place is about making. And what can be added to Welington Dotel, at this point, to make him better?

"Perfect," he tells me as I feed a ball to the machine and it shoots into the rubber mat, belt high. He smiles, the smile that he has learned makes people like him, kind, confident, and nervous all at once. I watch his fingers wrap around the handle of his maple bat, choking up a little, swaying. Like Hank, he swings hard at every ball, with an almost dangerous amount of torque. Even standing behind a screen, I duck and blink every time he makes contact.

"I won't hurt you, my man," he says, smiling as though it would actually be pretty cool if he did.

As a boy, I was preached stillness at the plate because that's how my father was taught, and the type A lawyers who always coach Little League in well-off neighborhoods, too. As though there were some strong display of mental focus in the ability to be stiff. It was the Latin players on TV who first wagged or spun their bats, who stomped their feet to what I assumed to be an internal rhythm while waiting for the ball. It created that sense of swagger that we were so quickly taught to associate with them—cocky, loose, raw. *Natural*, that was the best word. These exotic creatures, born with spring in their muscles, with a lust for physical competition, were *natural* ballplayers. That was the story I spun as an overmatched outsider on a predominantly Dominican travel team, the one I most loved to share with undersized white friends.

"Dude, Francisco—that's my coach's name, *Francisco*—he told me I needed to have a little more Dominican in me."

"What?"

"Like, be cool when I play, you know. Be calm, be confident, be slick."

"*Badass*."

And badass, too, were the stories about traveling to tournaments where suburban white coaches claimed that birth certificates needed to be checked because what seventeen-year-old is cut like that, while in the crowd local girls pretended to root for the home team but gripped the chain-link fence hard as they watched these questioned foreigners beat the shit out of their boyfriends and brothers. I watched, too.

I never once felt in competition with the Dominican kids from neighborhoods I never saw beyond baseball diamonds, only the other white players. While we were all teammates, there were two distinct types of showcase happening. The fight by the marginally talented collection of Bretts and Andrews looking to show off baseball intangibles and well-tutored SAT scores to college coaches was nothing like the sexy, boom-or-bust talent that seemed to dance in the infield—*so loose!*—and had long ago promised their mothers that they would pull them out of a condition of living that I would never understand, and how could they not keep that promise with all their God-given skill?

Welington Dotel plays with that smiling, easily stereotyped abandon, and thus everybody likes to smile back at him. The white players remembered him from spring training and seasons past and parroted him before he even arrived, adding a shrill, absurd quality to otherwise boring warm-ups.

"*Soda!*" they screamed in overdone accents from the outfield, a reference to Dotel's apparently boundless, childlike enthusiasm for sugary drinks.

"Nice!" they shrieked when a player did something good in batting practice, Dotel's favorite American phrase that, in their versions, became something like the throwaway line of an ethnic neighbor in a seventies sitcom.

Dotel doesn't seem to mind in the locker room when they do impressions of him, at him. He performs their impressions back at them, mostly, bringing his voice up an octave to match their parody, though lately there have been moments when he's gone quiet, nodding into his bare chest when teammates address him.

The machine spins an old, frayed ball out, and Dotel lifts his left leg high, shifts his wrists down, loading before he springs. It should, I know, as most casual observers would know, slow his swing down, all this movement, and make him late to the ball. But the bat whips quickly, and the barrel meets the ball with a satisfying crack. The ball is headed for my face, and I drop to the ground as it hits the metal skeleton of the screen and rolls back at Dotel. He picks it up and looks at it as though he hasn't seen it before.

"Nice," he says.

Matt, the mailman, the most critical of the season-ticket holders, who attributes his strict standards to his army training, has never once criticized Welington Dotel, and that is an accomplishment. Matt has, in fact, taken to calling him "Sir Welington" and doffing his cap whenever Dotel trots in from the outfield. Matt tells those of us who sit near him that it's only men of Sir Welington's character, one he sees as defined by hustle and relentless cheer, who make it to the Show. Matt screams the same message to Dotel's teammates, though to them it is an unearned fatherly chiding: "Sir Welington is getting dirty like he wants to make it to the Show."

Matt has not read the articles, long hidden in Google holes now, about Dotel's fifty-game suspension for his attempts to push his body projection. I wonder if Dotel knows that I know. He has to be suspicious, watching me watch him. I hope he doesn't think I am digging, looking for needle tracks on the smooth, hard flesh of his ass when he exits the shower and pads naked across the locker room, the way my father used to look for tracks on my brother's arm over the table at a

Chinese restaurant, not to say "*Aha*," just to quietly confirm suspicions that would never go away.

At least Dotel's pockmarks would be productive, making him more of the kind of man he wants to be. In late 2006, at twenty, he was suspended for testing positive for steroids, one of 249 minor leaguers who quietly lost a chunk of their almost careers while we fans watched the morality trials of the twenty-five major leaguers who were caught, calling talk radio programs to opine about the devolution of American values. I won't even know about all these Dotel specifics until a year from now, reading L. John Wertheim and Tobias Moskowitz's *Why We Win: The Hidden Influences Behind How Sports Are Played*. Dotel never tells me that I'm not the first writer to come asking questions, that as he tries to explain to me all the things that make him special as a player and a man, a behavioral economist is asserting that "the true face of the steriod era? It might look a lot like the smiling mug of Welington Dotel."

But for now. Thunk, swish, crack, ping. There is a rhythm to us. I lose track of how many times we repeat the process, each of his swings sending hissing line drives back into the screen. He will not step out of the batter's box, will not de-focus except for the fraction of a second after he catches one just right and turns to the door as if he heard someone come in, even though nobody has.

We finish the balls.

"Thank you," he says to me. "Thank you. You are my man."

We scoop up the balls in handfuls and toss them in an old shopping cart, bend, toss, bend, toss, as if we're harvesting something. He holds up his right hand to display four balls held, with relative ease, tucked in between his fingers, because he thinks I'll like that. He's right. I show that I can't quite hold three with the sausage fingers that my father swears were the main thing that kept me from being great, blaming himself for the genetic sabotage. Dotel smiles at that. He holds his hand up, and I realize that it is an invitation to touch, to compare, and that brings a current of titillation, though I'm not sure exactly why. We press together, and he wins and smiles.

It is that time when things really begin to change, the middle of the season. Since I'm new to this story, it is hard at first to recognize that no one is guaranteed to stay put. Nothing is permanent. The first guy who left got moved up—Dennis Raben, a slugging first baseman. Tamargo announced it in the clubhouse after a win, and I was the only one surprised.

"Good game," he barked. "Oh, and say good-bye to Raben."

All eyes turned to him, so huge, almost glowing with his farmer's tan. He smiled, which meant the good kind of good-bye. I thought they might mob him; he was well liked, jovial. But something close to a reception line formed. His teammates were stiff, shy. His closest friends, Jones, Catricala, Brandon Bantz, gave him quick hugs, tousled his hair a little. Nick Franklin, who had taken to calling Raben "Dad," put both hands on the larger, older man's shoulders and looked uncomfortable. Raben told him he'd see him soon.

Everyone else shook his hand. Danny, Hank, Sams, all in a row, each saying something forced like "Yeah, brother" and then glancing down. A bunch of pitchers who seemed to realize at the same time that they'd hardly ever spoken to Raben went up to pay their respects.

"How does it feel?" I asked him at the end of the procession, that most ridicule-worthy of sports questions that is, often, the only thing I can think of.

"Crazy," he said. "I've never moved up before."

He looked around the room at a bunch of young men who never had either. They looked back at him, realizing that. Tamargo, who had moved up plenty long ago, gave a short wave, said, "Well," let it linger there, and left.

I don't remember Welington Dotel saying a word to Dennis Raben that night. He may have been the only one not to say anything, not out of dislike, I don't think, but what to say? He stood, framed in his locker, naked, looking straight ahead at the clothes that he'd hung neatly, his deodorant, body spray, lotion, cologne, watch, BlackBerry, family picture, lined up across an eye-level shelf. I remember thinking how little space he needed, how little conversation or eye contact, anything beyond a locker with the dimensions of his body.

"Where is Dotel?"

"What?"

"Dotel?"

"Oh."

Sams makes a gesture with his head, up and away, over there. Sams is walking off the field after a dismal batting practice, face knotted in some mixture of confusion and rage. He is holding a bat still, occasionally glancing at it as though the wood were to blame. He does not want to talk.

I glance to where his head directs me. Players walking in clumps to the clubhouse, some laughing, none of them Dotel. The center-field wall. The smoke rising from smokestacks unretired and out of sight.

"No," he says, the way one would say it to a dog. "He's gone. Too many outfielders on this team."

"I was watching him take batting practice yesterday," I say, whining a little.

Like, *Say it ain't so, Joe.*

Like, *Come back, Shane.*

"Yeah," Sams says, at least a little happy.

I imagine that Dotel's release was, at least, spoken in Spanish because Tamargo would have the ability and the tact to do so. You should not have to strain to figure out the last words you hear from an organization, nodding when you're not quite sure what to do. And I imagine, no, I know, that Dotel took the whole situation in with the silent grace that a fan would want him to have.

I asked Tamargo once, "Do they yell at you? Do they cry?"

No, they do not cry. And that is a rather stupid question. There is no rage, either. Even the throwing of a chair or of a punch is somehow unmanly in this context, and everything that these men have been taught about how to be takes hold, instinctively. Still, I don't understand how someone can smash his plastic helmet on the cement of the dugout floor until it cracks as a response to hitting a fly ball to center instead of a home run, but repress every instinct to make noise one last time when he is told that he is insufficient, when it is ended.

From my first arrival in the clubhouse, ducking away from all the proud, nude men, I have wanted to see the act of their demise. I can say, and all the fans can say, that the draw of watching pro sports at this level has to do with watching someone realize how great he is, witnessing his baby successes, feeling intimately happy for him and then somehow connected to his happiness, if only through proximity. And that's kind of true. But ultimately, I can turn on *SportsCenter* for immediate and distilled transcendence. And victory, in someone else's games and someone else's life, can't sustain interest on its own. No, I have that opposite urge, too, more visceral and satisfying. I like that I can be up close to watch powerful people be rendered into nothing more than anyone else, a kind of bloodless snuff film.

"You can't see that," Tamargo told me early on, and I sulked a little, and he glared.

I am glad now that I didn't get to see the moment Dotel was cut. He is a real person discarded. And I don't want to have seen him trying not to fold into his folding chair. Or to be present for the car ride to Quad Cities International, two duffel bags in the trunk, a bag of bats next to me in the backseat, BJ, the trainer, driving in silence, all of us focusing our attention on the sunrise that hasn't yet come. Nothing about the scene would have been unexpected. And I would have sat there hoping for a crack that would never appear.

"He knew," Tamargo tells me. "Of course he knew."

Did he? Or maybe the better question is, what did he know? He hadn't played in twelve days, I know he knew that. He counted. But the way he smiled. The confidence with which he hit the last ball of the day, each day, heard it ping and leave a dent in the metal cage. The way he said, "I'm ready, I will stay ready," and the way it was true. The way he always spoke in *whens*, never once a nod to the precarious nature of his assumptions.

My wife is pregnant. She's a good girl. She's waiting. When I get to Seattle, it will all be perfect. You know the schools where the kids wear suit jackets—that will be where my child goes.

And on his last day, when Pollreisz opened up the door to the batting cage, interrupted his fantasy of a little boy named Dotel junior wearing a prep school blazer, he went back to hit again.

"I've got ten minutes for you," Pollreisz said. "You too tired?"

And he said, "No way, not me, come on." And Pollreisz said, "Attababy."

They simulated a game. Pollreisz barked out the fantasy. *One out, two strikes, man on first.* Dotel waited, slapped a grounder that maybe would have skipped past the second baseman if this wasn't just a room with Astroturf flooring, green mesh, broken chairs, the husks of sunflower seeds spit-stuck to the walls. Then hit and run, then sac fly, finally swing away, Dotel catching the ball cleanly, dropping his bat, and watching his shot as though it could travel through the ceiling.

"Catch that, Asshole," Pollreisz said, Asshole being the name of the hypothetical opposing outfielder whom he likes to conjure when one of his players does something well in simulation. Dotel laughed. They stood together, and Pollreisz said to me, "What do you think, partner, is he ready?"

"Ready," I said.

"Ready," Dotel said.

And Pollreisz was the proud coach, slapping his prized stag's chest. And I was the admirer, believing. And Dotel was the player, loose and hulking, preordained to perform.

That was yesterday afternoon, and it felt sincere. Maybe it was sincere; maybe nobody was fooling anybody or being fooled or being lied to or professionally cuckolded. You do not stay in the game if you do not automatically react to adversity by keeping faith. Terry Pollreisz is a sixty-three-year-old man who showers in a group and wears pants with elastic waistbands at work. He crams wads of original flavor tobacco behind his lower lip, spits as though the act of spitting indoors still gets him a little high. He wears cowboy boots to his car after the game. He believes, vocally, heartily, in *goodness,* in people's indefatigable ability to *earn* things. Never mind that he would be standing by the door hearing Dotel's soft good-bye in six hours: Is a man not entitled a chance to work? And Dotel, with his idol's smile, his pride, his blistered palms from day upon stubborn day of extra practice—was that muscle memory or just denial? Was it admirable, the consciously constructed last image of himself working, the need to be remembered as such? Or was it that there was nothing else to do but swing?

He told me that tomorrow he would hit a home run and then we would talk about it, how he knew it was going to happen. He walked out the back door to the parking lot to call his wife, the patient one waiting to bear him a child who would know only opulence. The last I saw of Dotel came from a distance. He was leaning against the outside cement wall of the batting practice building, underneath the paintings of faceless white men in old-timey uniforms with calf-length stirrups, and those ever-bland, ever-cruel words, *Field of Dreams,* painted there as a dramatic finishing touch to the 2006 stadium renovation. Maybe he wasn't looking at anything; maybe he was just still for a moment, content. He was facing the riverboat, freshly painted, never moving. And today is tomorrow and he's gone.

Written into Midwest League rules are two distinct seasons, a second chance every year. To prevent teams from being entirely out of contention by June, the standings begin again after the all-star break. The first and second place teams from each half qualify for a play-off berth, so, unless a team is terrible all year, it's got a decent shot at finding something to play for. It's like bowling with bumpers. Such a forgiving system makes the value of each game less, each half as crucial, which is why it is hardly ever talked about, I think, the way the good trophies on windowsills are arranged to block the ones that say "Most Improved Player" engraved on a fake-gold plate. Clinton's disappointing first half simply spawns a disavowing of the recent past and a resilient hope for the near future.

Matt, the mailman, is sitting a few rows back, in the shade, because people worry about him fainting when the direct sunlight of full-on summer mixes with Old Style Light, a big body, and the general stresses of passionate fandom. He yells louder, and it seems to hang in the humidity, not amplified, just lingering. He is furious that Welington Dotel is not here, that the rest of these slow-moving, heat-fearing slackers are still on the field nearest his home while Welington Dotel has been insulted with exile.

"*This* is what I have been saying," he hollers, eyes straight ahead, everything *this*. "We go and give away Sir Welington, the best damn leadoff hitter we've got, a guy who should be playing center field in the Show."

He won't be. But perhaps he deserves to be. And even if that's not exactly true, he certainly deserves to have somebody claim it.

The players glare up at Matt, and he glares back. Their goal is so indelibly not a mutual one now, each betrayed, the players incredulous that they could be chided by strangers for not getting dirty enough, as dirty as a guy already deemed unworthy by the organization. The fans just as disbelieving that sometimes the players not trying the hardest for them are the ones left. Matt Cerione, trotting in from center, feels the sting of being underappreciated by someone whose sole purpose at the field is supposed to be appreciating him. He is so much *better* than those watching, and clearly better than Dotel. How could this fat prick have the balls to not want him? But Matt, the mailman, is positive that he knows what this team needs. He has been here longer than any player, assessing talent for more seasons than most of the front-office staff. It comes down to the fan's dilemma, easily ignorable until moments like this. His irrelevance. In a few weeks' time, this tension will boil over when Cerione trots after a double, doesn't gallop the way Danny maybe would have, the way Dotel would have for sure. And the mailman will be leaning over the railing telling him everything that's wrong with how he plays, how he lives, telling him that those who don't run hard don't make it. And Matt Cerione will say, "You don't know anything, you fat fuck. You bitch. You fat fucking bitch."

Mailman Matt will deflate into his seat. Cerione will disappear into the dugout, the sound of his muffled expletives buzzing through concrete.

A few days earlier on a highway in North Dakota, Dan, Tammy's husband, had a heart attack, had time at least to call 911 before slumping against the giant gearshift of his truck in a ditch as the sun went down. So that is something *real,* and we in the stands had been talking about how the first thing he asked for in the hospital when he regained consciousness was a cigarette and how scary addiction is, and how God reveals himself in the spaces between life and death. Heavy stuff. Also, there was a stampede at a parade in nearby Miles, and skittish show horses stomped on twenty-four people and Deb *saw* it, her daughter *saw* it, and how do you get a kid to forget that? Also, there's Julie's son, getting ready to head back to Afghanistan. And Cindy's husband, the bomb defuser, already over there and with something different in him now that makes him not want to come back.

But those things are distanced, an ache, not a stab. The shattering of the unspoken alliance between bleachers and field, the permeable but still present wall extending up from the top of the dugout, that is what will really hurt. The loss of the time that people claim to remember when fans wouldn't have been made to feel shame. And Mailman Matt will get patted on his ample back, hear whispers of "That was out of order" and "There wouldn't be a game without fans like you." And hours later in the clubhouse, Cerione will sit on the trainer's table, his body sore from the pains of a season, and he will talk about the lack of care for him, about playing for the fans, leaving it all out on the field for *them*. How can people be so unappreciative?

I will hear both and think that maybe both are right.

So tensions are high.

At least Hank gets to play a little more now, a rebirth in the making, maybe, or a first birth, the shedding of a cocoon. Steve Baron and his abysmal batting average have left, sent down to Everett to do some growing up. It's just Hank and Brandon Bantz, ordinary and persevering, entering their mid-twenties, splitting time behind the plate. Think Costner's Crash Davis or Robert De Niro from *Bang the Drum Slowly*. That's what I am thinking at least. They are on the field together in Cedar Rapids before the game, identical except for skin color, talking with a lovable, weary humor. They've been hitting. Hank two days ago, a hard grounder down the third-base line, driving in two. And Bantz yesterday, a double in the left-center-field gap, a triumphant dirt cloud rising as he slid into second.

It's Hank's turn today, mostly because Erasmo is pitching and it helps him to have a guy mumbling Spanish back at him during mound visits. But no matter, he will perform. I will watch. Hank and Erasmo stand on the bullpen mound and laugh together. Hank pulls his mask off and wipes the sweat from his dark, quiet eyes. I find him, in the most ridiculously meaningful sense of the word, heroic.

I have forgotten about Dotel. Everyone has. Hank, five feet away, readying himself to perform, fills the void for me, though *void* is too strong a word. Hank is here.

The team returns to the locker room, and Hank tapes his forearms. Then Hank and Erasmo leave the rest of them early, return down the cement hallway toward the light of the dugout, their spikes scraping, at first a staggered noise, then in unison. *Clackety-clackety-clack.*

Clack-clack, clackety-clack. Clack-clack, clackety-clack. Their spikes sounded like music on the concrete floor.

It was a chorus in all the books that my father read to me, *Keystone*

Kids, The Kid from Tomkinsville, The Kid Comes Back, World Series, marking the end of moments of action on the field, announcing reflection. When I first bought cleats, oversized and unnecessarily metal, I wore them down the street to get milk, listening to the sound of me on the sidewalk trumpeting my presence, trying to conjure childhood memories from the old Italian men sitting on folding chairs outside the Laundromat, wheezing totems of what I thought manhood should be.

I sit next to them now, Erasmo and Hank, in the dugout. They drink water and speak as though I'm not there, and I am happy for that, catching the odd word of Spanish, smiling as they laugh just because they're laughing, which, I realize only now, they hardly ever do. Erasmo is a giggler. When something is really funny, his eyes widen and creases like parentheses snake across his round cheeks. The sound of a still-pubescent nerd escapes, a gurgle almost, a squeak. He puts his hand on Hank's shoulder, says, "*Coño, Diablo.*" I begin to laugh, too, like a child at Thanksgiving who doesn't get the joke but loves the unhinged feeling at the table. It isn't hard to see them as the next logical step in American baseball lore, not from small towns in the middle of cornfields, but from Mexican L.A. and Central America, still looking the part of well-worn fables, dugout shadow across their faces, youthful and grown-up all at once, sitting close on a long, empty bench.

Terry Pollreisz pops his head out from the hallway, shoves tobacco behind his lower lip.

"*Hola,*" he says, and they smile at his effort.

He shuffles over to us, hunched. He tells me to leave. Hank looks frightened and then hopeful and then nods before anything has been said.

I don't leave. I linger by the doorway. Pollreisz's kind growl gets silenced in the space between, but I see him smile with his browned teeth. I see the white of his knuckles as he kneads his catcher's shoulder harder than usual. I hear Erasmo say, "*Lo siento.*" I see him give his former teammate a half hug, arm across Hank's back but body pulling away, unsure, the moment they touch.

Erasmo walks over to me, gives me a little shove.

"We go," he says.

We go. Back down the cement hallway, his cleats clacking alone now, a scattered and weak sound. Erasmo runs his hand along the cinder-block wall. He will not initiate this conversation. I begin to ask, "What just—"

He cuts me off, a swipe of his hand across the throat—done, over, isn't it obvious?

It isn't, but the subtleties are not something Erasmo wants to talk about. Hank hasn't been cut, not like Dotel, but it feels like it. He has been sent, with compliments, to the purgatory of rookie ball, meant for prospects just signed, half a season of games in which they can dip their toes into professional waters. Hank has been sent there to be the backup to more eighteen-year-olds who have talent that he never will. It is doubtful he'll be back. Hank is told, "They need you."

These are things I know about athletes:

Player X worked fourteen hours a day on a watermelon plantation as a teen. No wonder he got so strong.

When you take a raft from Cuba, staring at circling shark fins, the World Series doesn't feel like much pressure.

This guy was just about to quit and go work on the assembly line next to his father, but then fate intervened.

From the grocery store to the Big Show.

He knows his father is seeing him succeed, even though his father is blind after that meth lab fire.

Returning to that village, no longer a starving fisherman's son, he gives out brand-new gloves and tells toothless children, "You could be the next me."

I don't remember which player was in which story, which sport even, which Bob Costas rain delay special informed me. I do remember crying at most of them.

He, He, He, He. Came from nothing. Suffered. Won.

"Don't talk to him about it," Erasmo tells me, the first time I've ever heard him be didactic. "It is no point to talk about."

When I sneak back toward the dugout, sneakers noiseless in the concrete tunnel, Hank and Pollreisz are still standing together, still touching. They're on the grass by third, looking out. They are, both of them, pantomiming. Swings, throws. Hank catches an invisible ball, transfers it to his throwing hand, pretends to nab a base-stealer in slow, absent-minded progression. Teens rake the dirt, ignoring them. AC/DC is play-ing over the speakers, Brian Johnson proudly proclaiming, "*I've got big balls,*" and the teenagers are laughing at that, making pantomimes of their own, pretending to lug testicles the shape and weight of a pair of cantaloupes. Above the left-field fence, an intern starts the hot tub, where drunk, young, possibly attractive people will watch the game tonight. It sounds like an outboard motor, and Hank and Pollreisz jerk their heads up to look. Hank isn't talking. He is standing straight, unmoving, seems to be concentrating all his energy on that. Eventually, Pollreisz says, "All right, pal?" because it's time to get ready for the game and this moment has to end.

Pollreisz walks past me, gives a suspicious glance, but still calls me "partner" anyway. Hank trails, dragging his spikes through the dirt. We leave the dirt, enter the tunnel.

Clackety-clack. Clack-clack. Then we stop.

"You'll be back," I say, hearing how false it sounds.

"Nah," he says. And then, objectively, "Well, maybe, but probably not."

When Hank walks in the locker room, everyone looks at him. He sits against the wall nearest the door, at his locker between Bantz and Danny. Jones is standing there, too, discussing testimony. A member of the Cedar Rapids grounds crew walked up to him after batting practice and asked for permission to testify.

"He said he saw a YouTube video of me from spring training talking about Jesus," Jones tells everyone. "He was, like, waiting to talk to me."

"Were you creeped out?" I ask.

He and Bantz don't glare; they just pity me.

"No," he says. "It's not creepy to hear faith."

They tell me the groundskeeper confessed to being a bad man, drunk and misguided, a waste of God's love. And then he saw something, that light, and he was saved, and he'd been working the dirt hard at baseball games ever since. He was going to be a grandfather soon. He wanted to tell it all, and Jones was the kind who had the chance to spread his story among the still faithless.

"Amen," the players say now.

Hank is putting on his shin guards, not looking up. Hank gestures that he needs to clean his cleats and is handed the spray. He works them over until the black leather is almost soaked, blacker than before. He

wipes all six inch-long spikes carefully, flicks excess dirt off his finger-
nails and onto the floor. He knocks them against the cement wall. *Clack.*

Jones spreads his long fingers over the middle of Hank's back, kneads
him a little.

Bantz is next, flanks him, grabs his hair, shoves the back of his head.

"Don't be sulking," he says, and they all laugh.

It's an after-school special. It's the black kid from Brooklyn, the former captain of the Dallas Baptist Patriots, and Hank, second-generation
Mexican, living out his father's most impossible aspirations while his
father toils in the vanity orange trees in wealthy people's Pasadena
backyards, paid cash for hard labor. The connecting thread is this work
ethic, something inarguably good and American. Hank doesn't want
any of it now. He cuts his laugh short and shrugs his shoulders, flinging
off the condescending hands.

"I'm done," he says.

"Done what?" Incredulous and smiling, even though they know
exactly.

"I'm out. I'm going home."

"No," they tell him.

"This is just one little thing," Danny says.

"It's weak to lose faith over something like this." That's Jones.

Bantz completes it: "Stay believing," less Journey, more New
Testament.

"I'm *twenty-four* fucking years old," Hank hisses, louder than he
wanted to say it. His teammates pull back in unison.

Danny manages a "So?"

"I'm fucking twenty-four and I'm supposed to start over?"

I think this the only context in the world where that statement doesn't
sound like a joke.

"Don't do that," Jones says.

"*Why?*" Hank's voice cracks, and the room is stilled. Some teammates
look over; some look away.

He stops himself. He lets the hands return to his back, bows his head,
and absorbs the kind dishonesty.

"You're all good, old man," Jones says, and all four of them laugh into
one another, Hank's eyes still on the ground. He suits up because he will
play tonight, even though any ember of consequence has been taken

from his performance. He could play to a level that he's never achieved, and still there is no way that he will play here tomorrow.

Hank announces, in an attempt at bravado, that he will get two hits tonight. This is met with unanimous approval, quiet but heartfelt, the way stern grandfathers shake hands in the important moments of life. It feels like a eulogy. Something mythic. Dave, old Dave, from *The Kid from Tomkinsville*. Or De Niro in *Bang the Drum Slowly,* ending in sad triumph as Michael Moriarty intones, "From here on out, I'm never gonna rag anybody." Or Kevin Costner in *Bull Durham,* finally done with playing, content to settle in a good town with a good woman, that expected, treacly conclusion. But that character set a record and got the girl and then he walked off, disappointment softened by glory. And that character could famously debate the merits of Sontag and tell long, looping stories about his wild life because that was the point, he was a baseball player but also something more. I have always loved the idea of losing when beauty is gained from the loss, when there is deep, orchestral consequence to what is ending.

Hank must believe in those things, too, or else he wouldn't have shined his cleats up. But real failure is muted and swift, especially in the minor leagues, especially at this level. There are no options to it, no metaphor attached. No wisdom to be gained.

This doesn't mean anything, Hank. I want to tell him that. This is something staged, constructed to be redemptive, so that there is a kind feeling with you in the middle seat on the 5:00 a.m. flight to Pulaski, Virginia.

I watch him play from the stands, sitting up for his at bats as always.

I lean over to Joyce, who is, of course, present, and say, "Hank is gonna be sent down."

She looks out at him. "Mmm, yeah. Seems like it should be about time. I don't have him yet. Remind me to get him before he leaves."

We will wait for him after the game, I know, and Joyce will grab his arm before he gets on the bus, ask for his signature on a ball, tell him he's been wonderful, tell him good luck. He will give a sardonic smile for the benefit of his teammates, but this might be the most appreciated request that Joyce will make all year, a memento for her wall, third row, fifth column under the big window by her kitchen table, the section reserved for those who still technically have a chance.

Hank and I are the same age. I have never thought of myself as old. In fact, my happiest thoughts, the ones that I force in at least once a day, revolve around youth, around the notion that whatever is happening now, I am incomplete. When I talk with the few younger fans, we talk about everything with open ends, no borders, a summer watching and then who knows? That is the appeal, or part of it. It dulls for three hours, sometimes four when the pitchers are wild, any feelings about anything outside the boundaries of one game, a drunkenness that extends beyond the cheap beer—a game as of yet untold, a life, then, that is in no hurry. It is a gift that the players give us, a sense of urgency that is theirs alone to shoulder.

In the first at bat of what may be his last game as an A-ball player, Hank swings at the first pitch. He slashes it, a line drive over third, slides safely into second, the LumberKings' first hit of the game. He is applauded harder than usual by his teammates. He scores on a single up the middle, sliding once again, dirt-adorned as he trots back to the dugout, having tied the game at one. In his third at bat of the day, he muscles a grounder over the bag, a probable out with a better third baseman, but no matter. He got his two hits. He's a man of his word. Freeze. It should be over. This is the moment he wanted.

He comes up in the ninth. Jones is on first, there are no outs, the LumberKings are losing 5–3. He gets ahead in the count. He gets a lucky, meaty mistake of a pitch. It is waiting for him, and he swings too hard. He grounds out.

He will propose to his girlfriend, he knows that much, when he is done playing. He will finish college in South Central L.A., the same Cal State satellite school where he started. Maybe he'll get it done in a year or two, working with his dad full-time trimming hedges. Eventually, he will be a cop. He likes uniforms and order, so he will be a cop. He will save. He will buy a house near his parents. There are worse things. Welington Dotel has nothing else, beyond unaffiliated independent ball and perhaps a winter stint in the Mexican League, no country that is fully his anymore, no written English, no high school diploma, never worked a job other than the one he just lost. But to be here, to be good enough to not quite hang on in an A-ball squad for one of the worst major-league organizations in baseball, you need to have embraced rigid, single-minded optimism. The kind that makes any other option so hollow and pointless that it hurts.

Hank is wearing his blue-and-white-checked collared shirt coming out of the locker room. He is wearing black jeans, black sneakers. His hair is gelled, and the wind, hard tonight, does not move it. He drags his bat bag across the parking lot, the heaviest piece of luggage that he will bring to the airport. Joyce moves, stands by his shoulder, as I knew she would, calls him Henry, asks him to leave ink behind, asks him with reverence.

I am glad that I resist the temptation to tell Hank everything about myself in the twenty paces he takes between the door to the visitors' locker room and the bus. And it is a strong temptation, because he will be gone and because he seems, even as he doesn't want to, so bare that he should be met with some unburdening in return. I am drifting, Hank. And I think that I am ill equipped. I find it difficult to think of life as anything other than loss, and I know that sounds big, too big, but it's true.

I want to tell Hank that I've been thinking about the term *nostalgia*, the root of it. How I learned that the word originated when a graduate student mixed the Greek word *nostos*, "return to the native land," with *algos*, "suffering, grief." I want to tell him that it was born to describe mercenaries who traveled Europe for a job until they weren't sure what they missed, that it was classified as fatal. I want to ask him, Isn't that crazy, Hank? To die from wanting to return. I want to tell him that I miss things that were never mine, want to return to a place, more of a feeling, that never really existed, and doesn't baseball always promise that there was once something purer?

I like you because you are sturdy, Hank, and there is supposed to be poetry, holiness, other overblown paeans to the way a dependable catcher is always squatting for some other guy's benefit. And maybe you were told that, too, so you live it. You were never not sacrificial.

"I'll see you soon," I tell him.

"Write about me," he says.

"Use my name," he says.

The Middle

It's HOT. We say that to each other four or five times. Danny is in his workout clothes—black shorts, black LumberKings T-shirt. He wants to take the shirt off, lean his bare skin against the wooden picnic benches, pretend he's at the beach, pretend the Mississippi is the Pacific and this is his summer after high school. He's not allowed to—*look like a god-damn professional*—so he settles on rolling his shirtsleeves up above his shoulders and pulling the bottom of his shirt above his abs, letting the sun hit some skin at least, running his fingers along the muscle mounds that cover him effortlessly. Muscles are a small comfort in the face of today's slight. The all-star game rosters have been released—Nick Franklin, Erasmo, two other LumberKings. Not Danny. He isn't angry, he says. He won't say that he's sad, either, because sadness is, well, too sad. It's just a bit unfair, is all. And, man, it's hot today.

There is a game to play: seven o'clock start time, nothing unusual. But the quiet and routine boredom hangs heavier, feels like smoke, thick, black, and chemical, with a smell and a taste. Danny smiles at a ginger teenager in too-short shorts passing by to set up the concession stands.

"Hey, do you think I could get a Pepsi?"

She turns in a hurry, looks at Danny and then the ground, says, "Yeah."

"Like for free? And you'll bring it to me?"

He knows that she'll do it, they both do. She smiles into her chest, says yeah again, walks off, her body clenched as she forces herself not to move too fast, returning with twenty-four ounces for him, asking, "Is that too much ice?" This is a perk.

Danny's wife, Chelsea, is down the street at the public pool. She does that a lot, lies by the pool during the many hours when he's at the park and she's not allowed to be. She moved here once it became apparent

Danny wasn't getting called up to High-A anytime soon. Now there is a limit to the different ways she can fill an afternoon. Sometimes she has lunch with a group of girls who lust after Danny's teammates or with her dowdy host mother and the host mother's church friends. Then most of the time she comes to the field early, drinks iced tea, sits in her California girl cutoff shorts, and lets her legs stretch across rows of empty plastic seats. When Betty and the others shuffle in and say, "Hi, dear," she hugs them and agrees, "Gosh, it's hot."

I have spent a lot of time with Chelsea because she is always there waiting and so am I. Other wives and girlfriends, mostly girlfriends, come and go, but she is the constant, committed fully and daily. Committed not just to Danny but to all of this: wifedom, fidelity, baseball, sacrifice, God, positivity, smiling. She seems like a missionary of sorts, a Mormon pamphleteer, far from home and with a job to do. She walks into the stadium both a part of it and above it, an outsider willing to be happy here.

She is told she is beautiful, every day, God, Chelsea, you look beautiful, because she always does, tanned skin, just enough of it there for us to see, not too much, jangling bracelets, intricate sandals with leather that snakes up her calves and makes everyone else tuck their flip-flops back under their seats. She responds with "Thanks" and "You're *too* nice" and "Cheer for Danny tonight." Everyone does. She makes rounds through the pockets of loyal fans during every game, ending up next to Betty and Tim, all of us, while people pull out photographs of Danny looking clean and ready and powerful, showing his image back to her the way she wants to see it.

Danny runs through his numbers that Chelsea has already reminded me of—batting in the high .270s, a surprising eight home runs, and, most important, second in the Midwest League in steals, a ranking that would be higher if Danny played every day. He tells me that now, outright, more outright than any player has been with me: *If they let me play every day, I'm the best leadoff hitter in this league.* He nods once, fast, punctuating the sentiment. He sounds very close to believing it. I agree. He smiles at me, not quite trusting.

Then he veers off, brings the conversation somewhere nicer, lying flat on the picnic bench, looking straight up at the sky. He's telling me that story again, the one about when he was eighteen, which was only three years ago, but he tells it with distance in his voice. He doesn't address the money outright, but it's there, more than $300,000 the summer after high school, paying for a sweet car and money for his parents, covering a big chunk of his older brother's college tuition, which made him feel so awesomely benevolent. And then he went to short-season rookie ball in Arizona, tore the place up as if everybody else were moving in slow motion, stuck in the mud. He proposed to Chelsea and they married, and they went to Hawaii for six weeks. He played invite-only fall tournaments during the mornings, and then they lay on the beach and talked about how there was nowhere else they had to be, so comfortably alone, tossing each other into oncoming waves, collapsing gleefully into the sand.

I heard this story yesterday from Chelsea, sitting at this same bench, waiting for Danny to get dressed after the game. Same details, the beach, the warmth, Danny's on-field success, as if nobody was capable of stopping him from becoming who he wanted to be. Same tone, same panic underneath the perfect memories. Same quiet, unsure anger, both feeling let down, cheated for the first time.

Danny sits up, slurps his Pepsi like a little boy, greedy, easily sated for an instant and then not at all. He feels, or reaches to express feeling, which is what I would do, what most people I know would do, and that lack of complete stoicism, his willingness to at least voice hurt, is a relief on this day when the first half's best have been decided and announced. Sometimes the drone of suppressed emotion can be the most unforgiving aspect of the clubhouse. So many things happening to these players, so much stubborn silence. Sitting next to a young man, raw and bruised, I think of a baseball camp I went to a month after my brother died. I think of the men who coached me there, the water bottles they filled with spit, the cup checks they conducted, strolling through the lines of players in the morning, picking crotches at random, and bringing the handle of the bat up to clip the bottom of the sack, the undefended boy shrieking and then nodding when informed, "Now you will come to the field prepared."

I remember in pregame warm-ups when one boy called another boy a faggot and then a third boy with big, wet eyes, not me, said, "Don't do that. That's an awful thing to call someone." I remember the boy with the big, wet eyes running laps while our coach yelled, "Shut the fuck

up and don't ever act like you're better than your teammates again."
Despite the baseball played there, camp was something not comforting,
something truly frightening, a place that was meant to hurt me. And
it was the first time I had ever played badly, leaping away from inside
pitches, apologizing to teammates for mistakes, and then apologizing
when told not to apologize. At night, I read *Harry Potter* with a flash-
light under my comforter, didn't fall asleep, but still dreamed of the
ability to become invisible, the ability to bring those unjustly lost back
to life. Before my coaches told me as much, it was then under the covers that I began to allow for the realization that there was something
hysterical and needy in me that could never be an athlete in the way I'd
been taught to believe I could. That easy tears *did* somehow correlate
with an inability to win.

Danny is not that boy, of course, not thirteen and in a pubescent,
mourning free fall, not taking asthma breaks during wind sprints or
making secret calls home to be told he *is* good. But in a locker room
rigid with the absence of outward doubt or fear or melancholy, he is the
closest thing. He is that someone who cannot help but express that he
wants more, a cardinal sin in both Dickensian orphanages and minor-
league baseball clubhouses.

He begins to describe feeling small. Or not so much small, but less.
He tries to piece together why he isn't an all-star, and I'm glad that I can
be a yes-man for him right now, my presence like his wife's or parents',
or Betty's or Joyce's, those dedicated to the idea of him and without the
need to be impartial. Yes, .280 is pretty darn good. Yes, nobody is faster
than he is. Yes, I watch him every day. I see him run like nobody else.
Other people should see it, too.

Erasmo is an all-star. He is the only starting pitcher from Clinton to
get the distinction. In the clubhouse, the other starters, all friends, are
playing cards and unloading a torrent of mutual complaint. Erasmo
is not a part of that conversation, nor is he celebrating with his Venezuelan friends, because they, too, have not been recognized. Erasmo is
alone, his laptop warming bare knees. He is looking at the same pictures
of himself that he always looks at, this time under fresh headlines that
call him "all-star." His Facebook page is up, covered now in Spanglish
messages from Nicaraguan journalists who want the first quote about
his achievement.

Erasmo gets no bonus for his all-star inclusion, nor does it guarantee anything other than a lack of a rest. Still, he is elated. He is an all-star in America. The game is to be played six hours away, and the team hasn't paid for bus or plane tickets. Nick Franklin will drive the two other American-born all-stars, bass thumping out of his car, slick lines cooed at teenage girls at rest stops, briefly free from any responsibility. Erasmo will get a ride from Ted, the general manager he's never spoken to, sitting in the backseat with Ted's tween son, flicking his eyes back and forth to their conversation. But none of that, the kid, the smell of strangers' farts in a closed vehicle, the endless miles of drive-thrus and corn, will rob him of the feeling of expansive, crescendoing satisfaction.

Erasmo is a pleasant surprise. Low overhead, easy upkeep, the unsqueakiest of wheels.

Tamargo told me just the other day, pointing at his best pitcher running sprints alone, *"You'll see him in the bigs someday."* If so, he will be the greatest kind of investment, a career maker for whatever low-level scout first saw him. Fifty grand up front, with no negotiation, no other options. Two years in Venezuela, cheap room and board with a small salary, moving up to the United States ahead of schedule. And he'll keep moving up, never dominant enough at any level to get a big head about it. Special attention, personal trainers, psychological counseling, these extra resources will not be necessary for a boy who never feels comfortable speaking beyond his responsibilities, describing himself as anything other than one of many. Give up less, get out more. That's the ideal.

Archer Daniels Midland picked up a town that needed lifting. The company turned it into a town less dying than it had been, and so the town is tied to it, pulled tighter with each construction project and tax break. It is not a unique relationship between power and weakness, I know, just easily visualized here, the way that lives can so casually be lived in the shadow of an institution or an idea or both.

The strikers and Clinton Corn sapped the life out of the town, out of thousands of lives ultimately. Even before the massive corporate structure of ADM found root in Clinton, the strike organizers noted how Clinton Corn was a part of Standard Brands, a conglomerate controlled by J. P. Morgan in New York, and how the powers that be within the company had become "increasingly remote." The strikers encouraged all Clinton residents, all their people, to boycott what their town helped make, a list of fifty-three products—Planters peanuts, Baby Ruth candy bars, Royal cheesecake, Acadian Canadian whiskey, Dr. Ballard's pet food, Jujubes, Blue Bonnet margarine. And on and on, seeming like everything you could ever think to ingest.

The products were still made, of course, only this time by non-union workers willing to walk through pickets to a job because, in a poor area, even lowered, non-guaranteed factory salaries are better than you can find anywhere else. Those striking workers who refused to give in were driven away, or they collapsed and went back after too many unemployed months. And within a year of the strike's end, Standard Brands had merged with Nabisco. And by 1982, the factory was losing money and had given up on Clinton, and sold the plant that it had fought so hard to control to ADM. ADM drastically cut the numbers of workers, poured money into new buildings, newer machines. ADM grew.

Clinton, unlike most towns of its size, isn't anything close to a square or even a fat, lopsided circle. Clinton is close to ten miles long and never more than a few miles wide, a sliver of brick and smoke packed tight in between the river and a state's worth of farm. Its survival and identity are defined by what can be done with the commodities on this little strip. Look at a map of Clinton, zoom in, zoom in more, and see how the block of buildings connected with tunnels and tracks that make up the ADM factory has swollen into a tangible presence among the rest of the sprawl, a proportion that makes me think of the scale of a figure drawing, head on body.

The head is eating the body. Over two hundred homes have been lost in south Clinton. Eminent domain was never actually used to take people's houses, but the residents had no reason not to know they were being forced out. The company and the city government did successfully petition an Iowa court to approve the legality of eminent domain in this instance. The threat was there, and that was all that mattered. I spoke to south Clinton residents who said that the men in suits who walked door-to-door like Jehovah's Witnesses, except frowning, shook hands, promised a small sum, told homeowners they should embrace a gesture toward choice over a total lack of it.

So it became an issue of what their homes, some that had been their parents' homes and their parents' before that, were worth and who would make that determination.

Forty thousand dollars. That's what I'm told many of the first houses were appraised at. The deals were quick and quiet, so it's hard to know for sure.

There was a second round of buyouts, the offers increasing a little, more incentive added when the city sold south Clinton's school, its playground, its church. What's a home with nothing around it?

You hear stories of people getting better deals. Non–south Clinton residents grumble about the odd shrewd negotiator squeezing a brand-new home across the river out of the company.

Plenty of people were never approached with an offer. Now, just a narrow street or two removed from the barbed-wire fence and the "Private Property" sign, the smell and the light and the heat, their houses are worth practically nothing. No more offers are made. If a home-owner breaks down, approaches the company and asks to be bought out, sure they'll help him. It is, to use baseball jargon, the ol' squeeze play. Joyce's friends the Brodericks, Ed and Mike, they are still making noise. Consequently, they haven't been offered anything for their homes along Twelfth Avenue South, half a block away from the house they grew up in, now half a block away from the polymer plastics section of the factory. They do not expect an offer any time soon. Because the factory will make their homes unlivable and nobody else will buy them. Because you don't live in a place like that unless you're holding on to a memory of what it used to be or what you want it to have been. And someday, Ed concedes, the unchanging living conditions, the losing battles, it will all be too much. They'll be squeezed into submission, and that's when ADM will be kind enough to buy their houses at market value, which will be insanely low, but inarguably just. Ed is sure he will be remembered as the guy who held out to the end looking for a sweetheart deal.

It's about controlling the narrative.

In 2006, Clinton made national news, with environmentalists' articles pointing to it as an example of something wrong. The coal-powered ADM plant produced twenty thousand tons of airborne toxins in a year, while the EPA's standard for a plant being a "major source of pollution" was a hundred tons of any one toxin. A group called Environmental Defense ranked the Clinton plant the twenty-eighth largest emitter of carcinogenic components in the country. Now I read local articles proudly pointing out that pollution has been drastically reduced, something that should be celebrated, even though drastically reduced from drastically dangerous still isn't ideal. In the local paper last year, when the Department of Natural Resources registered Clinton as consistently flirting with the boundaries of legal particulate levels in the air, citizens were assured that local industry was constantly working to reduce emissions, that it kept its own air-quality monitors, held itself accountable so that others didn't have to. An ADM spokesperson assured residents that the company did in-house testing and that all of its emissions levels were compliant, though no numbers were given. The focus was then shifted to the personal responsibility of each citizen: How can *you*, the specific *you*, the individual living in town, do your part for your neighbor's lungs?

These are articles that I read alone at night after the drive home, nine Google tabs glowing onto my face, oddly frustrated, still searching. I'm not sure why I keep driving through south Clinton, looking up at all the gray steel and smoke. Perhaps because driving by the factory after games feels surprisingly appropriate and because this issue, ever present to me, seems so easy to forget for anyone other than the people living in it. And the Baseball Family. They don't forget either. They speak of the things demolished, flattened, eaten, in the same gentle voice with which they frame baseball games from seasons before I was born, stories of fans now gone.

When Joyce drives into south Clinton to visit her friends near where she grew up, she is followed by white cars with ADM's logo on them, the green-and-white leaf floating against a blue diamond, bucolic to the point of profane. They do not say anything to her, but the questions are there in the steady distance between her bumper and theirs: What is your business here? What motivation could somebody have to visit other than to gawk or ring some alarm?

Nobody has followed me, but I usually drive through at night, after the games, sometimes after dropping Hank or Erasmo off at home, sliding again through the empty downtown, slowing for the potholes under the railroad bridge, reemerging in a place that feels as if it doesn't exist.

I got out of the car once and entered one of the vacant houses through a hole in the plywood on the porch door. I don't know what I expected to see besides the nothing I saw. Of course it was nothing. No sign of the family who lived there or the things they had accumulated. Nothing was left behind, that's the point.

I thought of Betty and Tim and Tammy and Joyce describing the value of things. Tim wants to build a museum in the corner of the stadium, fill it with all that he's saved. That is what we talk about in the stands when the game isn't interesting. Tim describes how important it is to have something to commemorate this place and what has happened in its confines, before it all goes away. Because everything does go away at some point. Tim always makes sure to acknowledge that.

The signs on the south Clinton houses are all the same, cut maybe from the same board. The wood is painted white with red-stenciled lettering that makes me think of grade school: *ADM Poly Is Not a Good Neighbor.* In what seems to be an affirmation of their point, the signs are losing their whiteness, covered in soot and coal dust, some of them fuzzy and tinted green from an unexplained chemical effect that I see on the sides of houses, too, like a collection of worn pennies.

I don't know if anybody who isn't looking sees them, though. The houses and signs are blocked from view. They face the train tracks and the factory, the trains with no passengers to look out, the factory with no windows, no open gates, nothing to suggest that anyone can see.

Danny looks away from the field, tired of it. He looks past the waterfront, the lighthouse, and the riverboat and focuses on the shoreline of Beaver Island. You used to be able to ferry to it from the dock in south Clinton. The ferry is long gone. ADM rents the dock from the city but is trying to buy it outright for five million dollars that the cash-strapped city could use now, in the process losing the long-term income generated from ADM's lease.

"That's nice over there," Danny says.

"What is?"

"All the green."

He's quiet, then continues. "I grew up in a pretty brown place. The green is beautiful."

He's right. There is something heartening to the lushness, the depths of the hues, a rounded, sensuous color unlike anything you see traveling west into Iowa.

Beaver Island is a ghost town. Skeletons of houses are still there in neat rows, the outlines of properties that were once farmed. Some of the LumberKings fans, not many anymore, but some, were born there.

"People used to live there," I say.

"Nuh-uh," Danny says.

"Yeah," I say. "Farmers and stuff, I think."

I know all this because Tim keeps promising to take me to Beaver Island. He describes it for me, how he camps there with a friend who has a boat. He waits until the LumberKings are on the road and packs fishing gear. They anchor in a protected inlet, jump ashore. They catch walleye, trout, other kinds I've never heard of. I think of them in ancient black and white—I think of Huck Finn's Mississippi—the only image I had before I came here. Sometimes they sneak the fish into games in a little red cooler, hand out newly cut steaks to us in the stands the way Betty gives Danny his candy.

"I want to live on an island," Danny says. "Wouldn't that be cool? Like nothing on the island but you?"

"I think I'd be scared," I say. "All that quiet."

He considers this. He leans back against the picnic table, runs his hands over his abs. I watch him do so, the familiar desire present to touch them or even slap my palm down and feel it bounce off his skin. Sometimes I am guilty of a middle school type of envy—does he really appreciate the way he was made? The natural perfection that I would call athletic genes, that he would call God's hand? He doesn't work out that much, he is always eating, but his body is an efficient furnace. He has to worry if it's not enough for the majors. I sulk because it's still more than I got.

To see him and not hear him, Danny is everything that I ever imagined myself developing into on the most optimistic days of my childhood. He is a lot of people's boyhood fantasy of adulthood, a lot of people's adult fantasies of adulthood, too. He plays baseball with a grin, sliding headfirst, popping up, and running again, as though devoid of bones, packed full of only muscle. Chelsea meets him after the games in her cutoffs or a sundress, with bare legs that should make me ache but don't. She is beautifully desexualized in a way that I've read about in all the old baseball books written by men—the exact model of the kind of woman who makes a ballplayer settle down, the opposite of the kind who makes him stray.

"I think I could be a farmer," he says. "It's one of those jobs where you still get to use your body. That might be fun."

He laughs because it's ridiculous, but maybe not.

"I bet it's hard," I say. "I've never done it."

"Me neither."

This is almost a friendship conversation. Or it's the kind of conversation I have with my actual friends who are all far away from here and have never done anything with the pressure or persistence with which Danny will swing a bat tonight. It is a conversation of indecision, the maudlin self-pity of young men who feel they deserve more. It is a conversation of the purely naive, staring out at fields that look the way fields have always looked and ignoring that it takes two thousand acres to turn a profit now, all corn or soy never meant to be eaten, that young guys like us don't just walk up to a patch and plant a livelihood, that half of Danny's biggest fans can talk about their families' farms that are no longer. But never mind the truth, we are having this conversation of indecision that mirrors most of my internal conversation. Danny is not an all-star, he's not being treated as anything great, so he could be anything at all or nothing at all, like everyone else, like me.

It's a thought that he is not supposed to have. The moment you can be anything else at all, you are not aimed toward being great at one thing. It's why nobody in the game will ever tell any player it's time to stop until his official release. Because the moment the conversation starts, chances are a career is over. That is simplistic, sure. As though there were something divine and implacable that makes an athlete, hard to have, easy to lose. But to play the game or to love those who do, it's the half-lie that must be believed.

Clinton Corn was first unionized in 1937, the same year Riverview Stadium was built, a twin birth, or rebirth, of the idea of a proud and contented American blue-collar town. This fact, that world, should feel totally removed now, so many years later, unrelated to what I see every day. It should feel like what it is: history. Can something be a myth if it once really existed, this functional town, gritty and prosperous, the nation's game plunked happily in the middle of it? Or did it ever really exist the way it is remembered?

I don't know if the things Tim tells me are true, but I don't think they're lies. Tim is a fantastic rememberer, in the creative sense. The whole Family is. Baseball stories mix into town stories mix into stories about love, about shenanigans, about specific moments when everybody in a neighborhood that doesn't really exist anymore would go from house to house, stopping to sit on lawn chairs out by the street, every door open, the nights endless. Tim tells me of himself as a boy, heavy but fit, slow but powerful. He was a boy in these bleachers, almost where we are right now, a boy, too, in the summer on the farm where his mother grew up, a boy on his paper route—of course he had one—biking through Clinton smelling something sweeter coming out of the smokestacks. Because Clinton made candy then (and then booze), delicious and relatable items for parents to boast to children about.

What a great, true claim to make: *We're the town that gave the first Twinkie its flavor!*

Yes, better than: *We're testing chemical reactions to create pioneering corn-based plastics products!*

Clinton does not have control over what is produced within its boundaries, but that is not unusual. When Tim or Betty or Tammy speaks wistfully to me about what the town once was, the various things that have befallen it, that qualifier is always there. "It's not especially bad," or "It's like most places, I guess," or "It's the kind of story you hear a million times. And we're luckier than most." All of this carries a mixture of pride and humility that I find, in my all-powerful East Coast judgmental capacity, to be charmingly midwestern. It's also true.

Clinton is in the middle of everything still, used for production and transportation, then overlooked. But it is still used. It is a factory town that has a factory that turns a seventy-million-dollar profit. No matter how much of that profit is tangibly bestowed on the city, that's still truth. It is a corn town in a country that subsidizes corn. That must be a good thing. When I speak to local politicians, they tell me it's a good thing. When I speak to people with money or influence, they tell me it's a good thing. I sat down in the editorial offices of the *Clinton Herald*, a newspaper over a century old, stubbornly located in the bare heart of downtown, and the editor told me Archer Daniels Midland is a good thing. She began to look at me quizzically and then finally with spite as I pushed forward with my questions: But what about the air? And what jobs, new jobs, have really been created? What about those houses down there that are gone, the few people left living among the nothingness?

Those houses were an eyesore. And where would anyone be if the factory picked up and left?

In the middle of things now, I start to feel as if I'm asking the wrong questions. Maybe I get turned shoulders, one-word answers, because I want there to be something sinister to the newest master of this town, to the calculated capitulation toward corporate control, and the erosion of a generic blue-collar Eden that I never lived in but love to read about, love to put in writing—*erosion* and *blue-collar* in the same sentence, a campaign slogan for every bright-smiled politician born in a small place. And when I speak to council members who, for decades, have never been voted out of office, or to the mayor, or to the editor, baseball is always tossed in as part of the assurance that the town has been allowed to keep its roots while moving boldly into what will be a prosperous twenty-first century.

Just look at that field out there. Retouched, clean and clipped, and still a time warp to something beautiful. People ask if I felt how special it was when I first stepped out on the infield. I did. Me and Dave, all that unsullied snow. And then it's a deluge of talk about beer and brats and corn and fishing and work ethic and hard hats and home runs and good memories and progress.

To call something unfair is weak, so is saying *unfortunate* over and over in interviews, leading subjects with *Isn't it unfortunate to lose your history?*

Maybe a neighborhood like south Clinton needs to be lost, the way most players need to lose because too many people want to win, and if they all did, then success would be nothing. Maybe it is a neighborhood not supposed to exist now. There were houses built a century ago in between the river and the industry. Packs of men walked just a few blocks to mills that were dangerous and volatile but always hiring, just down the hill from the mansions where their bosses lived. It was a complete ecosystem, and now it isn't and that's that. And you have to be a bleeding-heart fool or the kind of person who bemoans the loss of everything quaint to argue with the logic.

"South Clinton, everything down there, that's not a town that we want to be anymore," I am told by one councilman. "There is no place for it."

But what is there a place for? There is no place for a downtown. Or, rather, the place is there, the facade, but nothing fills it. And so there's no place for local grocers who offered credit to union members on strike. There's no place for the activists who were bred here, the churches that doubled as meeting halls, the radical ministers and labor leaders, almost all of them now dead or moved or, worse, just silent. I listen to their voices on old tapes at the State Historical Library in Iowa City, charming relics waiting for inclusion in a dissertation.

Erasmo is pitching tonight, and we're watching, as always.

Tim and Tammy are talking to me, saying something different.

"I don't want you to think we're stupid because we're here," Tammy says.

"What do you mean?" I say. "I'm here, too."

"No, because we're still *living* here," Tim says. "It's not like we couldn't go somewhere else. But family is here. The things we love are here. Somebody has got to stay."

It is the first conversational allusion I've heard to the "brain drain," though when I speak to historians, sociologists, and over-compassionate easterners about this place, it's a common theme. And months before I ever met the Baseball Family, I had an idea of them in mind, a single word to sum them up: *stayers*. It's a judgmental word, stark and nearly religious. A population defined by devout inaction, not diggers or movers or players or doers, but instead the opposite of all those things.

I've been reading *Hollowing Out the Middle*, a book dedicated to looking at the struggling midwestern town. Perhaps the most succinct point in it, one that didn't seem cruel until I came here, was that the towns were killing themselves, pouring resources into their best performers— the smartest, the best athletes, those pushed toward achievement from a very young age. Those people respond to the care and attention by succeeding elsewhere, becoming "a boon for someplace else." But then that posits, implicitly, that the dwindling number of people living whole lives in Clinton do so because they weren't tapped for something better.

I interviewed a man who'd done well in finance out east and had returned to his native Clinton after retiring. We spoke in his loft in the Van Allen Building, a landmark, a reference to its builder, a man I should have heard of. He showed me pictures of the old lumber mills, the old churches, the old tugboats, his grandfather in his factory team baseball uniform. He told me that ADM cannot be blamed for not hiring Clinton natives for newly created jobs. This is a new industrial world. Gone are the days when the underskilled could wander down to the factory and punch the clock that same day. The people today are unqualified for the industry that defines their town, one now geared less toward bodies and more toward expertise.

Tim once worked part-time security for Clinton Corn, hated it. Then he worked the line at a smaller factory for seventeen years and didn't like that much either. He didn't like the facelessness of product assembly, didn't like the twisted roots that his hands had become. Finally, he quit. That would have been a moment to leave Clinton, but he kept going to baseball games, kept dropping by his mother's for dinner, kept telling Tom Bigwood that things were going to be fine when they weren't. He got a job as a school custodian, the same job his father got after that errant steel beam knocked him out of factory work when Tim was a little boy.

Tim has been to more LumberKings games, has sat in this stadium more, has yelled himself hoarse more, has made the players feel holy more, than maybe anyone. In the past he would have driven to see Nick and Erasmo as all-stars. In the past there would have been his Crew, a caravan of *we* going to support their own. But people die. Most lose interest. Tim won't be driving to Fort Wayne for the all-star game this year, two states to the east, just to be lost in a stadium built to hold eight thousand, in a city with a quarter of a million, a place with no tradition, just gourmet concession stands.

Instead, free from the responsibility of watching, he'll spend some time on Beaver Island with friends whom he's known since he can remember. I will imagine them. I will imagine them wandering through the ghost town. They will rest in the shadows of wooden houses, empty and rotting but still standing, on patches of dirt still fertile, growing weeds. They might cobble together a fire with sticks, smoke lingering in the thick trees around them, not even a half mile away from ADM. They will be peaceful and validated and ghostly.

Tonight Tim wolf-whistles for Erasmo, his new ace pitcher. He claps along with his mother and father and sister, for their all-star whom Betty calls *E-rissimo*. For his part, Erasmo is playing up to his new title, surrendering one run in the first, then seeming personally insulted by that surprise and bearing down. He looks older, and this is the first time I've noticed it. It doesn't seem right that he can change over the course of half a season. But he's twenty. His jaw isn't so round anymore as he sets it, takes a sign, fires for a strike. We are watching him change, and it only reinforces, I think, how nothing else is changing around him. He gets the ball back from the catcher. He sets, stares, throws again. Strike. I am watching, chewing sunflower seeds, terrified of his forward momentum.

I don't travel to the all-star game either. I take a break, go home to sleep in my childhood bed, read my childhood books, sit in the backseat of my father's car on the way to the cemetery for the tenth anniversary of my brother's death. People lay pebbles and tell stories from when he was my age, all potential. My father says that he'd never seen somebody want so much, but I keep my head bowed toward the grass, manicured into a sterile beauty, and how can I not think of an infield? What was it that George Carlin said? Two biggest wastes of space, cemeteries and golf courses. You could add baseball fields to that, just as falsely pastoral and dated and futile. I feel my throat close as I lay a pebble on a head-stone that has no titles, just a Beatles lyric. It is not a crying throat close, instead a panic attack. The kind that has been sneaking up on me as I drive to the games, drive from them, as I sleep and prepare to return to the field the next day, all the moments when I'm not actually watching.

I don't think my brother's death means anything to me anymore in terms of grief. All gentle feelings of loss have faded and were ambiguous even at the time. What has lasted is the disappointment. Somebody who wanted things furiously as a young man and never got any of what he wanted. A reach and then a failure, an end, ashes. A reminder of reality juxtaposed with the books that my father read to me at too old an age, those about a game.

I close my eyes during the car ride home through Long Island. Then I flee into my bedroom with the door closed, lie under Thomas the Tank Engine sheets, black-and-white photographs of Mantle and Mays on the walls around me, plastic trophies on the windowsill, where they will always be. I leave home the next day, drive with college friends to Atlantic City. We dress up in the fanciest clothes we own. I wear cuff links for the first time in my life. We look for coke and fail. We take drinks off the trays that waitresses bring around in the casinos, tip with rumpled one-dollar bills. We say, "I love you, bro," dangling ourselves on one another's shoulders at a rooftop club, and we watch men's hands far older than ours tickling the hems of short skirts that we call trashy and pretend we don't want to fondle, too. We are all somewhere between twenty-three and twenty-five, somewhere in between college and everything else. We are children born into varying privilege who have been told that we deserve something from the world. There is the Goldman Sachs friend who buys us shots as we pretend not to resent the power of his chosen adulthood or at least pretend that the resentment is based on principle, not jealousy. There's the rest of us, unmoored.

We walk to a twenty-four-hour diner, past the whores who make everything feel like a movie set, who call out to me with my scared eyes and round face, "Wanna learn something?" We boys laugh to each other and can't meet their eyes. We ask each other, what if we did it? What if we tried on that type of guy for a persona, the one who high-fives as he fucks a stranger for money, doesn't care if she appreciates all the things that make him him?

I am no good at playing adult.

One of the whores looks like Chelsea, I think. Or a false and deteriorating version of her. She has the wide-open eyes, the youth, the teasingly pious dress, though less pious, more teasing. In my drunken moralizing, she is sacrilegious. She is an affront to the real Chelsea, the ideal, so unlike anybody I ever met before her. I want to fuck this stranger to feel like a monster or help her to feel wholesome. I do neither and walk by, giggling. I go to eat a burger at a window table, chewing and pointing as one friend vomits in the gutter. The rest of us say, "That seals it; this is the best night ever." I want to go back to watching.

The all-star game is played, time passes, then some more, and not much has changed. The team is getting a little better. Things are moving forward, but Danny is stuck. He isn't playing poorly. He isn't playing great. He isn't benched, but he only starts half the games. He is alone, though, that is the main difference. After games it's just him and his host family, old folks in bed by ten, long before he gets home. Chelsea is back in California looking for off-season jobs. She has an interview to be a breakfast monitor at a Days Inn.

Danny and I were going to go see *The Expendables,* which looks epic, but we're late because I was at Manning's Whistle Stop, hiding from the rain, drinking Old Style, and scarfing down frozen pizza. He was at a fan's house having a steak dinner and missing home. They played pool and said grace. He called Chelsea and put her on speakerphone, and she talked to everyone for a while.

She reminded Danny that he needs to start being proactive, making calls for part-time winter work. He was a salesman at Staples last off-season, red T-shirt, pleated slacks, a name tag saying, "Hi, I'm Daniel." In five months he sold more than anyone else on staff, set a new branch record, commemorated with a plaque bearing both his photograph and his name.

We're too late for all the epicness of Sly Stallone and "Stone Cold" Steve Austin sharing the screen, and Danny refuses to pick up the movie in the middle. We see the next available show, *Scott Pilgrim vs. the World,* a semi-animated hipster opus about a drifting Canadian boy a little older than Danny, a little younger than me. The theater is nearly empty, just us, an elderly couple who may have remained in their seats from the last movie, and two teenage girls who clearly don't like high school.

We watch Michael Cera's impossibly narrow shoulders.

We listen to him kick at his sheets and say things like "I just want to lie here."

We watch two pale men awake next to each other, kiss on the lips, and go for coffee.

We watch a mass of freaks vie for a purple-haired girl's affections—a skater, a vegan, a chubby lesbian who only wears black.

Danny is writhing at the weirdness. He whispers questions to me, the first time he's seen me as somebody who might be able to answer something: Why would a straight guy lie down next to two gay guys? What makes a bass guitar different from a guitar guitar? What are these people's jobs? Is that what your house looks like?

He wants to know if I, too, have the kinds of knickknacks, band posters, instruments, and books that we see on-screen. He wants to know if I understand these people in glasses identical to my glasses, strewn about on beanbags, talking constantly, never doing. Maybe he has never known anybody who fits the role of lovable white male movie protagonist, outside a war movie, a church movie, or a sports movie. I like to think that there's a yearning in him for such aimlessness, but how can I know that? His type of hero is better, doesn't need irony or music trivia proficiency. I come to games for that.

He misses Chelsea. He texts her. I smell his cologne and hair gel, more pungent from the rain outside. He bolts right after the credits, calls Chelsea from the parking lot. When he hangs up, he says, with a touch of true sadness, "Man, this might be the last time I'm ever at this theater." Then he catches himself, smiles, says, "I said that last year." He looks back at the Clinton eight-plex, and so I do, too. It's a movie theater. The names on the marquee are misspelled in places. A kid is taking a cigarette break outside.

"You should take a picture of it," I say, not sure if I'm kidding.

He shrugs and I drive him to Walmart to buy toilet paper.

He stands in front of the Walmart sign, the shimmering red, almost extraterrestrial, hovering above the stretch of black parking lots around us. He looks up, turns his palms to the sky, gives a high-pitched, holy hum, and then breaks into a soft giggle.

"This is the place," he says.

And it is. Most of my greatest intimacies in the baseball season have occurred here. Clinton's Walmart is a super one, complete with clothing, groceries, home and garden, an eye doctor, a Subway, a gas station, a Tire and Lube, and a bank, where you can deposit checks directly for store credit.

Danny even recognizes some employees, says hello, says thanks when they tell him they heard he's doing well. He doesn't know that a year ago a ten-year lawsuit was finally settled, begun by Clinton Walmart employees, extending throughout the entire state, becoming the collective action of ninety-seven thousand current and former Iowa Walmart workers who all were victims of a "uniform scheme of wage abuse." Some of these people saying hi to Danny were probably part of the group that took a stand over being screwed out of minimum wage, and when the victorious dust settled, Walmart paid out $11 million total, or an average of $113 per employee.

There are similar grumblings happening among ADM workers right now, though we don't know it yet. In the coming months, they will officially file their own lawsuit against two small companies that subcontract hourly labor at ADM, complaining about a lack of fair overtime pay and the fact that in a factory so big the punch clock is half a mile from the exit, that there are always extra tasks, off-the-clock work, that they must do on the walk out to their cars. And another suit will be filed a week after the baseball season is over, by the Brodericks and forty-five of their remaining neighbors. They will claim that the factory is so big, so loud, so bright, pouring so much unidentified runoff into what looks like an Olympic-sized pool across the street from their windows, that they can't sleep, that they can't live, not in a way that makes them feel human.

What does this have to do with us? With Danny? It's just a group of people dwarfed. But the scope of dissatisfaction is palpable, affects so many people whom we walk past, looking for toiletries. Danny pushes a shopping cart like a little kid, running, riding, turning on two wheels. I trot to keep up, and he talks back to me, a tumult of complaints and truths that could never be voiced in the clubhouse. He talks the way he does to Chelsea, only Chelsea really, and I think the words come so fast because of the realization that she isn't here and that she is the only one, has been the only one since fourteen.

He was yelled at today for trying to steal a base on his own, and rightfully so. He tried to steal third with the team losing, the kind of selfish move that sends Little League coaches into embarrassing, hat-stomping fits. Tamargo didn't exactly stomp his hat, but he was furious, and everybody saw him glare at Danny, who refused to lock eyes. Everybody noticed that Danny was pulled from the game, too, for committing that cardinal sin of putting himself above the team. Danny recognizes the hypocrisy. He is *trying* to be noticed. That's the whole point. If he isn't noticed, then he isn't worth anything, and then he isn't on any team at all. And the thing that makes him noticeable is his speed. Thus, he will run. He *should* run. Nick Franklin, he points out, makes bad decisions all the time. Tamargo hates Nick Franklin, Danny assures me. Hates him. But Nick isn't some regular guy like Danny. Nick has, as Danny puts it, the right to do anything he wants.

Danny's eyes are wide, his voice hushed as he says it, but nobody is listening, and these aren't exactly secrets just because they're never voiced. Tamargo is middle management, and he knows it. This is his team to run the way he is told to run it from a thousand miles away. Nobody pretends that Nick Franklin doesn't matter more. That the further you are from Nick Franklin status, the more you become just a guy with a really poorly paying job who complains loudly about it to his wife and mumbles under his breath to everyone else.

I want to see Danny run. That's what I want. I want to see him run.

It is such a clear thought, acute and dominating and sudden. I want to see him sprint through Home Cleaning Products, through Waste Disposal, hands raised as he coasts into Lawn Care along the back wall that must be ten base paths away from here. He doesn't break out into a full sprint. He doesn't stand in front of the discount mowers, fists in the air like Rocky. That's too much.

I have to remind myself that Danny is still some version of a star. He still plays in a professional baseball stadium because no matter what has happened in Clinton, there is a professional baseball team here. It's still fun to watch, maybe more so for the accomplishment of lasting and never changing while other institutions erode around it. And Tim is a little tanked on Mike's Hard Lemonade because he's trying to get away from the carbs of beer and the boozy citrus tastes pretty fucking good against the heat. And Danny is on the bench today, but the day before he hit a line drive home run over the left-field fence, and nothing feels better than that. And in the seventh inning lull of a sloppy, slow game, something remarkable happens. Two bats extend up over the top of the dugout, as though floating. Latex gloves have been blown up by an unseen mouth, taped to the handle of each bat. Somebody has made them into arms.

"Look," Tim yells and begins guffawing as everyone else notices, too.

The bat-arms begin to clap, and Tim takes the cue, claps along with them, screams at his people to follow suit. They do. The bat-arms move faster, whipping a thousand people into something like a frenzy. Then the bat-hands switch tack, begin waving back and forth in time with the rhythm they created. This is too much, and applause breaks out. I find myself laughing like somebody far less sober than I am. I find myself crazed. My shoulders bump into Tim's. We rock into each other, saying, "What the hell?" Joining the chorus of fans who have forgotten that a game is being played and only want to know who is making this simple, wooden robot clap.

The game ends, and Danny emerges holding one bat-arm in each hand. I am wholly a fan as we all cry out that we knew it, we knew it was him. Betty is overwhelmed by the silly kindness of the gesture. Danny turns and hands her a bat. She hands him a picture she's been saving, one she took weeks ago and printed out, him standing in that classic baseball pose, head high, one hand resting on his bat like a cane, the other on his waist.

Of Monkeys and Dreams

IT'S THE MIDDLE OF THE SEVENTH INNING. The LumberKings are slaughtering the South Bend Silver Hawks. Yet again, and not surprisingly, it is hot. We talk about that fact in the stands. But today brings tolerable heat, nothing too bad, not one of those days when "hot" is the only thing to say, not like the one last week when the stands were packed because the ADM work floor overheated to 137 degrees and people got bused out early, taken to the game to drink and not be angry. So things are good. And despite the LumberKings' overall trend of losing as much as they win, there is a sense of optimism. The team is on a two-game winning streak. The season is more over than not and Nick Franklin is still here; there he is, nibbling at a leather tie on his glove, waiting to take the field. Tim is saying that there is a good feeling to the bunch out there right now, saying that this one feels as if it has the potential to be a dream team. He is providing no proof.

Also, three sheep are running onto the field, displaying pure terror as we begin to cheer them. They break away from one another, one sprinting right at the bleachers, toward the noise, one grazing behind second base, as though if it behaves normally, all this will go away, another trotting along the outfield fence, trapped. We watch. They are all novelty. They can do nothing but be, and I think that their appeal—grazing on a *baseball field*?—will soon grow thin.

"Here we go, here we go," Tim says next to me.

Two sheepdogs sprint in from right field, saddled. Monkeys are perched atop the saddles, little hands clutching little reins, torsos flailing as the dogs gallop.

The monkeys are capuchins, of course. What other monkey would let itself be slipped into baby-sized leather chaps? These are monkeys to worship. Even the name, "capuchin," originally referred to a group of friars. People saw brown fur, white tuft on the head, and they thought it looked like a brown robe and white hood. They were holy, humanish little things.

Somebody screams, "Oh my God, those are *monkeys!*"

Somebody else says, "Thanks, Captain Obvious," but the derisive laughter that should follow is muted because something amazing is happening, which is way more interesting than scorn: fucking *monkeys* are riding on dogs as if they're *people.*

"Get ready for the greatest show on earth," Brad tells us from the PA booth.

The show is the herding. While we are transfixed by the improbable animals, an extended-cab Dodge Ram pickup creeps onto the field and parks between home plate and the pitcher's mound. On each side, the word "Dodge" is written big, all capitals, part of a sponsorship agreement. Also, there are two American flag decals, a bald eagle's head blown up to the size of a beer keg, and the stenciled slogans "Grab life by the horns" and "Be the best of the best." Two real American flags fly above the roof, and the four white wooden walls of a miniature cattle pen rest on the flatbed. "Wild Thang" Lepard leaps from the pickup, and Mitch runs out to help him assemble the pen.

Wild Thang grabs a microphone and faces the twelve hundred or so of us scattered in the stands in front of him. He asks, "Are y'all ready to see something you won't believe but that is 100 percent, God's honest real?"

Hank is standing on the top step of the dugout with a plastic smile. He unwraps a strawberry sucking candy that Betty gave him, pops it in his mouth, raises his eyebrows as if surprised by the sweetness. He showed up again a few days ago, walked into the locker room with his two duffel bags and his bats. He found his old locker untouched, his jersey, the arbitrarily chosen 31, hanging, clean and pressed, the way it had been throughout his brief demotion.

"We kept you here, Hanky," Danny told him. There were smiles and shouts, a lot of soft sentiment that made everyone quickly uncomfortable. Hank nodded and tried not to give such a childishly wide grin, such open admission of being truly, vulnerably touched.

I was standing next to Pollreisz in the hallway next to the trainer's room talking about crossword puzzles, a shared hobby that we get too much mileage out of. He hit my shoulder and flicked his head toward the kindly drama happening among his charges, toward Hank.

"*That's* what it's about," he told me. "When you are the kind of man that the team wants around, we keep a piece of you."

He was speaking metaphorically.

Now, on the field, I stare at Hank like always. He's in better shape than he was at the beginning of the season, one of a handful of players who can make that claim. Instead of preparing to play each day, he has prepared his body to look more worthy of playing. Sometimes I see him running his hands down his torso and grinning to himself. But his shirt, his 31, is just as pristine as it was in his locker. This strawberry sucker is his eighth, I've counted. His hands are getting sticky, but it doesn't matter.

Sams is next to him, benched as well, three inches taller, maybe three inches wider than Hank, so next to each other they look like an evolutionary progression out of a high school textbook. Sams is staring at a sheep that has wandered toward them, puzzled, maybe a bit frightened. He is flexing his forearm. I can see it from the stands, contorting with sinuous lines and then snapping back as he clenches his fist, then unclenches, then clenches again. Sams's right forearm has a black ink tattoo on it, spelling out *Rivalino*, his middle name. He told me once that it means something powerful, something royal, he doesn't remember what exactly, but it is important to him, that general feeling, and so it is embossed on him. A crown dots one *i*; there is a cross, as well as other symbols of great significance, hidden somewhere in the word.

He touches this tattoo often, does it now as the sheep, rigid and unblinking, glares at him from the grass along the third-base line. It is his most visible marking, also his most opaque, but it isn't the big one. The big one spans his back, shoulder blade to shoulder blade, enough room for bold, capitalized script announcing a decree: *Live Your Dream.*

"What's it mean?" I asked, the first time we spoke, as he hurried out of the shower in a cold early April clubhouse. It was a question that should have been laughed at—no meaning could be more obvious. Another man with another profession would have pointed that out. But this game, the clubhouse, they're spaces free from irony, and Kalian Sams reached a hand around to feel the words, raised with his goose bumps, and told me, "It's *everything*," while teammates nodded.

On the field, Wild Thang makes a guttural, military noise, and something in the monkeys or the dogs or both tightens. Muscles perk, eyes focus. They gallop with purpose toward the sheep, who, even after nearly three hundred shows a year, are somehow not ready for this shift in the drama. Shrieks of laughter are swallowed by shrieks of fear as the monkeys ride their beasts up close to the sheep, who twist and buck, and for a moment it seems as if one will get caught in between two species of stomping legs, that we will be left with the most hopeless image of all, a monkey in people clothes motionless on the outfield grass of a minor-league stadium. Betty grabs Bill's arm and closes her eyes. Tim screams, "Ma, you old softy, nothing is gonna go wrong!"

Dreams, from the beginning, were erotic. Or, if not explicitly erotic, still undeniably sexy in that they were linked with the fulfillment of what is desired. The granting of wishes that awake, open-eyed, seemed far-fetched.

See Middle English folklore: This lady was the same / That he had so dreymd of.

Even when not literalized with the female form, the dream, as a concept, was still a success: *Good is to dremen of win.* "Good" meant "God" and "win" meant "joy," but also "striving." And that faint sense of desperation became clearer later, when dreams were found to be metaphors, and even then, the desperation was hidden in the subtext, never in the intent of the speaker.

Shakespeare: We are such stuff as dreams are made on.

Tennyson: Like a dog, he hunts in dreams.

It is stupid, probably, pretentious, definitely, to be thinking of Tennyson while looking at Kalian Sams's back. To impose literature and metaphor onto a game and a group of people that want to be taken literally. But it is difficult not to grope for something a little deeper in a space where clichés are not clichés and things are taken so literally that it's impossible to know if I'm being fucked with because, most of the time, even when I should be, I'm not.

My dreams, when I remember them, are horrible. It is, I know, not directly related to Sams's ink, but when I dream of women, they are those I know but with contorted faces. They are on top of me, and they are disappointed. They are asking questions that I cannot answer, and sometimes, often, my body is heavy, almost permeable, as strangely familiar hands prod my skin and tell me to be better. I yell in my dreams, and it is always silent.

The players never seem to be afraid to fall asleep, but it is hard for them, I know that, far from home, always under pressure. On nights when I stay out after games with the players and it's too late to sleep in my own bed, I crash on their floors, pressed against the legs of rented coffee tables. I see light from under Hank's bedroom door until I finally fall asleep, and when I open my eyes in the morning, the light is still there, and I think he never wanted to turn it off. Sometimes I hear whispered, unintelligible conversations with his girlfriend; sometimes I hear the creak of footsteps in circles, of a heavy body doing push-ups on a thin floor. And Erasmo and Mario and Noriega, lying like a bar graph in their one-room apartment, how can they not be in one another's dreams, the sound of close, tense breath ever present, turning into wind and warning when they finally fall asleep just before the sun rises?

But this is not the dream on Kalian Sams's back. Nor is it the dream that is the answer to almost every casual question I ask anybody just to break the silence of waiting for the game to start.

How's it going? *Living the dream.*

Is it hard to be away from your newborn son? *This is my* dream.

Don't you think you should get paid a little more? *If dreams were easy, they wouldn't be dreams.*

There is stubbornness to it. Honor, maybe, but plodding obstinacy, too. That is where Tennyson comes in, dogs dreaming of the hunt, the way they look as they sleep. Twitching, pawing at the air, a conclusion-less effort that does not allow them rest.

I can find only one person who stood up and said the phrase "minor leagues" before a Senate Judiciary Committee during baseball's antitrust hearings in 1997. He was Dan Peltier, a career journeyman, parts of nine years in the minors, 108 games in the bigs with Texas and San Francisco, one home run against the Cleveland Indians, the highlight of it all. Peltier began his testimony as a baseball player is taught to speak. He acknowledged how much the game had given him, called himself lucky, reiterated that quickly. He was lucky to have been able to play a game for a living, the way so many want to, and he was especially lucky to have an accounting degree from Notre Dame and enough saved to begin an adult life at thirty. Then he spoke of reality. In A-ball, he made $850 per month. Take out a good $50 per month for clubhouse dues, an archaic system in which players have to help the guy whose job it is to wash their jockstraps make a living. Subtract rent, which he was responsible for. Subtract food. Unlivable.

Baseball salaries are different now. The highest-paid major-league player in 1997 made $16 million less than Alex Rodriguez does right now, a goal too lofty for Hank and Sams to even consider as they hang bored on the dugout railing. Minor-league inflation has not caught up. Hank makes $200 more per month than he would have in 1997, and in rookie ball the salary is still $850 monthly.

If it was easy, it wouldn't be a dream.

It doesn't matter that this sentence doesn't make sense.

Tim is wearing a bright yellow-green tank top from 1991, custom-made, advertising his Roadkill Crew in hard-angled lettering above a cartoon picture of what looks like a possum, eyes marked with *X*s, tongue out in gleeful death. If the color of the shirt has faded in twenty years, I am frightened to know how bright it was originally, just how proud and blinding it must have been when a row of fifteen identically neon shirts walked into an opposing stadium to cheer the LumberKings, no, not the LumberKings then, the Clinton Giants.

Nineteen ninety-one was a *dream* season, a dream in its symmetry and smooth story lines, a dream in the way that it can be relived, retold, take on significance in the context of two decades' worth of new happenings. And things are scaled differently in dreams.

The Midwest League championship trophy is a humble one, intentionally so, I think. A thick, polished, dark wood base, a square plaque

embedded in it with the logo of each team. On top of the base is a
bronze man the size of a deluxe GI Joe, gloved hand on hip, throwing
hand hidden behind his belt. He is nothing like any of the young men
who have held the trophy for the last half century. His carved pants
are ballooning, with pleats in them, the kind that can only appear in
pressed wool. Nine inches' worth of old-time ballplayer.

"It felt huge" is how Tim describes it to me. "It felt life-sized. It felt
like I was holding me over my head, made of metal.

"And then I remember walking into the office that winter and seeing
it and it was nothing," he tells me. "And I thought, my God, what was I
thinking? How did it feel so big?"

The giant-trophy moment happened in Madison on a cold night in
September, on the pitcher's mound after storming the field without
anyone telling him he couldn't, in the middle of a team of winners,
before following the bus on dark highways home for three and a half
hours, banging the side of Betty's old Dodge and howling.

Tim has, of course, seen more than a few stadium sideshows since
that last championship night. The racing mascots—Charlie the Tuna,
that inexplicable stork that hawks pickles, and other famous felt faces—
who swing by midwestern minor-league stadiums after performing in
Milwaukee or St. Louis. Also, those creepy guys in blow-up suits that are
meant to be half animal, half sports legend—Monkey Mantle, Harry
Canary, Ken Giraffey Jr. The Coors Light Girls came last year, and Tom
Bigwood was ready. He walked down the aisle to his seat in slacks and a
button-up shirt, his hair soaking with mousse and combed to the side.
And he was pretty trim because of the racking pain that his tumors
caused him every time he ate, so it was like looking at some new person. It was the only time Tim had ever seen him like that, so obstinately
fancy.

Tom Bigwood always wanted to be a player, I know that. Which
shouldn't be surprising, a guy watching baseball while wishing, dreaming, of playing. All of us are him to some extent. But Tom was never
good, never played schoolyard ball or Little League or high school,
never bar-league softball with friends on Sundays. And maybe that's
why his fandom was so unfiltered and endless, because it was cut with
no jealousy, no illusions.

"He was so big," his sister-in-law told me in her living room three blocks from the stadium. "So he never had to think, *Oh, maybe I could,* and then find out, no." She asked him, right before he died, trying to get him to talk over the noise of his labored breathing, "Tom, if you could be whatever you wanted to be right now, what would it be?"

And he said baseball player. Or maybe race-car driver. But probably baseball player. He couldn't fit in those cars. He'd laughed at that, she told me.

Tim doesn't know about all that. But he does know that Tom knew how lucky these boys are. These ones, he points to the LumberKings on the field trying to warm up, Hank and Sams right in front of us, watching.

"Wouldn't you be them right now if you could?" he asks me.

Yes, the answer is yes. If, right now, I was given the chance to drop out of graduate school, tell my girlfriend I would be gone for a while, plan ahead for a five-year cushion of poverty and probable failure into my thirties, I would, without hesitation, abandon any other potential life I've worked toward. I would justify it, without a second thought, as the ultimate dream. In the face of such hyperbole, everything else becomes bland and heavy and unnecessary. But just because these players have done what many of us also once wanted to, because they've taken ownership of a collective dream, do they deserve to sacrifice for that privilege? The common answer is yes.

Sometimes, at bars in my liberal college town west of Clinton, I play pool with white people with dreadlocks, and they ask me how bad the shithole is and I laugh. I say, "I wouldn't want to live where those guys live," not talking about Clinton, talking about sleeping in tiny apartments, packed so close to other bodies, and the hardness of half-deflated air mattresses on tile floors. Every time they say things like "yeah" or "must be smelly" or even "cuuuute," like how you call grandparents cute, or mom-and-pop shops, anything that's dead or dying. And then sometimes they say, "Lucky," or the ones who were mistreated by athletes in high school say, "Maybe they should try something new. Like adulthood."

I am sending texts now, to three friends.

"Monkeys on dogs. Minor-league rodeo."

I'm trying to take a picture with my phone to send, but there is too much movement. Tim glances down at me and says, "*Watch* the dang thing," and I am ashamed.

Chuck and Mailman Matt are saying that those monkeys are strapped onto the dogs. Betty is saying, "*Hush*," the point is that the monkeys can really do this. Tim is agreeing with his mom. It's like the fireworks on the Fourth of July. The sputtering and fizzling were laughed at by some, but Tim and Betty ignored those misfires. They pointed to the beautiful, arcing shots, the ones that exploded the way they were supposed to and drifted through the sky until embers touched their reflections on the river. It was beautiful, Betty reminded all of us, and Tim agreed, yes, it was, it was worth waiting for. It was a proper explosion. We were lucky to have seen it.

When the sheep are all herded, it is time for the origin tale.

"These dogs began over on the border of England and Scotland."

Wild Thang is stroking a pup's head with one hand, holding the mic in the other, breathing hard.

"They've got words over there that you ain't never heard before."

We wait for those words.

"Koombai," he says. He nods, somber. He offers no definition, but the dogs and the monkeys spring into action.

Terry Pollreisz pops out to stand next to Hank and Sams, puts a liver-spotted hand on the center of Hank's back, as usual. He leans in and says things into Hank's ear and Hank smiles, laughs with effort. I imagine that Pollreisz is telling him something cattle related. He looks to be pantomiming a lasso. He likes to tell stories, and his players like to half listen, hearing only the age in his voice, the general weathered, tame tone that his words always seem to take, boring but calming, too.

Pollreisz got to be a professional baseball player for one year, in 1969, and has since lived a fulfilling, accomplished life in service of trying to revise that failed moment. He played nineteen games in the minors, couldn't hit, began to doubt himself as a player and a man, was of legal draft age and unmarried, was deemed not worth waiting through Vietnam for by the organization, was cut, and then felt worse than he ever had, felt a panic that spread over him.

He told me about it once, though, standing in the batting cage as men a third his age hit. His blood pressure spiked so high that the army wouldn't take him, and at twenty-two, in a family of high school superstar athletes and veterans, he was washed up and useless to his country. It made him, he told me, doubt everything about himself, made him come to the conclusion that he was not worthy as a person, so quickly and quietly rejected from the only things he had ever equated with success. Eventually, he righted himself and got a master's degree in education, taught U.S. history and coached high school baseball in a rainy green town in Oregon, won a state baseball championship, was hired to coach the University of Portland baseball team, did so for twenty years, had an office with lots of pictures in it, had a wife and children and grandchildren, had a house near a creek with decent fish, was, by his own account, a settled and satisfied man. All of which makes his willingness to quit, sell his home, uproot his wife from her job as an administrative nurse, move to the suburban sprawl next to a spring-training complex outside Phoenix, and spend six months a year on the road, back seizing after long bus trips, seem so inexplicable.

"Do you miss your life?" I asked him.

I think of how quickly he answered me as I watch him watching animals dressed as ranchers getting more applause than he ever did.

"God, never." He was so sure. "All of that was nice, but it wasn't this."

He is as stooped as many of the Baseball Family's aged, though you can tell that what was once there was exceptional—long legs, broad back, hands that even with their arthritic contortions are substantial and imply a capacity for the endurance of pain. He shuffles out to coach first base only slightly faster than Bill shuffles into the stadium, trailing little Betty by a good four yards. It is a wholly different dynamic when he approaches the fans before games, not bright and improving like the players, but something closer to them, a face and a body ebbing. It's difficult to know whether he is someone to be envied.

"In 1962, a little boy was born," Wild Thang tells us. "And that little boy's only dream was to own one of these here dogs."

He is kneeling now behind home plate, where Hank should be crouching. Two exhausted border collies flank him. Also, one of the monkeys, finally off his saddle, has scampered up to sit on his shoulder, staring at the crowd, too panicked to move.

"And that little boy," Wild Thang continues. "That boy, he loved a monkey by the name of Curious George. It all started there."

He stops to let us absorb that.

"This has been my life," he says. "These animals are my . . . life."

It is a good pause. And in it I am able to realize that the music has changed seamlessly away from the honky-tonk rock that worked so well with small, galloping animals. The second movement in Wild Thang's symphony is something like taps. Also a little like a stripped-down version of the theme from *Independence Day*. The scene is absurd, but we are all hushed, I think because Wild Thang has so fully embraced the meaning of this moment. Into the microphone, panting but resolute, he sounds as if he may be starting to cry, and even if he isn't near tears, the tone is so intimate, this man kneeling as though in prayer, wearing the home team's jersey and a cowboy hat that must be older than I am, surrounded by his animals, his *life*, giving thanks.

He sounds almost mournful when he continues.

"God has given me a talent, I know that he has."

What a thing to know.

"I'm here with y'all tonight," he says, and waits a moment for the appreciative smattering of cheers. "Tomorrow night I'm in, um, Davenport. Come Tuesday, I'm in Oregon. And the next week, Montana. And the next week, Myrtle Beach, South Carolina. And for me to do that, to be this man, to drive all these places, it takes people like y'all. Y'all, in your town, coming out to these games."

It sounds as though he has more to say, and we are waiting for it, but he holds back, just enough to seem as stoic as we wanted him to be.

"I just want to thank y'all. May God bless you in the way he has blessed me."

He stands, stiff, and walks with his animals to begin a circle of the field, stopping so that everyone in the crowd can take a last picture of monkeys sitting on dogs.

You can argue that one comes to every sporting event to see something new, each game unpredictable. But most sports have a clock ticking down, a beginning and then a set amount of minutes until it is over. Baseball is untimed and languid. Though this is no great revelation, it's still satisfying in an existential way to know that the game will never constrain you with a predetermined end.

When will you be done? friends ask everyone here. *When is it over?* my girlfriend will text. And I can answer honestly: *I have no idea.* I have *no idea* what might happen with two on and two outs in the top of the eighth, a wild pickoff move to score the tying run or a walk to load the bases and a pitching change because the manager saw something scared on his boy's face. If anything feels honestly dreamlike in baseball, in the action, the team, the crowd, the field, the itinerant entertainers, it is that we don't know when it will be over while we're in it.

And even when there is a final score, we can be stubborn, we can keep the game from ending. No wonder baseball is so weighted with literature and film versions. There are always stories left that we can tell, myths we can make, myths to fill in the spaces, observations that soon become hyperbole that then become outright lies, but so what? We can surprise ourselves by how we remember it, never exactly as what it was, a dream retold in the morning, boring probably, but at least open to interpretation.

With the invention of cell phones and the Internet, then the relationship between the two, Wild Thang has become famous. He is on his way to YouTube superstardom. It feels good to believe in a bayou boy who always wanted a life like the Man with the Yellow Hat. But also just his confidence that this was preordained, always an end point, an unquestionably substantive life to live. And if he says it with enough certainty, it is true. His wife is back in Mississippi. She is a *good, no, a great woman,* staying with his son and all of the things he has given up *nobly* not only to provide for them but to commune with a worthwhile existence, sleeping some nights at truck stops, nestled in the straw in his trailer, warmed by the body heat of three species that he dreamed of as a boy.

Variations of tonight's speech have been spoken in places that look exactly like this one in Illinois, Delaware, Montana, and have gotten hundreds of thousands of hits with titles like: "Cowboy with Monkey Gives Crazy Inspirational Speech!!!!" And now people know ahead of time what is coming to town, and he surprises nobody with his entrance or his sentiment. But he still speaks every time and for longer, a whole life's story about struggle and triumph and dogs and monkey training and the gulf oil spill and triumph again. I see Jason, the guy who videos everything in Clinton, leaning over the opposing team's dugout, smiling, turning his left wrist to zoom the lens. This will be his all-time most viewed video, the only video that brings thousands of visitors to his YouTube page, more than Nick Franklin's home runs or Kalian Sams's home runs or Danny Carroll's, or Hank's two-run bloop single to right, which got 147 views, two likes, and zero comments.

Tim is a dreamer, he has told me so. But I think that he is using the word differently, the John Lennon way, though without that cheeky venom that colored Lennon's free love. "Dream," in the stands, with Tim, means something kind. He is a gentle, sedentary man, and so he prefers to dream.

He tells me a story from thirty years ago, right around the time that a young Wild Thang, just a humble rodeo clown then, began his pilgrimage to find the animals that would become his life. It's from the strike, that year of loud, angry stagnancy. Tim and his friends were of a younger, hungry generation in Clinton, coming into adulthood in a deep recession, jealous of the union men who had some and still wanted more. And the company had ways of being more persuasive than a group of old guys holding signs could ever be. The strike began at midnight on August 1, 1979. By August 2, the *Clinton Herald,* as well as local papers in other Iowa counties, in Illinois, in Missouri, ran a full-page ad listing every new position that had opened up at the Clinton plant, along with its hourly salary, and at the bottom of the page an extra bonus, forty-six cents per hour for out-of-towners to cover cost of living.

Tim had plenty of friends who were scabs out of necessity. Because they were making $5.00 an hour doing part-time shit as everything began to close, and $8.79 an hour, as was advertised, is the start of a life, and how is it bad to want that? Tim looked me in the eye in a way that seemed important when he said that he couldn't do it because he knew some of those striking men and he knew their families and he felt the collective deflation of his home that the losing effort was beginning to create. Or at least that is what he tells me, and so I believe it, and I look at Tim with melancholy reverence. He appreciates the things that deserve appreciation. He never worked a steady job at ADM, has never made what those guys make, but he does not want to be complicit in a corporation that would so happily crush people who were there first. All of it was a choice. It's important I know that. He did the right thing, stupid maybe, but sacrificial, and why shouldn't he be proud of that? Why can't that be an achievement?

"At times," Dan Peltier told Congress, "the minors seem to be a series of acts of desperation."

There is a bluntness to these words that, when I read them out loud to myself, I realize I never hear, day after day after day in the clubhouse.

Of course, then he ends with "Despite these observations, I would not give up my experience in playing baseball for anything. There is no greater feeling in the world than the first time you get called up to the majors, and there is also no greater low than the day that you get sent back down. Knowing what I know, I would still do it all over again."

I want to feel that certain about anything, but I don't trust that I can. Who can? What real person that I know, that I love, has ever been that certain? I was brought up on doubt, the expectation of failure eventually validated because failure always happens. The only time that reality wasn't discussed was during televised baseball games. And after my father told me that my brother's problem was delusions of grandeur, that he actually thought he could be somebody amazing and that chasing a high was just an extension of incorrect logic, we turned on a baseball game. And he predicted a home run because his favorite player was due and had that look in his eyes.

Dan Peltier, the lucky one, the college graduate, the man who made the majors, and who now lives in the St. Paul suburbs with his wife and kids, got the chance to speak out, and he was still ignored. And a week before this season started, an article ran in *Baseball America*, the only reading material delivered to the clubhouse: "Playing for Peanuts: Many Minor Leagues Scrimp and Save to Survive." It must have seemed a bit obvious to the players as they read it. It skimmed through difficult realities—the 2006 collective bargaining agreement that had no minor-league players in attendance, the fact that most minor leaguers interviewed said they would not unionize, fearing punishment and eventual release. But it ended on high redemption: "Their air mattresses will sit in rooms decorated only by mold. And they'll gladly accept this sacrifice. They're chasing a dream."

I never manage to ask the players about reading those words midchase. I am always afraid that they will think I am taunting them when I ask them things that are never asked. And I am always feeling guilty that maybe I am, in fact, taunting, or at least condescending, trying to point out their futilities that they don't want to see, because so many of them carry themselves with swollen superiority that can only come from a young jock and that is a tempting thing to want to deflate.

The LumberKings are winning 6–0, an occasion that should be happy. I see Hank trying to make it so, yelling one-syllable encouragement to his teammates after Wild Thang has given his last wave and driven off the field, his sheep standing proudly atop the truck, his American flags fluttering. But Wild Thang's exit should have been the end of this game. It cannot be topped. Neither team manages a hit over the next two and a half innings, and the crowd sags. Even the Baseball Family, though staying dutifully until the end, is showing that sense of duty on their faces. Hank stays on the top step of the dugout. He grabs Blake Ochoa, the man starting over him at catcher, by the shoulders after he pops out in the eighth, says something supportive in Spanish. The same with Matt Cerione after he strikes out. And then finally to Danny, playing left field, the LumberKings' last hitter who swings at a fastball near his eyes and grimaces the moment he hears it pop into the mitt behind him.

At the end of the game, Danny, Hank, and Sams trudge off the field in a row, none of them looking as if they've won, none of them embodying Brad's ecstatic tone from the PA booth—*"How about those Lumber-Kings?!"* They pass us in the stands. Betty asks them to stop for just a moment; she wants to take a picture for that little girl who looks even younger than she is, who has a crush on Danny. They pose, smiling big, Danny in the middle, Sams and Hank flanking him. They rest arms on each other's shoulders. They look just right. They are always posing.

. . .

Hank and I are in my car days later. It is midnight and it is pouring rain. He found me in the locker room and said, "Can we go somewhere to get drunk?" I was not sympathetic but thrilled, tapped for something important. He played this night and went 1-5. The game was delayed because of rain, an hour in the clubhouse, then a respite from the wetness, more playing, continuing this time even as the rain returned, grew harder.

I am a bad driver, a worse rain driver, and an even worse rainy night driver. I clutch the wheel as we slosh past the factory, bright. Driving up to the mass, before the buildings become impenetrable, I think I can make out south Clinton through the barbed-wire fencing. I think I can make out the signs on the houses of those who refused to leave or were never offered a buyout—*ADM Poly Is Not a Good Neighbor,* lit ironically by the fluorescent glare of what they are protesting. I feel us starting to drift. A train is sliding by, louder than my radio. It would crush us so fast.

"Are you sure you don't want me to drive?" Hank asks. "It feels like I'm about to die in fucking Clinton."

"I apologized ahead of time," I say. We laugh.

We are going to Applebee's because a radio commercial announced that Applebee's is open until 2:00 a.m. on weekends now—*even more fun in the neighborhood.* But this neighborhood is dark, and it closes early because nobody lives here. Hank is unconvinced, sprints out into the rain to bang on the door. Nothing. We go to the Rodeo, a chain bar like Hooters but with a mechanical bull to go along with wings and flat beer. Closed. As is Legends Sports Bar. Hank makes an unintentional noise, a low, breathy groan. He says, "How can it be so fucking hard to get a drink when I want a drink?"

We drive on to the Wild Rose Casino because it is always open, the only center of early-morning activity and light beyond the factory. I ask him his mother's name and his father's, his brother's, his sister's. I forget them all as he says them. They all live together still. I will see their place in six months, drive out on a sunny Southern California highway far from here to eat his mother's empanadas and look at his sister's *quinceanera* pictures and hold his high school trophies that they still keep in the living room.

The parking lot at the Wild Rose is packed. I recognize some of the cars from the stadium lot. We walk in and squint into the lights that come from everywhere, a row on the floor even, leading from room to room, like airplane emergency lights except not pointing to any exit. We walk to the Coaches Corner Sports Bar, and it is closed. Hank gives his best smile to the off-duty hostess and says, "Miss, I'm a ballplayer. We just won and now I'm hungry." She says congrats, but closed is closed. We drift down the hallway, past pictures of pastures and baseball mitts and sawmills and money and the grinning faces of part-time models. It's only hard-core gamblers left.

We stand in the middle of everything. People shuffle past to the bathroom before going back to their games. There are so many stories being hollered in robot voices out of so many differently themed slot machines: *Win the riches of King Tut's Tomb! Yarrgh, a pirate's booty for ye!* So many things to make pressing buttons and hearing winless whirs not what it really is.

We leave the Wild Rose and run back to the car, puddles drenching our socks. Hank brings up how pathetic those people were, desperate like that, just wasting away their time and money on a Saturday night. I join his harsh laugh at the button pressers waiting for something that won't come. It is important to have somebody to look down on. He asks if I want to give up on this night or maybe drive to another town. He says it's okay for us to give up on it. I say, "Really?" He says that he understands. We drive to a gas station and buy a six-pack of tall-boy bottles of Coors Light. He begins to chug in my car and says, "This is cool, right?" He knows I am still somebody who would never say no to him, and that is a nice addition to his life right now.

We get to the parking lot outside his place. He doesn't want to go in for a while, so we sit and drink in the car. He is drinking fast, so I am, with stupid, college muscle memory, trying to drink fast, too. His phone rings, and it's his mother in California. He speaks in one-word Spanish answers, hangs up quickly, like a teenager.

"Does she like you being out here playing still?" I ask.

"Oh yeah," he says. "She's cool with it."

"Nice mom," I say.

"She knows that I'm living my dream, right?" he says.

He nods to himself.

I say yes and want to say more. I want loving voices to answer for me when I call, affirm that I am okay and that whatever it is I'm doing here is worthwhile.

He is booze-cheered and ready to sleep. He finishes his third beer and thanks me, says, "See you tomorrow, probably."

"Yeah, probably."

"You, uh, gonna be okay?" he asks.

I don't know what to do. I am the observed, the pitied, drenched and quiet, surrounded by candy bar wrappers and Cheez-It crumbs, the debris of all my time alone. And if he is doomed to me, albeit nobly so, what am I to him? Just a guy watching him, tailing him, asking, *Is it worth it? Is it worth it?*—the same questions since the beginning—and then driving home alone, returning alone to watch more. I cannot say out loud what I think, that I like the story of himself that he tells, that I'm attracted to it on an almost prenatal level, jealous and protective at the same time. I like stories, Hank. And I need to believe that there is a point to you.

He tells me to drive safe, shakes my hand, and looks me in the eye. He trots to his apartment, and I watch his shadow in the parking lot light, stretched enormous until it disappears.

Voices

I'VE BEGUN TO LEAVE BORING GAMES EARLY. I feel bad about it. I apologize to Betty and Tim and Joyce. I am forgiven, though Joyce is often perplexed that in a never-ending sixth inning of a stagnant game, I cannot find anything to be interested in. I have begun to think of it as a character flaw, but I can't explain the guilt I feel to friends or to my girlfriend, all the people I never invite here.

What's happening?

Nothing, really.

Well, why stay?

Now I'm on Highway 30, which will then turn into 61, which I will exit off onto I-80. The drive has become subconscious—when to turn just a little, how to hold my eyelids open for all the moments when I don't have to turn and the only things to sustain my gaze are grayer-than-usual clouds or a swaying FedEx truck on a particularly windy day.

The last vestiges of the town are behind me, so everything is black.

Dave's voice is on the radio, but he's already starting to fade into crackling that sounds like when you hold a conch shell to your ear and pretend it's the ocean. The first time I met Dave, that day with the tour and the snow and the Mountain Dew, I asked him for a sample of his Radio Voice, capitalized, the official one. He gave a polite smile, unnatural and short-lived. He said, "No Radio Voice. That's a common misconception."

"Oh," I said.

"There's a lot of misconceptions about broadcasting," he continued. He shook his head at hypothetical misconceivers. "I just go out there and speak, and it's the naturalness that people respond to."

This, I have surmised, is a lie. Dave's Radio Voice is part infomercial, part film noir private eye. It is nasal yet strong, something that has to be intentionally dated, meant to come from a man in a fedora, chewing on an unlit cigar. Dave sounds tired tonight, but he doesn't waver. It is something like the hundredth game of the season—who knows exactly?—one that, even fresh in my mind, not actually over yet, I cannot distinguish from any other game. Dave's is the stamina of the voice and the mind, not the body, the need to keep consistent as each day stretches into the next. Other than proclamations about Nick Franklin and Erasmo Ramírez, Dave hasn't had much to raise his voice for.

Tonight's game is tied, he reminds any listener. It's been a long one, lots of walks and lots of errors, lots of runs that feel accidental, that leave everyone but Joyce unsure of who scored when. This is where the art of the baseball broadcaster comes in, and I imagine Dave's neck straining, nervous but prepared as he tries to fill up the air with practiced, natural chatter.

Gabriel Noriega takes the plate with men on base in the eighth.

"Well, here's a kid who's been struggling," Dave announces. He sighs into the microphone, a heavy, almost pornographic noise that can't have been intentional. "He's nineteen, folks. When you're nineteen and there's pressure on you, it's hard to adjust to professional pitching. This is a tough spot to see him in at the plate, though. But, you know, this is the kind of moment that could change the season around for a guy."

Untrue. And there is not much conviction to the words. Dave takes another long breath, and without his talking I hear the panicked squeak that my car makes somewhere in its bowels every time I hit the smallest bump. Kevin's voice breaks through the coverage, warbling and ecstatic.

"Let's go LumberKings!"

"Well, Kevin Cheney is still here, folks," Dave announces.

Kevin Cheney, not to be confused with the chicken-dancing Kevin, is the sometimes tolerated, sometimes beloved mentally challenged man who is allowed into every home game and given one free cheeseburger with extra pickles each night. He is kind and proud and will announce at various intervals that he is the number one fan, which nobody will disagree with. It is perhaps condescending but also wonderfully contained, the satisfaction he is allowed to feel here, a localized sense of purpose rivaled only by Dancing Bobby in his scoutmaster's outfit in Burlington. That doesn't matter right now. Kevin is in Dave's air, cutting into a soundscape that is Dave's own. And Joyce, too, I hear her—"*Come on, Gabby*," as if she knows the boy. I know that Dave doesn't like the intrusion.

I slow down along Highway 30, even though there are never cops. I let his voice hang in my car a little bit longer. It seems right. He gets thirty minutes pregame and fifteen minutes postgame and the game itself. He gets those moments on 1390 KCLN, one of the few stations small enough to serve only Clinton and its surrounding rural sprawl. Before he begins, there is an endless block of brassy, lilting pop songs from the 1950s and 1960s. When he stops, depending on how late it is, I've heard an antiques appraisal show or more music or nothing. There's no way to know how many people are listening.

"Maybe nobody," Dave has said to me. He is squat, average to look at. His hair is cut short like most of the players', but his is beginning to gray, even in his mid-twenties. He wears a wisp of a goatee, just on his chin. His mouth is a flat line. He doesn't look like his voice.

We were silent together for a moment, and then, uneasy with his own words, he said, "No, that's not true. People listen. Thousands of people."

Betty listens to Dave every night the team is out of town, and she tells him so. And she tells me things like "Oh, it was a heavy, humid one out in Bowling Green. Dave said they were sweating through their hats."

I can't see Gabriel Noriega miss a breaking ball in the dirt, but I know what Dave sees. I hear Dave describing Noriega's body lunging. He calls him eager and off balance. He says it with a tone that is caring but disappointed, ultimately unsurprised. Something paternal. And so I picture Noriega wincing as the ball falls under his bat, the way his young head must be pulled, prematurely, toward left field, as though this pitch is going to be the one he really gets into. I picture Dave wincing, too. He takes it hard when the team is losing.

When Dave's voice runs out, I ride with Delilah. I found her by accident. So few things catch my broken antenna in between towns, and the night is silent except for disappointing fuzz. So when I heard anything in my early drives, I stopped searching and willed the signal to stay. Delilah entered my world with majesty, her overblown entrance music like a batter's walking up to the plate. I heard a slow, mounting drumbeat, with one hammered guitar chord over it, a sugary soprano sax riff, and then *De-Li-Lah*. I was enchanted.

"Was this one of those days?" she asks me. "You know the kind of day I'm talking about. It's long and it's hot and all you want to do is come home and put your feet up and have a glass of lemonade?"

She knows. She chuckles because she knows that she knows.

I switch back to 1390 KCLN, just to give Dave another shot. Sometimes I can hit a pocket when I pass DeWitt, the closest thing to a town for a good ten miles, where there are so few wires to interfere that the signal fades back in, just for a moment. Dave is barely audible tonight, though. There is angry static. I'm guessing the game is over. The only words I can make out are "tough" and "tomorrow," noticeably strained even as they are swallowed. He's got fifteen minutes of recap ahead of him, which I won't hear and which he will cram with prepared material, interviews saved from earlier, and a little bit of time allotted for analytical ad-libbing, a display of his personality because in this business you've got to have personality.

I return to the clear signal. Delilah tells me about her children, the young ones, her boys. They had a baseball game today. "Isn't it always the way?" she says. She wishes that we could have seen them. But she knows we can imagine it—we've seen it with our own babies, haven't we? They grow up and they take their brother's old mitt and they put on a hat and everything is so perfectly the same.

She chuckles. She says, "Oh," and then lets it trail off into contented nothingness. She plays the *Dawson's Creek* theme song, the one that promises a lot. She likes that song. It is kind and inoffensive and evocative. I've heard it a dozen times by now, at various intervals on the highway, the easy music stroking the blackness. I sing along, loud, until the song ends. She will be with us from seven until midnight.

I make sure to tell people about these moments over drinks. They are less uncomfortable when not secret. If spoken about, preemptively joked about, they're no longer overpowering, embarrassing intimacies, the thing that I wait for and must experience alone. I can nod to the fact that I know how ridiculous Delilah is and, thus, the whole scene of me and her and the car and the loneliness is the hilarious construction of a self-aware mind. I don't acknowledge to anyone that her patronizing soothes me. That it is the exact level of communication I want. That I am relieved when I hear her in the in-between, taking me home.

Linked to the LumberKings' Web site is the LumberBlog, an addition initiated and run entirely by Dave, a platform that he thought out thoroughly and that I imagine him presenting to the rest of the front office using phrases like youth culture and mixed-media presence, concepts entirely antithetical to untelevised minor-league baseball played in a Depression-era stadium. "Well, all right," Ted told him. "David, if you want to do it, just do it."

He did and he did it well. It looks sharp. Not just A-ball sharp, either. Slicker and far more up-to-date than any other blog in the Midwest League. He is holding steady at the forty-sixth spot on the list of top fifty baseball blogs in the country that another blogger has unofficially compiled, a commendation that he notes when he thanks us readers and listeners for the support. Tonight, after he signs off the postgame show, rereads his notes, and slips them into his computer bag, after he drives three blocks to his apartment, where he will look out the window at the McDonald's across the street and then the stadium lights powering down just beyond it, he will blog.

Sometimes he live blogs the world. When it's raining and a game is delayed, he tells us, "It's raining, folks."

When it's windy, "It's windy," and maybe he'll throw in a picture of the flag contorted above the right-field fence.

Sometimes he lets himself go. He blogs not about baseball, not about Walmart's super savings or the after-game karaoke services of DJ Dawg or the limited-edition pink home jerseys auctioned off for breast cancer awareness. Sometimes he gives us something of himself, outright. Take, "Behind the Scenes: Tools of the Trade." It's for all those out there who hear him and want to be heard the way he's heard.

He is thorough. "Speaking of my digital recorder," he writes, "it's a TASCAM DR-07 that I purchased from Guitar Center. Yes, that sounds off the beaten path for sports broadcasters, but the mini recorders that you buy at office supply stores just don't have the audio clarity that my TASCAM does."

He lets us know that he is not a snob or a trend whore. He does not use Apple products just because they're fashionable, and his HP has worked just fine for two seasons. His headset is "rugged" compared with the things you'll see other guys shelling out for. But he doesn't mind being old school. Neither should we.

If we have questions, his e-mail address is there, and he welcomes any and all. We're free to comment on the post, too, an instant missive for the public to read. If we comment, he'll respond.

The radioman is the world creator. The radioman interprets moments that almost nobody else sees, and maybe sometimes he invents them. Because everything else is blank. On television, for the fractional percent of announcers who make that leap to the screen, their art becomes ornamentation to the images of the players that everyone cares about and the graphics that can exactly quantify a player's habits, trends, worth. Some of the larger A-ball markets have occasional TV coverage of their games. It's a terrible idea, primarily because it removes the opportunity to imagine beyond the confines of ever-dull reality. One camera peeking over the wall in center field reduces the game to specific borders, a distance that is neither bird's-eye in scope nor close enough to reveal emotion. It's like watching a recently exhumed video of a child's talent show, the triumph instantly exposed for how small it really was.

But nothing is celebrated until it is lost, and world creation is no exception, trumpeted in the human interest columns of sports sections only now that it can be referred to as a dying art. After this season, when Dave Niehaus dies and thus vacates his longtime position as the Mariners' broadcaster, the job that Dave and every other man in the lower rungs of the Mariners organization daily, silently fantasizes himself doing, tributes will be written full of weighty quotes. Niehaus will be remembered as saying, "[Radio] is where the creativity is." Vin Scully is still alive, but only that kind of alive that leaves everyone waiting in anticipation of the explosion of legacy-defining that will follow his death. He says that the radioman is "the eyes and the ears, and the imagination, as well." Former baseball commissioner Bart Giamatti, the most eloquent of the game's suits, put it best, calling a major-league radio broadcast "the enclosed green fields of the mind."

When the LumberKings are doing poorly, I think I can hear Dave's mind, but the fields aren't green. I hear only mounting negativity in his pauses and occasional sighs. Players' girlfriends, who have to listen to the weak KCLN streaming feed on their computers to track their boyfriends, complain, when they come into town, that his voice can make them think that nothing is ever going to be okay, certainly not the career prospects of the itinerant men they plan to marry.

When I can no longer hear him, I imagine his night. I imagine him in the booth, staying longer than he has to. The visiting announcer will have already packed up his things, may already be a couple of beers deep. Brad will have already knocked on the window that separates the PA man's side of the wooden cubicle from the announcer's, silently gesturing that Dave should leave with him. He will have already been waved off.

Often a player is commended for the things he does when nobody is watching. This speaks to his better-than-ours motivation, even at a young age, the "intangibles" that bring a player favor and are always referenced, though never satisfactorily explained. Of course there is the unspoken reality that since the player is commended for doing things when nobody's watching, somebody is, in fact, watching. Dave is watching, for one. And Dave will report, faithfully, that a kid like Erasmo is always diligent, always doing extra work alone and unprovoked, a quality that seems so important in the morality by which Dave lives. But nobody will ever say it about him.

A broadcaster, especially at this level, where no team would think of paying for two of them, is almost always surrounded and almost always alone. He rides the bus with the players, but he sits in the front with his laptop and organizes stats that he will announce about the boys who lounge behind him, screaming until it all sounds like one voice. When I leave the park early and I listen to Dave, Joyce is there, too, and Kevin and the rest of the white noise, and I know that he is perched atop a thousand people, that they are all experiencing the same thing. But Dave is talking out beyond the stadium, to anyone, to a collection of people with no faces, a group of indeterminate size.

.   .   .

I talk to myself on these nighttime car rides.

"That's a motherfucking dead deer," I say, when I pass exploded car-casses on the side of the road, trying not to look at the eyes, if they're still there.

"*Yeah,*" I scream, when I pass a semi and duck in front of it because we've been racing and I just won the race, though the trucker, who I can never see, doesn't know it.

Sometimes I imagine eye contact when a car comes up behind me after minutes of nobody. There is just enough light for me to see the shape of a face through the rearview mirror. I imagine that she is young, heading back home from college, something like that. She is tired and she wants contact. Through her windshield, bouncing off my mirror, we see each other.

It's too late to call home, which is what I still call my parents' home. If it were earlier, I would call my father, and he would listen as I described the field. He would give off low *wows* as I told him about the slope of the outfield fence again, the splinters on the wood, the chalk mixed in the dirt. He likes the details. He likes the way the seats clump in a semicircle around the infield and how everything else is empty space, how open that must look. He likes the notion of the river beyond the fence, and the train tracks, these enormous tropes clustered around a game unchanged in my retelling. He will talk to me still with a patience that is embarrassing because it means that he senses I need it. The stories I tell him mimic the ones that he told me to make me fall asleep as a boy.

Imagine it. Imagine it until you can't imagine anything bad, and then you will close your eyes, and then you will wake up okay.

I want to talk to Dave about fear in those moments when we do talk, whether we're sitting by Joyce watching batting practice or on the bus, at the front, turning our necks to look for inclusion when there is a burst of laughter. It's something that mounts over the course of a sea-son. When there is so much watching, so many moments in which you are not the primary actor, thoughts become louder. We are close to the same age, Dave and I, though I hardly ever remember that. Despite his self-imposed responsibilities and the distinguished grays in his hair, we're in the same space in our lives, out of college and not yet thirty, old enough to worry, young enough to try to look at the players as peers even as they're treated as part baby, part full-on adult, never equal.

We talk about the players when we talk.

We share anecdotes, and if something I say sounds too personal or juicy, too much of a brag or a challenge to his authority, I feel sorry for it.

"Sams needs to start hitting curveballs," I said to him at a recent batting practice.

"Obviously," he said. "Some guys, you know, it's just those little adjustments that need to be made holding them back."

"Mmm," I said.

"Who knows what'll happen," he said.

"I've noticed that if you throw him a first-pitch strike, it's a guaranteed out," I said. I was proud of that one.

"Oh, you've noticed that, too?" he said.

We turned to watch Sams together, and together we analyzed his failures. We were far enough away not to see his face as he fouled off easy batting practice lobs and saw Tamargo turn his back with some combination of boredom and disgust. We glanced at each other and exchanged a knowing, worried look. We did not say what I know I was thinking and what I hope and guess that Dave was thinking, too: that it would be painful and somehow wildly unjust for Kalian Sams to fail here. This man flown in all the way from Holland, with shoulders that look like a pair of bowling balls resting on a seesaw, who can hit a ball far enough to make you giggle for lack of a better response. And still he is tenuous. He could soon become past tense, a few pictures on baseball cards sold on eBay for thirty-three cents, a stat line that no longer changes. And what does that say about those of us who follow him?

Sometimes, Dave, I wake up right after I fall asleep because it feels like a hand that's even bigger than the hand of Kalian Sams is choking me. I drive to minor-league baseball games to find something remarkable. Or maybe I just want to watch because watching slows time, removes rush and responsibility from those of us not playing. Sometimes it feels like I'm trying too hard, I'm reaching for meaning, and I want to be remarkable, or at least validated in what I think is worthwhile, and that feels like pulling at a fishing line that doesn't end and is always weighted, yanking it toward myself until red tracks of blood run across my palms.

I want to ask Dave if he thinks that his voice stands out.

Overlooking the field, he got personal for a moment without me asking anything. He told me that he was searched for three times on his blog, by name. He can track every hit he gets and does so in the morning, slouched in his desk chair, drinking Diet Mountain Dew. Sometimes people are searching "Mariners" or "Iowa baseball" or, often, "Nick Franklin shortstop," but three of them typed in his name.

I thought Delilah was only an Iowa phenomenon, but I was wrong. She is everywhere. As I exit onto I-80, past the largest truck stop in the world with a population near a thousand on any given night, then a new thousand the next night, she is talking to me, here, and she is saying the same words to people in Boston and Seattle and Jacksonville and Palm Springs. After a commercial break we all hear her drums, her guitar, her soprano sax, then "De-Li-Lah," as usual. Her voice intones with a question.

"Have a long shift at the—" There is a pause, not long and ungraceful like when the LumberKings fail and Dave's sighs linger. Then: "John Deere factory?" It's been prerecorded from a list that she must be given by her producers, the most iconic employers of every region where she is syndicated. And the Quad Cities survive off tractors. "Kick your boots off and relax with me," she invites her laborer fans. Clinton isn't big enough for Delilah to speak directly to it, and "Archer Daniels Midland corn-processing and polymer plastics plant" doesn't have the "John Deere" ring to it.

A caller tells Delilah that she used to be full of doubt and now she isn't. She tells her that her boyfriend never wanted to commit, he just wasn't ready, but then one day he was. It was a miracle. And now he's perfect. Things worked out.

"Isn't that *amazing*?" the woman says. "Isn't it *amazing* the way life works. I just thought I should tell you."

Delilah is no fool and she seems dubious, but she congratulates the woman and calls her sweetie. I can hear the woman smiling. There are the sounds of a child who should be asleep in the background. Delilah plays a song just for this woman and her perseverance, her final, maybe delusional happiness. It's Christina Aguilera's "Beautiful," a perfect song for the moments when Delilah isn't quite sure how to handle a vapid caller but still wants to be nice. Anything can be remarkable when Delilah plays the right song.

I look down to turn up the volume. I look up to see the eyes of something. It's too small to be a deer, bigger than a rabbit, though. Whatever it is, it's alive for a last second and its eyes are wet and black and I am the last thing it sees before the squelch that is louder than Delilah, louder than my engine. And then I am past it, and it makes no more noise. Delilah says that music is the language of angels. When you are listening to her, you are eavesdropping on something holy.

The truck stop by exit 271 is lit up in a harsh, alien glow. I stop here when I have to pee, mostly, but tonight I stop because I want to stop. I want to stand still and look at the blood on my bumper and then close my eyes. The semis are strewn along the grounds, not parked in distinct rows, just wherever. Nobody is in the hallway at the truck stop. One of the lights that run horizontally across the ceiling is broken. It makes a sound like a radio with no signal. I look out at all the trucks, and I know men are in them, sleeping or masturbating or just staring ahead, but there are no lights, and I let myself think, for the moment, that I'm the only person inert and off the highway for miles.

In the bathroom, a man is bending down over the sink to splash water on his face and then looking up at his reflection in the mirror, beads of water hanging off the edges of his beard. He does it a few times, slowly, and doesn't look at me. I wonder who he listens to as he drives, how many times stations fade out and change with voices like Delilah's extending across state lines, linking places and days.

Tammy goes to most games with her family still, but her husband doesn't anymore. Dan was part of the Roadkill Crew, the wheelman a lot of the time, with Tammy riding shotgun and Tim howling in the back. He drove to Arizona for spring training for a few years, watching the sunrise on the fire-orange hills as they got close while everyone else slept. He organized all his vacation days at ADM around Clinton's away games. But he's quit ADM now. He hated it there for twenty-five years, the hours, the way his lungs hurt, the burn on his shoulders and arms after an afternoon inside the vats with a jackhammer, getting sludge off steel. He had been a complainer, or at least he had complained to Tammy about the stuff he saw poured into the river and the way things were inside the factory, and she had made a stink until the plant manager told Dan to shut her up. Dan is a truck driver now, finally. Before the heart attack, and again right after the doctors cleared him, he lived a life hopping between places like this rest stop, no longer stationary, looking forward to the next game's beginning. He is, Tammy says, who he always wanted to be, nobody's employee, unmoored.

I try to think of myself as that kind of man, my face drawn and tired from staring down the whole country as I hurtle through it. I try to think of how many people I would see and nod to, exchange a word with, that I would never have to speak to again. That is all I think of these days—I *could* be that. I have the capacity to be that. The sound of an engine starting comes from outside, the whining chug until finally the clutch catches and then a roar.

It is a beautiful act to put language to the game, making it better than it really is. I want to think that for sure, and I want to tell Dave that, too. It is a noble thing. It is making something, even if it doesn't last. Dave's earliest precursors narrated games before they could produce clean, live audio from the stadium. Before teams sent radiomen to away games, they would get transcripts and sit in a windowless booth, overlooking nothing, and they would call the thing with urgency. They held miniature bats in one hand during broadcasts, and when a batter made contact, they voiced it, slapping their wood against the thick cardboard of empty teletape rolls. They simulated crowd noise and then pitched their own words above it, heightening the ambience that they'd created, yelling behind the fabrications to make you feel it. There were the facts—the ball was caught in right field, the score is tied at one—and everything else was theirs. They had the power to make people imagine what they knew to be true.

Ted told me that at the winter baseball meetings in Orlando, the LumberKings got 650 résumés and tapes from men looking for Dave's job, a job that wasn't vacated and might not be any time soon. Voices with names quickly forgotten, hoping that something in the timbre of their home run call would give them the right to move to Clinton, Iowa.

All Dave wants to do is leave. This was supposed to be a springboard, an entrance leading right to an exit. He is in his fifth year now. This past winter was the first when he didn't return home to his parents' house in Wisconsin and spend the off-season doing ticket sales for the Milwaukee Brewers, his voice clean and precise over the phone, wasted on repeating package deals to one listener at a time. Instead, he stayed in Clinton and called high school football games, tried to dramatize the stumbling movements of pimply sophomores to their grandmothers sitting at home.

Dave and I pretend to each other. We feign assurance. Dave knows everything. And he tells me everything he knows as though I should know it, too, as though anyone should. He has shaped a life around memorizing and interpreting players who can do things that he can't. I look for that certainty. For talent that is certain, for scores that are official. For images that live up to what I expect them to be.

I tell myself again that the idea is to transcend, a word that does not gain clarity as I overuse it, but in fact grows more obscure. Still, to transcend. That vagary is what to reach for, found maybe in the clubhouse, the stadium, all of it. The broadcast. I've read quotations of men who said that watching baseball live for the first time was a disappointment after having listened to Harry Caray for years, because his version was so much more. And then they got to the park and everything had limits and the players were mortal men, maybe a little taller, a little faster than the average. That seems impossible, here and now, that sense of awe. Dave just wants more people to hear what he knows. I think we both want to look down on each other.

Brad and Dave, the local voices, go out after the games sometimes. They go to Manning's Whistle Stop, across the street from the stadium. Brad has been going to Manning's for a long time, it being the closest bar to the public address booth that he has manned since he was seventeen. Brad will tell me months from now, when we're driving together across three states because the LumberKings are still alive when nobody expected them to be, that he could have ended up at various places along the route. South Bend, in particular, offered him a job to be their public address man, and they would have set him up with other duties as well—stats, maybe some radio. But who knows? Sure, they promised him things, but what does that mean? We will pass the South Bend exit on our way to Ohio, and Brad will point.

"There," he will say, though all we'll be able to see are trees and a towering Burger King sign. "That could have been me in there."

It will be me and him and Erin in the car, Erin, exactly my age, getting her first experience with a microphone in her hand this season, working as the field announcer, celebrating the winners of the miniature John Deere tractor race and the rubber-chicken toss. Erin and I will look out the window at Brad's possibilities and say, "*Wow.*" I will ask Brad why he didn't take the gig, and he'll give a long, proud sigh. He'll tell me that he is a *part* of the LumberKings. He has a good job at the county landfill each day and a thousand people listening to him every summer night, telling him so the next day at the grocery store. I won't be sure if all that is true. Because the current version of Clinton and baseball is not like the one that I'm always told used to exist, that I am so ready to mourn. The field was the center of a town that had a center, a perfect keystone. It made sense, or at least it does now that it's gone. And Betty remembers her grandfather's farm, the horses, the way he would listen to the radio broadcast of the baseball games while milking his cows and she'd sit on the hay and watch him listen. But Brad is too young to remember any of that—the old teams, the old town. He never got to live through the times that he wants to remember.

I will not say any of this to Brad, and he will look past the Burger King sign and smile.

We are watching *SportsCenter* now.

I'm at Manning's because the players ditched me, promising to make me a part of their night and then showing me that they still have the power to leave me. I stood outside the clubhouse in the rain for an hour and finally ran in, finding only Tyler, paid to do the team's laundry, rubbing grass stains out of their pants. "Gone," he said, and I said nothing. I knew Brad and Dave would be here, and they are, drinking whiskey, in no rush to leave. The best players in the world are on the screen in front of us in six-second clips of their best moments from today. We say their names out loud, each one.

In a clip from St. Louis, Albert Pujols hits a home run.

Brad says, "Peoria Chief, Albert Pujols. That was in 2000, I think."

"Yep, 2000," says Dave, though he wasn't here then.

Brad simulates his decade-old announcement: "Now batting for the Peoria Chiefs, third baseman Albert *Pu*-jols."

Then it's Joe Mauer on TV hitting a home run—"Mauer," we say. He was in the Midwest League, too. He played against Clinton. Then it's Ian Kinsler on the Rangers, who was a LumberKing not long ago. Dave rode the bus with him for the two months that he was kept around.

"Nice guy," Dave says.

"Mmm," Brad says.

SportsCenter turns to a joke clip. A man runs onto the field drunk and takes a serpentine route, avoiding security with his arms raised in triumph. Dave tells us about how he used to work for the Brewers' grounds crew when he was still a college kid, thin and fast, he was really fast. A fan leaped onto the field, and Dave sprinted across the grass in front of, what, forty thousand people? He caught the man in shallow center, speared him, wrapped his arms around the man's waist, and didn't let go until he felt them falling together. He stood to a beer-fueled ovation. He asks us if we can imagine the size of a stadium like that when you're in the middle of it. We say no.

I tell Dave that I played summer ball in high school with a kid who's in AAA with the Brewers now. I say the guy's name and then say a nickname that I was never really friendly enough to call him. I ask Dave if he's heard of him, and he says no.

Are we all just trying to repeat the feeling of a moment when we felt most important? Yes. Obviously. But if that's such an obvious thing, why does it hurt to realize it, sitting here watching *SportsCenter* at Manning's Whistle Stop? What we've seen, what we've said, the way we saw it, the way we said it, hanging out there over the volume of the flashy ESPN anchors who just show us the choice moments and then yell, *"Boom goes the dynamite!"*

Dave thinks that I'm pushing it. That I'm talking too fast, saying "remember" too many times. *Remember how fat Kirby Puckett was? Remember how crazy Carl Everett was?* As if these were the former cast members of family Thanksgivings. He doesn't want me here, intruding on his bar, his game, his knowledge. He looks around under his

LumberKings hat, at Brad and me, at the unused pool table, at the obese basset hound that the bartender has left tied to a stool. He says, "Fuck."

I leave by eleven. Delilah is still on. It's Friday night, girls' night. All the ladies are invited to get metaphorically cozy by Delilah's hearth in a well-hidden compound somewhere in Seattle. A crackling fire is evoked, though it is eighty-five degrees here even in the rain, and who knows what they're feeling in Tucson or Honolulu. But it doesn't matter, because we are friends who have never met, me and the girls, and I imagine us in a room that may or may not exist, and I imagine Delilah like Aslan from *The Chronicles of Narnia,* with her golden mane and her Jesus complex.

I am in between again, in the dark. I am allowing myself to feel some heightened magnitude in the potential of a black horizon with nothing on it. Delilah speaks of nothing like it's everything, and that's why it resonates. She doesn't ask her callers where they're from or how old they are, so unless that information is offered up, they are nobody and they are all of us. She tells us that she is so happy to be here with us, that we're all together. She tells me she hopes that I am feeling good, that I am realizing what a special thing it is to be me on this night. I let myself believe her.

The Night

WHEN NICK FRANKLIN TRIED to hop into my front seat, Hank said no. Nick looked at both of us, seemed to understand, and ducked into the back. Hank is something like my protector, maybe something like a friend. Nick is sandwiched in the middle now between Luis Núñez and Fray Martinez, his other two new roommates, complaining about the odor from whatever product it is that Fray puts in his perm.

Fray, a relief pitcher, was terrible again tonight and is quiet. He is always quiet but usually listens and tries to smile in the moments when he understands things. Not tonight. Tonight, after he seemed unable to throw two strikes in a row, after even Clinton's most loyal began to mutter and boo, he is staring down at his bilingual Baseball Chapel pamphlet with drawn, fast-blinking eyes.

Nick speaks.

"Hank, Hank, Hank, Hank—"

"*What?*"

"Where are we going tonight?"

"Oh, you're coming?"

"Yeah, man, why do you have to say it like that?"

Hank is smirking a little. Nick doesn't like to be smirked at. He recovers quickly.

"You're just worried because I'm gonna walk in and all the girls are gonna be like, *Oh. Oh.*"

Nick repeats himself a few times, making a circle with his lips, making a wave of his eyebrows, delighting in the approximation of what will come over every young woman's face tonight when they get a look at him. Fray Martinez inches away from this display, glances up from his cheaply printed prayers, looking for an explanation.

We stop at Walmart for Coors Light and energy drinks, Stouffer's TV dinners and Pop-Tarts for tomorrow. Nick stands and waits by the door, texting, maybe his father, maybe telling him no, it's fine, he'll be good tonight, really, it's fine. Fray Martinez is trying to pay for his eighteen-pack of Coors but is left staring, frozen, at the clerk who says, *"ID,"* louder and louder, as though volume were the problem. Hank puts a calming hand on his teammate's shoulder and says something. Fray pulls out a Dominican driver's license, which does not clear anything up. Hank inserts himself between the two blank faces and assumes his usual position of smiling translator.

"Dominican," he tells her. "Dominican Republic? The island? And see it says right there: twenty-one."

"Oh. Baseball?"

Fray smiles and nods vigorously at the mention of his profession.

Hank walks away to have the stilted girlfriend conversation that develops as the days of no privacy mount: *Hey . . . lost . . . yeah . . . nope . . . not sure . . . I will . . . you too.* I follow him out into the parking lot, and we lean together on the hood of my hatchback. He smiles as it groans under our weight, and I jump away to protect it.

"It's a piece of shit," I say.

"It runs," he says. "It's stupid to ask for more than that."

He doesn't say it with venom, just flat honesty. We watch the rest of the players file out into the glow of that neon red sign that is the same everywhere.

"Can I drive it?" Hank asks. "Your car? I'm a way better driver than you."

This, too, is not cruel, just true.

"Of course," I tell him.

"That's what I miss the most," he says. "I have a Jeep at home. It's mine. I drive myself everywhere."

"Sweet," I say.

The other three cram in the back, this time with Franklin telling Núñez to sit in the middle. Núñez mutters, *"Coño,"* eyes the wunder-kind whom he now backs up on the field, realizes that this isn't a fun or winnable fight, and defers. The beers are stacked in between Fray's long legs, and he places his Baseball Chapel pamphlet on top to keep reading.

It's always about perseverance, always a challenge, always brief, one page English, one page Spanish, so that the stoic redemption is absorbed by all.

God uses trials to help grow our faith.

Dios aprovecha estos momentos difíciles en nuestra vida para que nuestra fe desarrolle.

God uses trials to discipline us when we aren't living for Him.

Dios usa las pruebas como instrumentos de disciplina cuando no andamos en Sus caminos.

The translations are stilted and too long, the product of an organization that's all-American Baptist, running its message through a Google function and assuming that the gravitas holds up. It reads like how the Latino players sound when they do their mandatory biweekly Rosetta Stone sessions, forced formalities that will never be natural no matter how hard they try to assimilate—*May I purchase some milk? Excuse me, where is the nearest library?*

Hank hits a bump on the cracked Clinton roads, and the beer clinks in between Fray's legs, drawing concerned whips of all the heads in the car. Fray looks contrite.

The baseball players are primping now. There are pre-torn jeans and fake-rhinestone T-shirts being tossed aside, picked up, and then discarded again. There are hats, not worn and dirt streaked like their LumberKings hats, but hats of major-league teams preserved in almost plastic newness, the brims subtly curved by expert hands.

I have nothing to change into, so I sit with Fray on the rented living room couch, watching a Kate Hudson romantic comedy while he slicks and buffs his Jheri curl. He finishes eventually, wipes his hands on the couch, and puts all his tools back into an ever-present prized possession, a leather, monogrammed toiletries bag. Fray likes alcohol and he likes women, or, more precisely, the way women look at him, his giant frame contrasted with full, soft lips and eyes that always seem to be pleading for something. Núñez, the other Dominican left on the LumberKings, likes to go out as well, and from the doorway to his bedroom Hank yells to me that you can always count on a Dominican as a wingman. Fray understands this and smiles.

The most fun of all the players, it is universally agreed, was Welington Dotel, with his willing, hilarious butchering of English slang, with his limber dance moves. American girls loved him here in Clinton, everywhere really. He's probably back in Oregon with the dimpled blond girl who loved him the most and married him and then got pregnant. He is off being a twenty-four-year-old small-town American father with conversational English, facing an entirely different ocean than the one he was born surrounded by.

Núñez puts on a pristine black fitted cap that Dotel left behind and cocks it to the left.

"I am a sexy motherfucker," he declares. He dances alone, with no music, his socks making muffled scratching noises on the gray wall-to-wall carpet that accompanies cheap rent across Iowa, that I recognize exactly from the apartment I arrived at a year ago.

"Do you talk to Dotel still?" I ask, hopeful. "Are you gonna call him tonight to say whatsup?"

"No," Núñez says. "He's gone."

"You have his number, right?"

"I dunno. I think so. He's gone."

Núñez shrugs and looks over to Hank, as if maybe something had been lost in translation.

"We don't really stay in touch," Hank says. "If you're here, you're here. If you're not, we don't have time."

Núñez nods. "It's his bad luck," he says with a sly smile that fades quickly, absorbed by the unadorned white walls and the bare lightbulb, nothing cheerful in the room around him to support the sentiment. We are all still, all quiet. All thinking that Núñez has been with this organization four years, that he, too, is a Dominican who has done nothing but play for all his adult life and is now playing less and less, watching more and more. He will be living in Brooklyn next year, out of baseball, not a citizen, posting a lot of random videos on Facebook. I might see him on the subway in two Christmases on my way to a party, and we will just nod at each other through a Saturday night crowd. Or maybe I will nod and imagine reciprocation from him. Or maybe that won't be him at all because a young Dominican dude in street clothes doesn't stand out on the A train the way he might in a LumberKings uniform.

Fray will be gone in a few weeks, yanked home with a visa issue that nobody helped him with. He will return to America for spring training, then another season here, then he'll get cut, too. And then there's Hank.

I want them to all be memorable to one another, but how do you say that out loud?

"I think I want to get fucked up tonight," Hank says to break the silence.

There's a carton of thirty eggs on the counter that should be in the fridge. It shouldn't be here at all, in fact. Iowa eggs have been recalled from major chain stores because of a small *E. coli* breakout, something that has been headline news for weeks around here and, thus, has probably gone unnoticed by every minor-league baseball player in the area. I point to the carton and tell Núñez to get rid of these eggs. He shrugs and asks what else are they going to do for breakfast and why would eggs be sold at Walmart if they're bad for you? It has been the same through the oil spill in the gulf, through the passing of anti-immigration laws in Arizona, a blatant affront to a third of the team that elicited nothing more than shrugs and distrustful glances when I tried to bring it up in the locker room. And through a collapsing economy reflected in the lives of their families back home, and in every city they travel to. Maybe there is some grumbling about why in the hell would these Ohio teams have such beautiful, big stadiums and suddenly no fans to fill them, but that's all. Newspapers are not read, or printed material of any kind, save for the stacks of *Baseball America* that show up biweekly and make everyone nervous as they look for a boldfaced mention of their own names. And the bilingual God pamphlets. Locker-room TVs are set to ESPN, and only that. At home, screens are turned to Xbox fantasies, games that can be won and then turned off in a matter of forty-five minutes. There is a complimentary LumberKings calendar magnet on the fridge in this apartment so that the players can track where they will play and also what day it is, but the dutiful marking of the passage of time with wins and losses ended sometime in May.

Hank's recent brush with reality came in the form of a call saying that his father fell on a landscaping job, shattering bones in his knees, rendered unable to work for months. Even that cannot be dealt with, not really, until the season is over. It is life. This is life, too, but also something else.

Nick Franklin walks out of the biggest room in the apartment and holds up a pair of white patent-leather loafers fit for a television pimp from before he was born. He raises his eyebrows to ask for approval.

There's whistling.

"I like to look distinct," he explains to me.

We pour out into the dark hallways, out into the parking lot, past the shirtless man grilling hot dogs in his Vietnam vet hat, into my car, and into the night, toward fun. There is a small nuclear power plant down the street from the Indian Village apartments, glowing and growling. It's the first of three factories we will see at various distances, through barbed-wire fencing on the way to the bar, gradually growing bigger, ending with ADM.

"People work there," Nick Franklin says with gravity as we drive past. "Right now, people are working there."

"Turn the music up," Hank demands.

I fumble with the dial, which fades and rises as it pleases. I flush as they laugh at my lack of control. It is a level of innocent but ever-present pressure that still overwhelms me, so specific to being on a team or among one, the feeling of never being alone, never exhaling fully. Often my weakness, my sensitivity, is highlighted in the briefest of interactions—when a joke is turned on me, when a hard, cocksure hand pokes at the softest part of my flesh, the kind of matter-of-fact cruelty that these boys can take and are defined by, that leaves me gutted.

"Nobody's car is perfect," Hank says, too gently, next to me.

I finally get the radio loud, and Delilah bellows out.

Hank's head snaps toward me, part amused and part betrayed by her syrupy, middle-aged proclamations of love and faith that mark me as something other than how I appear. Núñez laughs in the back and, seeing his reaction, so does Fray Martinez. I am about to switch channels when Nick Franklin yells, "*Yo!*" And then, when he has everyone's attention, "It's *Delilah.*"

He is leaning forward toward the radio now, as though to protect the dial and protect the voice. His face is between mine and Hank's, half visible in the weak light of my dashboard. I see him, I think. Maybe for the first time. I see the slight slant of the Superman chin that I always assumed was without a break in symmetry. I see baby-ness around the eyes, the cheeks. I see excitement uncontrolled, and kindness, and youth in him in the semi-dark, hear it in his voice as he experiences Delilah. And, yes, it's just a moment, but he is so rarely ever really there.

"My mother used to play this," he says. "I thought it was just a Florida thing. She used to play it as I fell asleep."

I want to cry and to pat him. Pat him somewhere, his head maybe, if he wasn't wearing such a new, rigid hat, brim tilted to the side at a perfect forty-five degrees. Or maybe his back, a pat that turns into a rub, something not quite fatherly, but close.

"What the fuck is this?" Hank says, not thinking about patting anything.

"It's, like, soothing, you know?" Nick says. "Like old songs. Love songs."

And then he closes his eyes. Just for a moment, but still, eyelashes pushed together, face slack, no smirk or scowl, an impression of what he may have been like in a childhood that he is still balancing on. It feels as though something important has been revealed here, an interior I guess, which of course he has, but that has never seemed important. It feels like he has shared a connection, a trust, a commiseration about the slow melancholy of life with me, born from more than the simple facts that he is in my car and we both only just realized that Delilah is widely syndicated.

"I like to be quiet sometimes," he adds. "I like to sort of chill and think about things. I'm like that."

He gives a look that scans all of us. He sees Hank, who has become some combination of big brother and hired help to him. He sees these Dominican boys whom he cannot really understand, but who he feels should understand him. He sees me. For a lengthy moment, me.

When I was nineteen and had graduated from high school, I went to college, bought a hookah, got dumped by my high school girlfriend, smashed an orange against my dorm room wall, smoked a lot of pot, gained a lot of weight, wrote a poem that involved the image of myself as a snowflake, and did mushrooms with friends, hugging each one individually, making a solemn pact that no matter what happened, we would none of us become hamsters running on the wheel. And I missed being read to, not that it had happened in years. But for the first time, on a dorm cot, I mourned that embarrassing routine. I mourned the absence of a soft sound that never changed, of the unmistakable presence of my father next to me and the safety it promised. I missed it all silently, stoned, unable to sleep, listening to my roommate pummel himself and sigh as he came into a dirty sock. It was painful, I remember, but it was vivid. I know all of it still. I remember the ridiculous weight of those days, and for some reason I will swear that they were necessary. There is value in melancholy and uncertainty, in desperate, exaggerated memory. I talk about it with Tim in the stands. How it is important to remember the way something felt and smelled and sounded. To miss it. Sometimes it feels like I miss everything, Tim has told me, staring past me at the players on the field. And I know that he will miss them soon. And Nick Franklin misses things, too, so maybe he will miss his time here.

The players drink at the Lyons Tap because it's not the Main Avenue Pub, where the coaches are every night, shirts tucked into their jeans, stumbling outside to deposit green spit on the curb. And it's not Manning's across from the stadium, so quiet, so empty except for Brad and Dave at the bar with their whiskey and *SportsCenter*. The Lyons Tap is where you go if you want to dance, and hip-hop songs are played in between loud country, when girls who look angry at something take the floor to grind torn jean shorts up against big men, their backs arched, their bodies dwarfed, like kittens against a scratching post.

There is a DJ who has never adopted a DJ name and goes instead by Randy. As we open the side door, we are met with a rush of excitement as Randy hits his button that makes the siren sound, again and again, simulating a Caribbean carnival so far from the ocean.

I walk in last. Hank is in front, eyes swiveling. The rest fall in line, trailing the arc that he, a wise twenty-four-year-old former college student, he who has lived outside baseball, creates. We look, I think, like a bobsled team, maneuvering through a foreign course in tense unison. It was easier when Sams was in Clinton. Sams used to push ahead, his height and blackness and eternally exposed pecs a beacon to girls who remembered him and a harsh warning to boys who resented their remembering.

But as of a week ago, there has been no Sams here, leaving at least one baseball groupie sullen in the bleachers, squinting toward the outfield during warm-ups. I was out of town the day he was called into the locker room and told he was being sent down. I missed that last night when he wasn't in the mood to go out and drink shimmering concoctions and try to make girls hang on his shoulders with pleading eyes. When he sat on the couch with Hank on the chair next to him, holding cans of Coors Light while he packed, Danny there, too, drinking water and not meeting his now-former teammate's gaze. I'm sure Sams said something like, *Man, I'm quitting,* and everybody else chimed in with *No, you're crazy man, don't talk like that, keep with it.* Danny probably said something referencing God's plan, and Hank, though he never speaks such sentiments, probably nodded, keeping fidelity to a stern faith that makes even secular players devout. What an expected scene, everyone knowing which role to play, the outcome never changing.

I was sitting between Hank and Danny when the new guy, a relief pitcher, walked into the locker room and plopped a bag in the space that still smelled of Sams's European skin cream, watched them glance at each other over him.

"That's Sams's locker," Danny said.

"Where is he?" the new guy said.

"He's gone," Hank said. "We told him we'd keep it empty for a while in case they call him back."

"Oh," the new guy said.

There was a pause. I sat on a half-broken folding chair looking at a stain on the carpet, silently hoping to witness a moment of collective team remembrance, the creation of a hallowed space, once Sams's always Sams's, the kind of continuity that is promised in every baseball narrative I have ever devoured. A chorus of jeers erupted around the room. Why would anything stay Sams's? Should every fuckup who couldn't hack it be commemorated? What kind of kindergarten bullshit is that? There are, after all, only so many lockers. The logic was irrefutable. Danny and Hank gave up on the Sams defense, shrugged, and strutted toward the showers.

Sometimes, in the clubhouse, players still say, "Ah, *man,*" just as Sams always did when he was frustrated, his oddly high, accented voice now extrapolated into something close to a Cookie Monster impression. That's what is left of Sams in the locker room, an echo of what he never really sounded like.

. . .

We stand by the unused shuffleboard table against the back wall. Fray's puddle eyes take in the scene around him, shaded with a light too low to be a strobe, more of an ominous flickering. Automatic hunting rifles are mounted over his head, crossed in a modern coat of arms. There is an American flag. There are stickers demanding that patrons support the Cubs and the Bears, every branch of the armed services, a few local unions that no longer exist, but this bar is old.

"*¿Qué es Lyons Tap?*" Fray yells.

Núñez says, "*Lyon, como león.*" He pantomimes the animal, makes a mock ferocious noise. I can see Fray scanning the bar for some evidence of a jungle motif, but there is nothing, not even a safari theme arcade game next to the pool table.

"Lyons is a place," I yell to both of them.

They turn to me. Fray blinks.

"It's actually really interesting," I continue. "This place, where we are *right now,* used to be Lyons. The town of Lyons."

Núñez stares at me, then leaves to go to the bar, where Hank is already buying drinks for himself and Nick. I am left with Fray glancing up at the machine guns and the flag. I could tell Fray, without him interrupting or understanding, that Lyons was a destination. That the area of Clinton used to be so relevant, always growing, that it was made up of three separate towns. That Erin, who works at the stadium, told me once about her great-grandfather who came through Ellis Island with "Lyons, Iowa" stamped as his destination on his papers. "Can you imagine?" she asked. People in Germany, in little villages, hearing from across the ocean that where they needed to be was Lyons, Iowa? This was a fertile place. Black soil, wide river, flat land for the railroad to roll through.

It was like a heart, beating, with veins in every direction, veins sustaining a new country, pulling immigrants in, turning Americans out, pulling timber in, shipping out the lumber that would build cities that hadn't even *existed* before, not one house in them.

The wood blood that flowed all over America.

The wood blood that built Denver to the west.

Bob Soesbe, still a city councilman after all these years, told me that metaphor a five-minute walk from here. Bob, whose eighty-seven years were all spent within a mile of this bar, who lives in the home where he was raised in the 1930s, who watched his childhood friend shine as the star shortstop on the field along the river where Nick Franklin now plays.

There was a whirring, Bob Soesbe told me, though even he is too young to have ever heard it. A constant, percolating noise to everything in the town. Saws and straining tugboats, the train, the downtown, people moving, greeting each other, doors to homes opening and closing, even noises that simple and small.

Hank and Nick walk back from the bar and set beers on the table, and we all begin to chug them down, nobody wanting to be the first one to run out of air and surrender to a burp.

"You like Coors Light?" Nick asks me, gasping, eager.

"Yeah, it's fine," I say.

"Yeah, it's fine," he says.

We keep time with our heads to a thrumming, all-encompassing rhythm courtesy of Randy. I am happy that we are equally awkward. We are all nervous, young, straight men on a dance floor, seesawing our shoulders, bending our knees on the offbeats, rigid, queasy, riding an invisible ferry on a choppy day. I think of Nick fielding a grounder backhanded and lifting easily off the ground, rotating in midair, his arm whipping as his body twists, a continuous movement that lasts a quarter of a second but that we in the stands experience in strobing slow motion as a series of poses, each perfect, worthy of individual appreciation. He is so different from how I've ever seen him, here in this sticky-floored cavern, on a dance floor with no platform, no individual performers. He's been so well groomed for so many difficult tasks, yet not this one. He shuffles his shoes, trying to move them away from beer spills and peanut shells. We all look down at them. They are offensively pristine.

"I'm not a Coors Light guy," he says to me, attempting a tired knowingness. "It's so regular, you know? Bland."

"What do you like?" I ask. This is childish. I ask because I know that he doesn't know.

"I'm gonna get a vodka and Red Bull," he says after a pause. "That's my drink. I'm a vodka guy."

Hank sighs and says nothing. He holds his arms in tight to his sides and clenches every muscle in his body as hard as he can clench it without looking like he's clenching hard. He waits for people to notice, and I study the splayed, angelic shadow of a dead moth trapped in the shuffleboard light, not wanting to show myself as the only one to notice the clenching.

A blonde who could be as old or as young as any of us stumbles over and screams "*¡Hola!*" as she rests glitter-doused arms on his shoulders. Her hair smells like mango. She is wearing black tights that frame the curve of her ass crack and the muscles of her calves, eternally flexed because of stiletto heels that leave her helpless and, thus, embarrassingly appealing.

"Do you remember me, amigo?" she says. She leans or tips forward, and her mango hair grazes Hank's face. She wants him to remember so bad.

"Of course I do," he says. "How could I not?"

He lets his eyes move down her and up again, cataloging every detail. It was the exact right thing to say and to do.

"I was worried you forgot *me*," he says, in obvious but charming false modesty, so that she has to say, "No, no way, not you."

I want this girl whose name I don't know and will never know to rub glitter on me, too. I want her mango-smelling hair on my cheeks like corn silk. I don't want to want those things. I want to be above it, detached and mature, observing young, desperate lust. But I am young and maybe I am desperate. I wonder if I come back again, maybe without Hank, just me under the shuffleboard lights, if she would teeter over to acknowledge that we knew each other, had made a mutual impression.

It's not about acting on impulse. Not for Hank; he won't cheat. Not really for Fray, or Núñez or Nick, either. Hank sees his teammates watching this stranger, sees our eyes on ass and breasts, imagining those things bare, fake tanned and bouncing as she writhes. Up and down with him, under him. This won't happen, but that's not the point. We will all remember her most for wanting him. There is a woman at home who Hank loves and has for a long time, whose calls he answers always when she sneaks out the back door of a pet store in Duarte, California, to tell him that she misses him. I haven't seen a picture of her. I haven't been tempted to ask for a glimpse of his real life, his real love, the same way I never ask for pictures of the homes the players grew up in. Home is always quiet. Maybe it's boring. It's ordinary. Comforting to think of, missed after bad at bats, but otherwise forgettable. I forget her name.

She is in school for what Hank was in school for, but never finished: criminal justice. How to be a cop. They might be in a class together fall semester when Hank picks up some credits, depending on if he has time after doing his father's work. This baseball life will end, but that is not something to think about now, the potential for, at best, a routine, middle-class adulthood. I don't think I want that steady life, either, but I'm scared of not having it, and maybe that's why I admire Hank for being here, ever clenching, a baseball player on his tax returns, wonderfully itinerant.

"You gotta come to the games," Hank says to Mango Hair. "See us, see me." He can say that without complete fear now because he plays every other game, so if somebody shows up looking for a player, there is a fifty-fifty chance that he will be on display filling that role. He did nothing different in his play, there was no tipping point, but Steve Baron is still down in rookie ball, and Brandon Bantz just got moved up when someone in AA got injured. Now it's just Hank and Ochoa, a Venezuelan guy, also twenty-four, with a wife, kid, and as little future in this game as Hank has.

"Well, will you win?" the blonde says. She crinkles her nose to show that she's being playful, not mean.

"We're gonna make the play-offs," Nick Franklin chimes in, giving her his best cocky nod–wink combination.

Everyone agrees.

"Play-offs," Fray says.

The back door opens, and the Latin players, the rest of them, burst in from the street, a flash of unwhite skin under half-buttoned shirts slashing through the mob of stained denim and plaid.

I don't recognize Erasmo at first. He is not in his usual off-the-field uniform, the one he showed up with, horizontal-striped Old Navy polo and too-long jean shorts, the exact wrong thing to wear for someone who wants to look older and taller than he is. Maybe he borrowed one of Noriega's flashy shirts tonight because it is nearly bursting across his chest, metallic buttons in danger of flying off and blinding the petite bartender.

This is one of the first times Erasmo has gone out all season instead of lying alone on the floor of the Lafayette apartment, fan inches from his face, trying to fall asleep to the hum. He was the starting pitcher today. He gave up home runs, two in an inning, the last one so unmistakable that he grimaced at the ground and didn't even turn his head to watch it disappear behind the center-field fence. He is attempting, now, to blow off steam. Uncomfortably, it doesn't quite suit him, but he's trying. Someone hands him a Budweiser, and after eyeing it for a while, he tips it back and chugs so hard that when he has to pull away to breathe, suds cascade onto the floor.

"*Nice,*" he yells, "*nice,*" his eyes scanning the room, approving of everything, the beer spilling, the women, the mystery filth sticking to his shoes. His teammates laugh and pound his back, like the little cousin who just sneaked drags off a cigarette at a family reunion, dizzy and overjoyed. He dances alone, as he does in the locker room sometimes. He rolls his hips in little circles, bucks his shoulders, glances down at someone pressed up against him who doesn't exist. I see a couple of drunk dudes in oversized T-shirts pointing at Erasmo with recognition, and he sees it, too. He nods as if to say, *Yeah, it's me.* One of the guys, blond crew cut, tattooed knuckles, sharp, smiling teeth, pantomimes a pitching motion, and Erasmo smiles back, pretends to be an umpire, and signals *strike.*

For all his pragmatism, his quiet, lovable strain, Erasmo has an imagination, and I imagine it now, as he is unable to hide his satisfaction at being noticed. He is the center of this room, and everyone orbits him, that's what I think he thinks. This is the VIP section that we all stand in, the shuffleboard table a sign of status. He is Erasmo Ramírez. He is working, working, working, all the time working, and tonight is the night he finally reaps his rewards after previously reaping so little when deserving so much.

He drinks again, long and stubborn, his thick neck pulsing, and when he finishes he squints his eyes at the women on the dance floor, saying, "Hey, Mami," too quiet for them to hear. Mario and Noriega urge him on, louder, louder, bounce your come-ons off the walls, and he dutifully calls to the next passing girl, but the sound is lost in the processed blond mass of hair over her ears.

I hear a train outside, a screeching stop, the grumble of restarting. I feel the dance floor shake from more than rhythmic feet. The train is louder than any of us, louder than Randy, who switches gears into a country rock anthem, the kind of song that the players have learned to ignore at stadiums, engineered for baseball a generation before they were born. There is a mass dance floor exodus of those who are young and are even vaguely ethnic or want to be. They are replaced by those who have been coming to the Lyons Tap for a very long time and for whom this place and this song haven't lost any luster.

"Oh my God, I *hate* country," says Mango Hair to Hank but loud enough for all of us to hear. "It's like, come on, just play hip-hop."

She wants to prove something to him, that she listens to what he does. And that by extension she's only here in this town because of forced circumstances, like birth.

"I'm going to the bathroom," she says. She doesn't say, "Follow me, follow me," but we all hear it anyway.

Hank lets her go alone.

"She's nothing special," Nick Franklin says.

"Fuck you," Hank says.

This is interrupted by a rush of cheers for Erasmo, who has somehow danced his way into the pack where others are dancing, a sea of white forty-somethings, the only person not mouthing the words to the song, staying silent and concentrated. He is in the middle of two women, careening between their breasts.

"*Erasmo!*" His name is howled by the whole group, a dozen familiar fingers pointing at him, highlighting him. Inspired, he dances down low to the ground, lets one woman's ass bounce on his forehead, arms around her legs, face with a jack-o'-lantern smile. Others turn and look and yell, not words, just warbling exclamations to signify that something funny and memorable is happening, and they're around for it. Erasmo looks overwhelmed by his dance partner in a tank top that covers almost nothing, with a tattoo of a rose that looks so different now than it must have when she got it, all that time ago, on tight, unblemished skin.

She tells him things on the dance floor. I want to hear. I want to hear her tell him that she saw him on the baseball field. Tell him that she likes his shirt; it's classy like something a TV star would wear, or a magician. Tell him she has a car. Tell him that her kids are with her sister tonight. Tell him that they're nice kids but he doesn't have to meet them.

He tells her his name. I hear that.

"Erasmo," she parrots to him as they grind, her body arched so that her ass rubs on him while she whispers, upside down, in his ear. "Erasmo. Erasmo." Over and over until it becomes part of the beat of the song, and I watch her sweaty lips move from the edge of the dance floor, saying words, random words, just to hear them disappear.

Erasmo will take this woman home tonight, and I will imagine even more as I lie on the floor next to two players—the sounds of their sweat and bare backs making a ripping noise against a plastic couch, how she won't have to say *shh, the kids* because it will be just her and Erasmo, this serious boy with a real future, and she'll be able to call out his name as loud as she likes. Why is it important to me that she calls his name? He will walk home in silence, through the deserted downtown, and he will start to run, as he often does when going anywhere, the pound of his dress sneakers bouncing off century-old brick. She will come to games for the rest of the season. She will write on his Facebook wall, and I will eavesdrop on her Internet pleas all through the winter, while he lifts weights in an academy in a jungle in Venezuela and she is in this town in the snow.

> *U just crossed my mind. I wanted to say "hello."*
> *How's the baseball? U still practicing?*
> *I miss u so very much my friend.*
> *R u coming back this year?*

He will never answer, because he will have learned how to be an important person and he will never go back to Clinton, and sometimes I will feel like her, stuck, waiting, listening.

. . .

A fan meets us at the bar. He sits behind home plate every game and talks to Nick when he's in the on-deck circle. He is an avid supporter and, apparently, a formidable softball player, once a formidable high school baseball player, also a counter guy at the Pizza Hut down the block from the stadium who takes too-long breaks to hustle in and watch one half inning at a time. He is so, so excited to see Nick here, each of them in street clothes, talking as peers, even though he must be a decade older. His excitement makes Nick happy, and he puts his hand on the fan's soft back to feel his body tighten with glee.

"You like good beer?" the fan asks.

"Yeah," Nick says. "I like the good stuff. I'm not a Coors Light kind of guy, you know?"

Together, they order microbrews with hints of raspberry infused in them. Nick says that he totally loves microbrews. And raspberries. He swigs.

"I like your shoes," the fan says, and Nick smiles.

The fan ropes a woman he knows with an outstretched forearm and corrals her into the pack of players. They meet eyes and his say, *Whatsup, baby?* until hers say, *I don't want to be here,* and then his say, *Please.*

Out loud, he says, "This is Nick Franklin, the LumberKing." He doesn't say her name.

"Nick Franklin," she says.

"I'm sure you've heard his name."

"I don't really come to the games," she says, and then, "Sometimes I hear people yelling when I drive by," as an apology or a compromise.

Nick says nothing; what to say if she doesn't already know him? She, still nameless, is unimpressed, and that doesn't make sense. There's nobody here to buffer. Nick's parents, visiting for the third time already this season, are at their hotel, probably awake thinking about him, but they're not here. And his agents are in Florida. They'll be back in a couple of weeks, and then again once more before the season ends, assuring Nick that their phones just don't stop ringing and everyone on the other end of the line is saying his name.

Here, now, Nick Franklin has been swallowed. Here, now, strange bodies push and sway as Randy orchestrates from behind his console. Here, now, a wedding party just burst through the back door, bride still in her dress, dyed red hair, makeup running with sweat and happy tears, screaming, "This is *my* fucking night, bitches. I'm the bride. I'm the fucking *bride*."

The fan keeps trying to show Nick a memorable time, his voice straining through the music and the dead, thick air between all of us.

"You better talk to him," he says to his still nameless friend. "Nick ain't gonna be here long. Right, Nick?"

"Oh," she says.

"You're going to hear his name on fucking *SportsCenter*, and you're going to be like, damn, I could have talked to him."

There is gravity to this conversation that the woman didn't want or expect. She is drunk and willing to flirt, maybe. Not mull over hypothetical regret. She gives a defensive giggle and says, "That's nice for you."

"Oh, yeah, I guess," Nick says.

She says that a friend needs her, she's puking—can't we hear it?—and she leaves. The fan tells Nick that she's a total slut, and Nick says he's bored with beer. He heads to the bar and returns with a Bloody Mary, a pickle and two olives serving as a phallic, late-night replacement for a celery stick. Nick refuses to imbibe the same thing twice—bad beer, good beer, vodka. Pickle. He swigs and sways a little.

Some of the other players have made it to the dance floor, still in a group, huddled tight and performing their moves as much for each other as for any prospective women, yelling and laughing into each other's faces. Noriega, with an elastic body that allows him to cover an amazing amount of ground in the infield, bounces in perfect rhythm, and his teammates holler, surrounding him. Women, three of them, break into the circle, and everyone slides closer to Randy looming over the ones and twos, closer to the bass, where nobody can, or needs to, talk. They press tight, denim scraping, hands roving, eyes closed. Randy has switched back to hip-hop, and the bass is like standing in the stadium parking lot when a factory train goes by, sound that becomes physical and burrows in your stomach. The words of the song are commands, and everyone listens.

"*Teach me*," raps a woman's voice, dripping with a suggested orgasm. And then response, a calm, sneering man: "*All my bitches love me*."

A guy I've never seen yells in my ear.

"Get in there, brother," he says. "You've got to make yourself known."

"No," I yell. "I'm watching."

"I've got a girlfriend," I yell, too proud, leaning into him, my spit flecking his ear.

"She here?"

I don't answer, so he repeats himself: "Grab one. Make yourself known."

He smiles in commiseration, both of us clumsy and plain. I want to throw him into something solid that would make a pop when he hit it. I want to tell him that we are not peers, not equally alone, not equally overripe in our shirts that we bought when we were thinner, our faces that haven't been pressed into anybody else's all night.

"Look at *those* guys," my new friend yells.

He means the players, the sinews of their forearms crossing over bodies that they dwarf, the uniform stomp of their dancing feet as they move together, taking cues from one another, meeting eyes in celebration.

"They're LumberKings," I say, my voice a child's. "I'm with them."

Outside, in the corner of the parking lot, local boys in a pack smoke and dip and throw bottles into a brick wall to hear destruction echo off asphalt. They laugh and that echoes, too. They yell at Hank as he leaves the bar, a cacophony of curses. Maybe one of them was with Mango Hair, or maybe they just didn't like the rise of whispers and shouts at the edge of the dance floor, anointing these visitors as superior simply because they aren't from here and are better at one thing.

This is *their* bar, was and will be maybe for their whole lives. Hank's fists are clenched, and I think he might respond, but he looks and sees that everyone else has stumbled back to the car and it's just me, silent, withering. He walks away.

In the car, he yells, half kidding, that nobody from a team of *professional athletes* had his back, that he was left to be stomped by a bunch of hillbillies. Slumped in the backseat, Nick Franklin is lucid enough to remind us that he can't be getting into fights.

"Jesus Christ," Hank says to no one. And then to me: "Don't crash this car. If we crash the car with Nick Franklin in it, I'll be released and you'll be killed."

We all laugh, and that sputters out quickly as we all ponder how potentially true a statement it was.

"Delilah," Nick attempts to command.

I hope he won't puke. I turn on the radio, looking for Delilah as though she's Alka-Seltzer, but she's gone. It is nearly two in the morning, past her demographic. She's meant to coax mothers to sleep, maybe with their little boys tucked into the pockets of their armpits. She's not meant to be bumped out of cars going exactly the speed limit to avoid being pulled over.

"Not on," I tell Nick, and he says "Whatever" with such petulance that I want to laugh and then I want to hug him. My volume dial decides to stick at zero, and there is no sound. My car squeaks over potholes. The engine groans. I listen for a voice outside, even the buzzing of a sign turned on. There is nothing. There is no one. We all breathe, and we are all aware of it.

It is loud for the first time in the drive as we pass the factory. Floodlights on the ground point up at the metal, the vats and smokestacks, creating a glow that seems to emanate from the noise of corn being pulverized and burned and poured. We do not know what we are hearing exactly. The hiss is steam. What sounds like the ocean is some kind of heated runoff from the creation of biodegradable plastics hitting the walls of a newly built storage pool, smelling like poison, separated by fifty feet and a barbed-wire fence from those few homes that remain in south Clinton, the homeowners unavoidably awake, listening. The sound of manufactured wind comes from somewhere inside, I think, where the coal is burned.

We no longer hear the squeak of the car, the engine, our breath.

I told Tim that I couldn't watch the meteor showers with him tonight, or I should say this morning. He told me he'd be out along the side of I-30, turning off on one of the gravel, cornfield roads, then walking until free from lights or sounds. At three-ish, something amazing is supposed to happen in the sky.

I asked him if it was safe, walking out in the dark like that, alone. He said that nothing was safer. He said he'd walked home plenty of times when he was younger, from a bar or party in DeWitt or another town, fifteen miles of walking. Sometimes he'd howl, sort of how he does at the stadium when a LumberKing hits a home run, but different because there was nothing else around to meet his sound, dwarf it or bounce it back.

"I am the kind of person that bothers to look up," Tim told me. "You are, too. Aren't you?"

I'm not sure if I am. Or if I want to be. What does looking up get you? As we pass the former Laundromat with its windows smashed and the Democratic Party headquarters and the makeshift union hall, Nick says, "I'm going to be the first player to go twenty, twenty, twenty this year. In the country."

We all turn to him.

"Twenty home runs, twenty steals, twenty doubles. Soon. I'm almost there. My dad told me. And my agent." He holds up his phone. "I didn't even know."

This news, once he actually completes the trifecta, which of course he will, is going to reverberate. It will be spoken by coaches, by the scouts who descend for a weekend and call him kiddo, slap his back like family in front of everyone, certainly by the reporters who call his cell phone from restricted numbers, maybe even on some baseball show that buzzes in the background of the locker room, with somebody catching the mention of his name and screaming, "*Yo,*" so that all noise shuts off except for the famous people talking about Nick.

He isn't bragging now. He's sleepy, merely stating a fact, relaying what was told to him.

"Wow," I say.

"Oh, yeah, I guess," he says.

He begins to text on his phone, a new phone, the fastest phone with the most possibilities of any phone in the world. He loves that phone. He speaks of it with an exuberance that he lends to nothing else, that he cannot muster even for this bellowing accomplishment.

All anyone can tell me about Nick Franklin—parents, agents, coaches—is that the kid loves baseball. They say it with bulging, dramatic eyes. He understands baseball and continues to study it without a trace of apathy. That, I believe. He feels comfortable within it, he is interested in how good he can be at it, but love necessitates reflection, risk, pain, joy. I don't think that Nick has been allowed to feel any of those things. People feel for him, through him, but he—the most important piece of commerce that will ever sit in my car, hero of the stories that Hank and Fray and Núñez will likely tell in bars not far from where they grew up after their careers are over—I think he just knows how to do.

"Oh, fucking shit, fucking shit," Hank says next to me, after the factory noise fades. A train has beat us to the crossing right before the Indian Village apartments.

"Every fucking time," he says. "Every night, I sit here, I hold my ears, and I wait."

It is a long train, the kind that can block every exit of the stadium parking lot for half an hour when it comes to an arbitrary stop, even though it's legally required to move after fifteen minutes, in case it's blocking an ambulance or a house is on fire or a child is separated from his family, screaming pointlessly over the grain cars. Tim says that's never enforced, how could it be, what entity is around to tell these trains that trace the edge of the city, that flow to the beating heart of the factory, move it along?

My car stalls as we wait. The train horn, unnecessary, blows out, echoing on the river, so lovely and sad and benign when it is far off. Up close it is an angry howl. And there is the sound of metal on metal, the groan of some of the oldest train tracks in America, leading to one of the oldest, most worrisome train bridges crossing the Mississippi, a connection between East and West deemed a potential hazard fifteen years ago but untouched since then.

Trains are no longer repaired here. Now they just move through, and we wait for them. Hank and I try to count the cars over the din, but there are so many and they look so similar and the ground is shaking and we're drunk, so we quit and sit silently.

Fray Martinez leans his head out the window and looks up.

"*Bonita*," he says. He smiles.

Nick Franklin cranes his head out to look, too, and Fray is pleased with his interest. He points up.

"*Estrellas*," he says, barely audible over the train.

"*Estrellas?*" Nick says. "Stars."

"Stars," Fray repeats and gives a shy laugh.

"Moon," Nick says, and there it is, nearly full.

"Moon," Fray parrots. "Moon is *luna*."

They both nod. "The sky is big," Nick says as though he only just realized it. "*Grande*."

"*Sí*," Fray says. He looks surprised at the power of his voice as he continues, "*Grande, sí*."

I sleep in the living room, on extra blankets stacked in a pile, separated by inches from Fray on an air mattress, Núñez on the couch. Nick is talking to his girlfriend on the phone. She waited up. Nick is telling her about his home runs and his doubles and his steals. She, I assume, is saying something along the lines of "I love you, I miss you," because then he is saying, "Uh-huh." Hank closes the door to his room to talk to his girlfriend, and I think of Mango Hair, the way she seemed certain of his power, and I wonder if he is thinking of her, too. Lying among baseball players who get to feel desirable, I feel dull and I want to call home, but nobody settled is awake.

Núñez snores. Fray coughs and kicks at the dirty sheets that a teammate lent him. He is too big for his air mattress. I hear a rustling of paper, and it's the Baseball Chapel pamphlet. He reads by the light of his cell phone. He has waited until nothing else is happening, and he has grabbed at the words that should comfort. He whispers his clunky, translated prayers until his whisper quivers and he coughs again, and then he continues to pray and I continue to listen until he stops making noise.

The Numbers

LAST NIGHT, Erasmo was sharp, throwing hard, hitting ninety-three miles per hour for six innings. The game moved fast. He pitched, they hit the ball weakly to a fielder, he returned to the rubber, nodded, repeated. The stadium remained almost silent. Erasmo, when he is functioning at full capacity, is so good that he's boring. Fastball outside, fastball outside, a changeup wasted in the dirt, then a fastball inside, leaving the Wisconsin Timber Rattlers with their chests heaved forward, asses out, like cartoon elephants afraid of a mouse. That pose was the highlight of the game for the meager crowd in attendance on a sweltering Saturday plagued with shadflies moving in sinister clumps off the river, crashing and spraying deep purple blood off the Coors Light sign in left.

"Oh, I wish he would slow down," Joyce said above me in the bleachers. "It's a nice night."

Everyone agreed that Joyce was insane. It was not a nice night. It was choking and humid, bearable only by those who tally weeks toward the end of the season and begin wincing come August, because this will soon be over.

Even as the LumberKings pummeled the Timber Rattlers' pitching, with Matt Cerione hitting a towering home run into the Lumber Lounge, putting the game seven runs out of reach and finally rousing the fans to stand in the heat, Erasmo did not relax or slow down. He didn't even take Betty up on a personalized candy offer.

"He seems like one of the real religious ones," Betty said, as though there were a connection between anti-candy and pro-God. "He has a churchgoing face."

"Remember Salomon Torres?" Tammy said. "He was religious. He became a minister. Good guy."

"We used to barbecue for him," Tim said. "He was on the championship team in '91. We were with him before the last game, remember?"

Salomon Torres was the best pitcher in Clinton in 1991. He went on to play in the majors, kept at it until 2008. Now he focuses on his faith and his daughters. He hasn't been back to Clinton since, but he is a type here—sincere, brown, funny name, kindly relatable and exotic all at once. He, or the memory of him, is Erasmo, and Erasmo, the moment he did well here, became interchangeable with Torres, though he isn't aware of it. We watch his back as he returns to the clubhouse to ice, another number 50.

It is the next day, and we're stuck in the clubhouse before the ninetieth game of the season. Erasmo is dripping sweat, working the soreness out of his body, grunting his stats as he lifts, dips, squats. He knows every numerical way he can be quantified. He recites his wins and his losses, his strikeouts and his walks, how few he surrendered. He hasn't learned to lie and say that the only thing he cares about is team. He is upset because he hasn't been allowed to pitch a complete game, not yesterday, not ever. Never mind that the Mariners are trying to protect his young arm, complete games are recorded, and they show durability, both mental and physical. It is a blemish on the master list that he is sure someone important somewhere possesses.

I'm tucked out of the way, perched on a medicine ball, watching him dominate the weight room on his own, as usual. The strength coach should be looking at people's conditioning charts, and if he were, he might find names that are supposed to be in here and aren't, as well as proof that Erasmo should be resting by now. But he is looking at a used paintball-gun auction online. Erasmo has free rein to overwork. He looks in the mirror.

"Eight wins, four losses," he tells me again as he hoists and exhales.

People are looking over and listening, but he doesn't realize it.

"Not bad," he continues.

"It's *great*," I say.

"No, not great. It should be better. If we score more runs, I win more."

He says it not as an attack on the teammates sprawled around him. I don't think they or their potential reactions enter his thought process.

They haven't done their jobs, and it reflects poorly upon Erasmo. That is just true and there's nothing he can do about it and that's frustrating.

"I mean, come on," he says with finality. *"Come on,"* spoken quick and flat, is the English phrase that Erasmo has gravitated toward to express shame, derision, fury, the same way all the American players have taken to *maricón* to supplement their own native homophobia.

"I could be 12-2," he says.

"Well, I'm sure they know that," I say, too paternally maybe. "I'm sure they don't blame you or anything."

He says, "The numbers are what they see."

As though to emphasize the importance of numbers, he grabs a heavier weight. I watch his knuckles whitening against his skin as he strains. His hands are still a boy's, like mine, fingers short and chubby, knuckles indented when he is not straining, and that makes me feel good. That was the first thing I noticed when I met him and he shook my hand. Baby palms, dimpled knuckles. I thought it was charming in that moment of quiescence. But now he is always straining, and the stillness has rarely reappeared. There's always been some reason to grip.

Erasmo lived and played in Venezuela for two years, never anywhere you'd find easily on a map. A year from now, I will try to retrace his steps, which won't be easy. First, it's a plane from Chicago to Miami to Caracas, the capital. From there, it's a bus to Valencia, exiting the station past military police who stand near where the taxis wait, machine guns cradled like babies. I meet John Tamargo at his hotel in Valencia. He's been demoted, even though his new title sounds better. He is now director of Latin American operations for the Mariners, but all that means is that he is farther from home, farther from the majors, too, overseeing those with the most outside chance at success. To get to the Mariners complex, we drive an hour and a half, winding up hills, pushing farther into the jungle. We stop only at random police checkpoints, roll down the window, say "baseball," and are treated as unsuspicious, almost royal. Ilich is our driver, a former player, now a scout. He is one of the thousands who scour fields in every Venezuelan province, a network that ensures that if a player is nearing puberty and decent, he'll be noticed. On the drive all we notice are the girls, eighteen, I try to convince myself, who hop out of the brush by the side of the road with thermoses full of coffee and miniature plastic cups. They put their chests up against the windows and pretend it's an accident, and so we buy coffee.

Tamargo makes a low moan, says something about the *bodies* on Venezuelan women, I mean, Jesus Christ, the bodies.

"*Everything* is beautiful here," he says.

And he's right.

I have never been to a jungle before. The leaves are a different kind of green, and bigger, too. It gets cooler as we drive farther, a hallucinatory, horror-film mist over everything, and Ilich has to run his wipers, even though it isn't raining. It helps if I ignore the shacks dotting the hillside next to us, wood-bodied with recycled-aluminum tops. Though I find the blight romantic and expected, I cannot reconcile the size and newness of the satellite dishes perched atop the aluminum roofs. Or Ilich's casual comments about how the poor don't want to get themselves running water; they just want to steal electricity to watch MTV.

Incidentally, there's a small TV in Ilich's dashboard blasting reggaeton music videos. We watch polished, glitter-doused women smushing their breasts together as we climb into the mountains. Erasmo made this drive, I know, as alone and unknowing as I am now, but he was seventeen and joyous, fresh off being signed, feeling impossibly rich and validated. He'd packed his two suitcases that he'd been living out of at the academy in El Salvador and moved again, heading to be the only Nicaraguan on this team of thirty-five prospects, not knowing how long he'd be allowed to stay. I try to think of him maybe in this same car, looking out the windows, the farthest he'd ever been from home, but far from done, farther still from where he wanted to be.

Agua Linda is the name of the complex the Mariners rent. It's maybe twenty acres of manicured grass and a dorm fronted by a brick wall, so much more solid than anything else around it. Ilich gets out and bangs on an iron door painted bright blue to evoke water. The gatekeeper and his son wave as we drive in. We hear the sound of heavy hooves on wet grass, and to our right horses are trotting. The baseball farm occupies only half these grounds, sharing space with a horse farm, the stables facing the windows of the dorm so the players can make out the shadows of the beasts as they fall asleep.

I think Erasmo told me once that he liked the horses. That one day he would buy one. In the mornings here, after his runs, he would stroke their noses, and they would lick the salt off his sweaty arms.

Tamargo and I agree that the horses are beautiful, another *beautiful* thing.

"That's a fucking horse," Tamargo says. "Look at the size of that thing."

"Mmm," I say. And then, to welcome Ilich into this mood of wonder, "*¿Bonito, sí?*"

"*Sí,*" Ilich says.

Tamargo says it wouldn't be so bad to get a piece of land out here, huh? A hundred acres with nothing around but jungle and mountains. Buy some horses. Let them run. You wouldn't even know what year it was; that's the kind of life to want. Of course, Chávez might take the fucking thing at any time, so this isn't the best buyer's market, but still, someday.

Hugo Chávez, president of Venezuela, is a reviled figure in professional baseball. He is, at least nominally, a socialist in the face of an industry that is as purely profit-driven and as top-down as any on earth. Less than a decade ago, there were eighteen major-league teams with academies in Venezuela. Now, as Chávez's term has extended twelve years, there are eight. The Houston Astros were the first organization to invest as much infrastructure in Venezuela as in the Dominican Republic. Andrés Reiner, the Astros scout who first defined Venezuela as a place worth investing in, has since moved on to Colombia and then to Brazil, predicting that with a combination of poverty, love of sport, and a pliable, U.S.-friendly government, Venezuela's neighbors could become baseball's next El Dorado.

"Fucking Chávez," Tamargo says, still looking at the horses.

"*Sí,*" Ilich says.

These are, of course, issues that the players like Erasmo are not aware of. No, that's an unfair conclusion. They're issues not openly discussed. An apolitical life seems almost a necessity among athletes, especially those athletes who haven't reached any semblance of security, especially when the game becomes a life-dominating specialization from a very young age. Rationally, I can take all of this in and know that perhaps it is not the greatest help to the development of a human being, the single-minded drive with which these boys play. In this way, Erasmo is a forced innocent. When I first met him, it was all pity that I felt, as if he were some lost pup, agreeable, exploitable. But more and more, and especially when I'm standing where he once did, part of me is jealous. It's a monastic life, with fidelity to one thing. And so to watch Erasmo play baseball is to watch more perfection, more focused thought, than I will ever achieve in a lifetime of critical thinking.

A horse whinnies, and in the distance there is the sound of cleats on dirt, and Tamargo smiles at indistinguishable bodies. The Venezuelan Summer League Mariners are training before a game against the Venezuelan Summer League Pirates. At first, it looks like the scene before a Little League game—the baby faces, the small crowds consisting mostly of overzealous family members, the anonymous players cavorting in replica major-league jerseys. The main differences, of course, are in the thick Amazon tree line just beyond the outfield fence and the sometimes-stunning collection of raw talent on the field. There is something fierce in the concentrated eyes of the players, something that, in retrospect, I'm sure was noticeable in Erasmo and his Latin American teammates in Iowa, so different from those around them. Or maybe I just want Erasmo to represent everyone who comes to America from afar to play. It is easier to valorize and pity an unsubtle idea.

Either way, it's impossible to ignore how the VSL Mariners look at coaches as if they're deified, Tamargo in particular, who arrives every few months with those brightly colored index cards, the gatekeeper to the United States. He returns their worship with kindness. He roots for them, and I see on display the very best in his baseball knowledge, his ability to break down the smallest movements, to watch a swing over and over again and know when it has transformed into something worth praising.

"This is the way baseball was meant to be," Tamargo says to me, making these players signify what he wants them to. "These boys are playing for their lives."

"I'm hungry," Erasmo tells me, which is nothing new. He's done lifting for now, still soaked in sweat, needing to replenish.

"McDonald's?" he asks. "You drive?"

Of course I will. He is learning who will do what for him. He is learning that he's someone worthy of having things done for him. It's a parched Sunday afternoon that has followed immediately on the heels of a morning filled with lightning sheets over the Mississippi and street-flooding rain. It's one of those days when no player wants to play, when the idea of risking injury on a slippery infield in an A-ball stadium is a reasonable expectation only for brainwashed coaches' sons or crash-test dummies. But there is no way this game will not be played. A weekend matinee always draws fans, and right now Ted Tornow has put on his Wellingtons and manned the John Deere, plowing the soupy mud of the bullpen himself. Tamargo has already been to his office saying the game should be canceled and then wandered back muttering. As Erasmo and I leave, the other players are busy parroting their manager, exchanging monologues of discontent.

There is no discontent in the McDonald's. It's just us and the after-church crowd. We are the youngest customers in here by two generations. Erasmo puffs out his already puffed chest as we walk into the air-conditioning, pushing his team logo toward the crowd, but he gets no response from anybody. We sit and I hardly see his face as he hunches over a stack of three cheeseburgers, an order of large fries, two apple pies.

Around us, people sit in groups, each with close ties, all connected. Men with thin white hair and pressed white shirts shake hands and remember things from before we were born. I watch the hands of a couple to my right, brittle fingers entwined as though they would be uncomfortable unattached, his free hand tapping on her knee with no rhythm. Erasmo follows my eyes, notices the people around him for the first time, and looks momentarily surprised.

"Old," he says. "Very old. Like my grandmother."

"You miss her?" I ask.

He shrugs. "Sometimes."

"You must miss a lot of people," I say.

He shrugs. "Sometimes."

We sit in silence for a little while. He isn't as pleasant to me anymore. That's not necessarily a fair expectation, I know. But we spend a lot of time together, and at first he was happy to have the attention, and now he's busy. When I first drove him home in the rain, he was willing, smiling, and I set myself the task of finding the reality behind the rehearsed answers, as though I could free him from the fate of being blandly, productively likable. The first time I saw him, he walked onto the bus to go to Quad Cities in his striped polo and his too-long jean shorts. He smiled at me, a stranger, and pounded my fist. He walked down the aisle, and Chris, the bus driver, said with a strange pride, "Nicest boy you'll ever meet. Don't think he understands a word we're saying, but damned if he ain't happy to be here."

Chris is an overbearing man who treats the players with a concerned care, and though he tried to bar me from entering the bus at first because of my bearded terrorist potential, I've never found any malice in him. Erasmo was always his favorite, perhaps because he lets him believe that he smiles through an inability to understand, even though he understands everything. Chris gets off the bus when Erasmo pitches, finds himself a seat in the front row, cheers hard. But I can't ignore the heavy condescension in the way he speaks about Erasmo and his dutifulness, that adorably eager quality of a Sunday-school standout. And I don't like it when people talk about him that way, because it often so closely echoes how I sound when I describe him to others—a story worth telling because of the shit that he's mucked through, his silent perseverance, even though he is a goddamn professional baseball player, that identity that I still see as the pinnacle of awesomeness, and he has never once described any sense of having to persevere through anything.

The fact that he's from somewhere far away and *needs* to be in Clinton, that's the appeal. So the specifics of where he's from don't matter. On the first LumberKings trading card night, the Clinton fans got an Erasmo Ramírez card that claimed he was from El Salvador. He went to a sports academy there and was discovered there by scouts, but his only nationality is Nicaraguan. He was, of course, annoyed by the mislabeling and did, of course, nothing to correct it, fearing the reputation of someone who gets *difficult*—read *clubhouse cancer,* read *not worth it*—over inconsequential things. I still can't be sure who is aware of the mistake, since, when I sat playing cards with the white pitchers in the Quad Cities clubhouse, they nodded at him and called him, with confidence, Dominican.

"Are you excited to see your family once the season is over?"

"Maybe I will."

"Why wouldn't you?"

He raises one eyebrow at me and smiles over a cheeseburger.

"Who do I train with in Nicaragua?" he says. "I have my one friend; he goes to the field and catches for me. He asks me to help him, too. He's no good, though. He's just around. There's nothing for me."

"So no home?"

"Maybe. Maybe a month. I'm going to ask the team if I can go to Venezuela instead. Stay at the academy. That's good. That's where I need to be."

I don't know what the academy means yet, so the intensity of what he wants doesn't register fully. Later, when I'm snooping around the academy dorms, counting ten steps by eight across each shared cubicle, only a body's length between iron bunk beds, I will think of Erasmo and how intensely he wanted to return here. When the Agua Linda gates close at nine every night, no danger coming in, no prospect of exiting, I will think of Erasmo again. And when I see players feeding continuous coins into the two pay phones outside the mess hall, I will see Erasmo's face, his chubby hand cradling the receiver.

A stooped man with white wisps poking out under an unironic John Deere cap walks toward us, a round woman behind him. The man raises a half wave, and I think for a moment that he recognizes Erasmo, that he's coming to pay respects. But he shuffles past to the table behind us, populated by women in dresses that look like wallpaper and their half-finished milk shakes.

"Did you go to Clinton High, missus?"

"Oh, a long time ago."

There are laughs.

"Was it in '55?"

"Yes, it was."

The round woman steps up in front of her husband.

"I'm Janey's sister."

"*Helen?*"

A nod.

"Little *Helen?*"

There are noises that are happy and sad at the same time, trebly exclamations of what a small world it is, what a condensed but beautiful rush of time a life is. Erasmo and I watch.

"I *knew* that was you," as though she'd been searching forever and had a feeling just this morning that she was almost there. The faces haven't changed that much, it is decided. Amazing, isn't it? Wrinkles like fingertips after a bath, a little sag, but once you really *know* a face, you know it forever. It's a continuity that Erasmo gave up on at fourteen, when he first left for a dorm room crowded with itinerant jocks, one that I have fled, too, here in this town alone, but with much more trepidation. I think of Betty's words the first time we met: "Where is your mother?" I crave stagnancy sometimes. It's a choice, the selection of satisfied consistency above all else, one that is increasingly impossible here as the town shrinks and there are fewer opportunities to justify staying, but I don't want to see that. Kids leave now, if they can. They're told to.

Sometimes it feels important to try to get Erasmo to say that he'd like to stop for a little while, that he could be happy with some sort of settling. And for me, always so fascinated with those who are striving, worshipping them, pretending to live in emulation of them, it is tempting to change fascinations. To want a bland vanilla McDonald's milk shake and a present life set on the exact same backdrop as my memories.

"Can I be honest?" a Venezuelan journalist asks me in a restaurant in Caracas. "The major leagues, the Americans, sometimes I think they look at us, and by us I mean Latin Americans, as some sort of uneducated animals."

He is a pale man, this writer, doughy in a way that makes me feel solidarity. He is speaking to me in stylish English fashioned around a two-year stint in a digital journalism master's program in London. He is part of a Venezuelan upper class that can obsess over and profit from baseball without ever playing at a high level, that can identify the game's importance to the political, cultural, and national identity.

"Baseball is part of our spirit; it is who we are," he says, and he slams the table. Soup sloshes. "Nobody feels the spirit of the game like a Latin player, and they treat us like we know nothing."

"Yes," I agree. "I love that spirit." Or something awful like that.

It is a passion I have seen in every opulent place in Venezuela: the country club where the dentist who spends all his free time as a sports radio host told me of his plans to become a scout; the thirty-million-dollar Polar Beer baseball complex where the locally famous agent showed me his portfolio, pictures of young men with dollar amounts written next to them, saying that he's finding and making national heroes; the privately funded Venezuelan Baseball Hall of Fame on the second floor of a deluxe shopping mall, where pale historians tell me the narrative of the game; and now here in the only part of the capital where you can walk alone at night.

But I've never heard the grandiose talk from players themselves. And again, differentiation becomes nearly impossible. Boys become men become bodies. One of the most successful agents in Latin America told me while watching middle schoolers scrimmage under a Firestone tires sign that he planned to set up his new scouting office in the rural province of Oriente. When I asked "Why? Who have you seen there?" he said, "No one in particular, I just like how black they are. I like how black bodies project."

The Chicago White Sox manager, Ozzie Guillen, got in trouble while I was in Clinton for saying that Asian players are pampered through the American baseball system compared with their Latin American counterparts, given translators at all levels, not just clubhouse Rosetta Stone lessons. But he was right, I say to this reporter, who replies, "*Sí, sí,* Oswaldo speaks the truth." Japan, South Korea, Taiwan, they are relatively stable economies, and Japan's own professional league can make a player a millionaire at home. They don't *have* to be feeders into the promise of American ball.

Venezuela has been an oil country for a century, and so baseball came with American drillers and foremen, who taught the game to laborers. In Nicaragua, a country too small and too poor to ever produce a truly famous athlete, soccer reigns supreme, but more and more, like in all of Central America, baseball scouts will show up on small, dirt fields, and word will get around, and boys like Erasmo Ramírez will come to try to earn the chance to leave and go somewhere they can't quite define. Or maybe that's too simple. It's true, yes, the desperation to leave. But does that take away the possibility for Erasmo to be a kid who plays and loves what he plays? It is too blindly cheerful to say, *Aw, he's so happy to be here,* but just as pointless and narrow-minded to paint him a victim when, so far, he's winning.

. . .

Erasmo tells me, in monotone, of the years and the travels that led him into a Sunday afternoon, post-church crowd at a Clinton, Iowa, McDonald's. He has already told me because I always ask, and now I have asked again, hoping for more.

"Yes, it was my mother; she took me to the tryouts."

"She must be an *amazing* woman."

"I like her. She works hard."

"And she wanted the best for you."

"Well, yeah."

They rode a bus four hours to a field in Managua, the capital, not saying much, because he was nervous and so was she. He was twelve then, and small. He didn't look like anything special or feel like anything special, and while there was some surprise at the power coming from this tiny boy, he was told no, and he and his mother rode back home that night, the mountains closing in through the dark.

I ask if she told him it was all right then, on the bus, told him it didn't matter.

"She told me try again," he says.

And he did. He went home to a house that he describes as fine, in a town, Rivas, that he describes as beautiful and then describes as poor, before settling again on fine. He threw a baseball every day, and he also threw the javelin, a sport he loved and dropped quickly because what chance is there to make money, make a life, on Junior Olympics javelin glory? He threw until he was thirteen and only a little bit bigger, and his mother found out, somehow, that a man was back in the capital looking for talent.

"Who?" I ask.

"The man from Chicago," he says.

"That sounds like a Jimmy Stewart movie," I say.

"What?" he says.

A girl who must still have a while to go in high school comes by, sweeping the floor. She is wearing black polyester pants that McDonald's makes her wear. There is sweat in small circles staining the fabric behind her knees because it is hot and every time she crouches to wipe ketchup blobs, the fabric sticks to her.

Erasmo eyes her and says, "Nice." He raises his eyebrows until his eyes become even rounder, bites his lip, and nods, a cartoon image of what a man should look like when he fantasizes.

"She's young," I say.

"Nah," he says.

This persona is still in its infancy for Erasmo. This girl, so young that she doesn't even notice his eyes or hear the gravel of our voices, would be someone Erasmo might whistle at in stadium parking lots, never loud enough for her to hear, one who his roommates would then chide him for coveting, not up to their practiced ogling standards. And when it's just me and him and I try to talk about missing home and being frightened and all that, he just wants to go back to practice, or, failing that, wants to see if I'll accept him as the kind of man who understands the pleasure of young asses stuck to McDonald's-issue polyester blend.

I make sure not to mention my time in the stands with the local girls who come to games in Hooters T-shirts, slathered in lotions that make them gleam, smelling of liquor as they talk about Erasmo's teammates using nicknames, giggling while suggesting an infatuated intimacy that makes me ache with something between jealousy and guilt. Because those girls, when I point to Erasmo standing squat and calm on the mound, say, "Oh, he's a mystery," or, "Oh, him," or just shrug. I think about Erasmo and his middle-aged lover beneath him, her children's toys scattered in the background. I wonder what she means to him. The life that he repeatedly tells me the scaffolding of, never the insides, seems to have no room for mischief or fucking or loving. Maybe there was a girl he held hands with, felt up on the sand of a beach in Rivas when he was twelve and last had time. Most of what I think I know about him is imagined.

Our eyes follow her down the aisle of tables, past the high school reunion that is still going on, stopping to acknowledge that she *is* so-and-so's daughter, to bow her head and blush as old hands reach out to poke her, tell her what a woman she is becoming. She disappears into the bowels of the kitchen, the sound of her footsteps lost in the hiss of fry.

"What do you miss most?" I ask him in this pause.

A shrug.

"Your mother's cooking?"

"Yes."

"Your father?"

"Yes."

"Does he look like you?"

"With a mustache."

"Do they ever ask you if you want to come home?"

Finally, he looks at me like I'm stupid, with real emotion.

"No," he says. "What does any of that matter? I am here, I am working. They are there, they are not."

Erasmo's picture is on the metal wall of the cafeteria of the Agua Linda baseball complex in Aguirre, Venezuela. I am tired and nauseous from the way Ilich doesn't slow for turns or stop drinking his coffee on bumpy mountain roads. Waiting for needed breakfast, I see Erasmo. His face is the last one on the wall, glued on hastily a few months ago. He is under Félix Hernández, to the right of Asdrúbal Cabrera. Each of those players is in Phoenix at this exact moment, preparing for an all-star game that will be watched in every household with a television in Venezuela. There are others, too, on the wall, ten in total, from bona fide global stars like Felix to guys who played one season in the majors, icons when they return to their hometowns but merely a blip of half memory to anyone else.

"*Las Estrellas de Agua Linda*," reads a banner running in cursive across the bottom of the wall. "*Felix, Wladimir, Asdrúbal . . .*" The list continues on through first names, ending with "*y ahora . . . Erasmo Ramírez!*"

I imagine him when he returns to train in the summers. I imagine him after he has finished breakfast, looking at himself, pixilated but permanent. The players still here in the Venezuelan Summer League do not look at the wall as they eat their *arepas*, drink juice fresh squeezed by the staff of women from this little village, who live and work at the complex as some combination of maids and surrogate mothers. The players are reminded of what they could be during every day of their lives, so these pictures, taunting over each meal, are an unnecessary motivational tool.

I can't think of the wall as anything reaffirming. Erasmo, whose accolades are, so far, limited to Venezuelan League domination and an all-star selection in Class A, who has generated buzz ranging up to "Might be a pretty consistent middle reliever in the majors," has already been enshrined here. In fact, none of the players other than Hernández and Cabrera have established a consistent position in the major leagues. The Mariners have rented out Agua Linda for nearly a decade, and this wall reads like the tail end of a fantasy draft.

A couple of players can speak English, and they talk to me at meals, another American with a pad to write on, reporting about them and their talents somewhere in the most important country.

"How is Erasmo?" a boy named Ricardo asks me at dinner.

Ricardo was Erasmo's roommate when Erasmo first arrived in Venezuela. He has thick blue braces that do not interact well with molten ham and cheese sandwiches. His body is the opposite of Erasmo's, towering over me, so wiry that he seems elastic, but for all his lanky potential he is still in Venezuela and Erasmo is not. Sometimes they text each other.

"He is doing good over there, right?" Ricardo asks. "He is a star?"

"Yes."

"Traveling? In the nice hotels? All the girls?"

"Yes."

"He tells me I'll be there soon. He tells me I will love it. I know I will."

He holds up his phone, as though to prove that their interactions exist.

"We talked all the time when he was here, man," he says. "We didn't get any sleep. We had so much to say, you know? It's not always like that. Everybody here is here for themselves. We talk, yeah, but not really. Not like really listening."

Ricardo is charming. He has a quiet, rasping voice and a smile that make you want to protect him in a way that he doesn't need. But there is a slickness to him also, born of a life of being charming and told so. He is, I gleaned in my first hour and a half at Agua Linda, the favorite of all the staff, and when he sneaks into the cafeteria after a bullpen session to steal extra coffee, he is met with adoring coos from the women who have already begun to prepare lunch for forty. Maybe that's why, despite being a year older than Erasmo, he is in his fourth season in Aguirre, the last a boy is allowed before he ages out, finished at twenty-one. This is, of course, the speculation of someone who has never wanted anything as much as Ricardo seems to want to play baseball for a living. But he doesn't display the need and focus so obvious in Erasmo, a blunt and forceful emotion that pushes him through every new place where he is a stranger and there is a baseball field.

"I am lucky," Ricardo says to me. "My father manages a liquor store. My mother tells me to go to school."

So Ricardo reads engineering books in Maracaibo in the fall because he can. And he reminds himself that he should continue to do so when another former teammate, one who didn't get promoted like Erasmo, calls and says, I'm selling newspapers on the highway. This wasn't the life that was supposed to happen.

"The coaches don't talk to us about it," Ricardo says. "But I know."

"Does Erasmo give you advice?" I'm sure of his answer before he gives it.

"Just to continue working."

Erasmo's phone is buzzing in the McDonald's, and he is smiling at the screen, a text from someone he likes, maybe loves, far away from here.

"Do you miss home?" I ask. Again. There has to be some past worth romanticizing as much as it's worth running from. I want to believe that I am filtering a character for him, not imposing one.

"I want something else."

"Right now?"

"Yeah. Pie, I like the apple pie."

He smiles, guilty.

"I am so *hungry*. All the time, hungry."

I long ago finished my chocolate shake and small fries, and I have been watching Erasmo eat with a mixture of jealousy and awe. It doesn't bother him as long as I don't stop him. We talk about his parents a little. I know that at some point both of his parents worked in an office, a fact that he passed on to me with proud gravity. He said that he thought they were accountants, but when I said "Oh," he said, "Well, maybe. They sat at desks." Now, like many in the second-poorest country in the Americas, Erasmo's parents pick up odd jobs where they can. They call. He calls them more because he has a new agent who gave him a Black-Berry and pays for the international minutes. Nobody in his immediate family has left Nicaragua, and they will not visit him here. They will join him in Seattle if he makes it there, no, when, he corrects himself, when. They might move into a big Seattle house together, in the style of big Seattle houses. He asks me if I've ever been to Seattle. I say no. He says it's beautiful, says it's the place a family would want to live. I ask him when he got to visit, and he says never.

"Do you tell them about here?" I ask.

"Yes."

"What do you tell them?"

"That it's like anywhere. Like home, kind of. Maybe the same size. And there's water. A river, though, no ocean. Maybe I miss the ocean. I tell them it is safe and it is quiet. Safer than home. And quieter. They like that."

Erasmo had just turned fourteen when he went to El Salvador at the request of the man from Chicago. The man from Chicago seems to be a part-time scout. He was friends with the man from Miami, originally the man from El Salvador, who got a U.S. college scholarship and then got Salvadoran government funds to start FESA, an athletic academy that would give Central America new heroes to root for. The man from Chicago was looking for boys from Nicaragua. Most of the boys weren't much to see. Most of them couldn't break eighty miles per hour on a fastball. Erasmo and one other boy threw eighty-five, and that was the first number that really meant something for him. Eighty-five meant maybe worth it. The man from Chicago spoke to the short, chubby boy from Nicaragua and his short, chubby mother. He said that Erasmo was invited to live in El Salvador and play in El Salvador for free. Erasmo hugged his mother and kissed her. They didn't discuss whether he would go. They took the bus home through the mountains, and when they got home, he packed.

There are three boys from Curaçao on the VSL Mariners, and one from Aruba, places smaller even than Nicaragua. They are described to me by their coaches as raw, then as long shots. One was approached at sixteen after running sprints on the practice field of a Caribbean junior tournament. He went home and told his mother, and there was celebration, and then he packed up and left. His mother is visiting, and his little brother, too, in Mariners caps and shirts, and flip-flops, next to me in the meager stands. His mother waves a lot, and his little brother whines, tries to hide from the sun. They both wince when he fails, which he does often because he has just been turned into a switch-hitter and is still coltish and confused when swinging lefty.

"They tell me he's doing good," his mother says. "I haven't seen him in a long time, but they tell me he's doing all the right things."

"He is," a coach later confirms for me. "Good kid. Fast."

"Will he . . . will I see him in Iowa?"

"Oh. No, probably not."

There are thirty-five players on the roster here, ten more than on any professional team in America. The Dominican Summer League Mariners also have thirty-five. There is no room on American teams for the vast majority of those players. There was never supposed to be.

"He left school?" I ask the mother of the Curaçaon boy. "To come here?"

"Oh yes," she says. "And what boy doesn't want to leave school?"

She smiles, so I do, too. Her son comes up to bat and bunts the first pitch down the third-base line. His teammates scream, "*Corre, corre, corre,*" and the mother screams, "*Run.*" He does. He is, for three seconds, totally un-gawky, unquestionably a man, the power of those legs like the power of Erasmo's arm, both the surprise and the reason. The umpire calls him safe.

His mother jumps and cheers for him and waves a towel around as if a championship has been won.

"They tell me he's the best bunter," she says. "He's a major-league bunter."

The boy smiles on first, his smile hers. Erasmo's parents never watched him play, not since fourteen, I know that. Maybe it helps.

Erasmo is talking now, but I have stopped listening, gravitating instead toward the aged, post-church table, standing to shuffle to their cars. They agree that the burgers were good, as were the fries and the company. They agree to meet next Sunday, to do this again, and then maybe again, and indefinitely.

Erasmo is saying, "Continue working," I think, and I'm remembering my dead brother.

It is a reach to feel long-stale grief while watching Erasmo roll up his empty burger wrappers until they are something to grip like a baseball. This is about him, not me, but my brother is dead, and the last thing he ever lied to me about was watching me play baseball.

I do not tell Erasmo that my brother, nodding off on the phone, told me that he would come watch me. Told me that he still remembered the way our father looked at me playing, how it had been so long since he'd been looked at like that, how the field, a field, would be the place where a family that had never really existed before would exist again. Told me because, even as he slurred, he knew that it would be what I hoped for and could be convinced of.

In most of what I remember of him, he's talking about what he's going to do. Always future tense, always believable until it was impossible. He spoke about me the same way, and that was believable, too, and it felt important, having my own greatness and meaning identified for me. He told such beautiful stories of what would be. How can anybody be so dedicated to something that it ceases to mean anything? Erasmo doesn't elevate his quest to something huge, doesn't seem to allow much time for wondering at himself. It's about the need to become something, not the story of it. That's what is working for him, and it brings on thoughts about my brother, about my father, about me. That maybe we who love to appreciate and mythologize what we might do never fail to disappoint.

He does not want to talk to me anymore.

"We go?" he says, a pretend question.

We go. We pull up to the field where the whole LumberKings staff is out drying the mud. Ted is still running the John Deere back and forth over the home team's bullpen, trying to turn brown water into packed dirt.

"Do you want to call home?" I ask Erasmo, a desperate move to see if my questions, our relationship that I see existing and that maybe he doesn't, have made him soften for a moment to think of things other than what is in front of him. He shrugs.

In *The Kid from Tomkinsville*, the Kid takes the train. And even the

Kid is older than Erasmo when he leaves home. He sees his grandmother with the dust around her ancient face as she watches him leave, and he leans out to watch her watch him, and I was safe and home, listening until the chapter ended, then mewling, "Read it again."

The Kid misses Grandma, and he writes to her by the streetlight seeping into hotel windows. Grandma has a lined face and white hair, and the Kid knows she makes strong tea for herself when she is worried about him, and just to know that is comforting. They own a farm and he misses it. There is a town to miss, a contented quietness. I had never seen a farm in real life then, had never felt contentedly quiet, but I wanted to.

Now, before games, if the players won't talk to me or if things are slow in the clubhouse, I drive on the gravel roads out into the farms, play Christian radio, smoke bummed cigarettes out the window, and try to pretend I'm somebody that I'm not. Joyce told me once that if you're in an old enough car listening to old enough music and you drive far enough late enough in the season for the corn to become like blinders, you could be anywhere and it could be any time.

I walk the stadium in slow circles, tired of watching Erasmo's back-and-forth sprinting in the still-damp outfield. I find the wooden plaque with the names—*from Clinton to the Show*. I stand next to fathers and their sons as the fathers say things like "Do you see how possible this is?" I look for the first Spanish name in a collection of Duanes and Marvs and Eds and Billys. Angel Bravo, 1963, enshrined here and in the Venezuelan Baseball Hall of Fame on the second floor of that shopping mall in Valencia, and nowhere else. And after Angel Bravo there is Angel Mangual, Miguel Fuentes, Pedro Garcia, Carlos Velázquez, Leo Hernández, Germán Rivera, Alejandro Peña, and the beloved Candy Maldonado. And then more, into the 1980s, then the 1990s—Guerreros and Santanas and Escobars. Torres and Valdez and Rios and Volquez and López and Nieves and Chávez and Feliz.

Erasmo, just Ramírez to most since his first name has been written off as unpronounceable, lives with Noriega, Martinez, and now Medina, fresh off a plane from Caracas to Miami to Chicago to Moline, picked up in a dirty sedan by a guy with his name misspelled on cardboard, doing a favor for the team. Jose Jiménez, a reliever, lives in the apartment upstairs with his wife, who cannot speak English and has no visa to work and spends a lot of time looking out the window of her fanless apartment at the streets of downtown Clinton wondering where all the people are.

There are different ways to view the internationalization of baseball. The easiest, perhaps, is as metaphor. If baseball *is* America, its hard work, its organization, its productive and pastoral beauty, depending on how you feel like seeing it, then baseball players are the ultimate Americans. Now nearly 30 percent of baseball is Latino, and here comes a big leap into "What does *American* even mean anymore?" It *is* easy, though it brings with it difficulties, resentments like in a factory a century ago, hordes of brown men with their willingness to do anything, "totally raw" but "naturally athletic," taking over the game and remaking it in their image.

Then there is that paternal instinct, marveling at what these players can become but resenting every suggestion that they should not be grateful for what they've been given or at least enraptured by the beauty of this game we have exported. I have stopped asking pessimistic questions, and I even let them slip away in Venezuela, too, because the answers are cold and still hard to argue with.

Isn't it bad not to get an education? Education will give them nothing.

Won't it be hard to adjust to a new country and life on the fly? Rosetta Stone.

What happens when they don't make it? We made them richer than they were before. And they can always coach somebody.

What about being young and frightened and alone, far away from anything that makes you comfortable? We're making men here.

Yes, these things are true. And yes, it is unfair to want Erasmo to feel more. I come to these games for meaning and metaphor, and he comes here for numbers, the right algorithm to move on.

When the field dries and Erasmo finally stops sprinting and the game starts, a new guy is on the mound for the LumberKings. Tom Wilhelmsen is instantly adopted as a favorite, a twenty-six-year-old with the kind of story that runs for two and a half minutes during televised major league rain delays. He used to love weed, and he still loves Steely Dan, still wears a Fu Manchu mustache and has hungover eyes. He quit baseball when he lost his love for the game, and now he loves it again and he's married, newly focused, and his father is so proud. He made mistakes and speaks about them in interviews with a tired humor born from lessons learned. We, all of us in the stands, see ourselves in him if ourselves were six feet six inches and could throw a ninety-four-mile-per-hour fastball after seven years away from the game working at a bar in Arizona. He is the gifted and redeemed man who we want to be. And he's pitching a no-hitter.

It's a bit cringe-worthy to say that I am trying to figure out how to be a man. Maybe it is a lie. I don't know what I want other than to not feel like me. When Betty tells me I can stay at her place tonight if I don't want to drive home again, and Tim says I can stay with him, and Cindy, and Joyce, too, I freeze, not sure how to answer. I wonder if Betty would tuck me in. I want to be tucked in, and that hurts with how silly and small a desire it is. I don't talk about me. I point to the field instead, whisper, "*I think Tom has a no-hitter going.*" So we all turn to him, what he might do, his total self-sufficiency on the mound.

Tom Wilhelmsen gives up a single in the sixth, and we sigh. Tim says that the last no-hitter thrown here was by Domingo Valdez. Remember Domingo Valdez? Baby face, Tammy remembers. I watch Erasmo, on the front step of the dugout all game, leaning back, raising his eyebrows at the most explosive of Tom's pitches. After seven innings, no runs, ten strikeouts, Tom tips his sweat-drenched cap to the crowd, we few who waited through the delay, and we call to him. The game ends in a win. Tom Wilhelmsen is 1-0, hasn't given up a run. He's off to a numerically exquisite start, as is Yoervis Medina, fresh from Agua Linda, who along with Tom and Erasmo forms a trio of talent that people think could take the LumberKings to the play-offs. But none of that matters to Erasmo. They are nice guys, just like he is a nice guy. They all wear the same jersey. But their numbers, even the wins that they earn for the same organization, are lined up in tense opposition on that master sheet he imagines.

In a few days, Erasmo gets a new chance to improve his numbers, on the road in front of a drunk and rowdy crowd in Quad Cities. He is quiet before the game, not just with me, with everyone. He is expressionless on the mound as he warms up. And then he is magnificent. Over six innings, he throws decisively, takes the rubber, throws again, fast but calm, curveballs that snap, changeups that fool, fastballs that would look good in a major-league stadium. This is angry success. At the end of the fifth, he bounces off the mound, cocky, challenging the opponents, the crowd, his own teammates maybe. He smiles to himself before descending into the dugout, smiles at how good he can be, how good it is to be so good in front of so many.

I'm in the little Clinton section of the crowd, watching former marines who had been screaming, "You ain't a pitcher, midget," at the beginning of the game become grudgingly electrified by what Erasmo is doing in front of them. Dominance, we are watching dominance, and maybe none of us knew how much we wanted to see that. I'm thinking about my brother again because that is the only real difficulty that has ever anchored my life, and when you have luxury like that, all you want to do is savor the difficulty, the hard weight of it. I think of that last conversation again, about him watching me or promising to, about him slurring that he had never won anything, that he had never been looked at as great, even though I always looked at him that way. He lived for recognition and never received it, and that is so common, and that is why baseball is such a resonant thing. It gives special men instant, prolonged recognition. I realize that Erasmo Ramírez is being watched by more people throwing his twelve strikeouts than ever watched my brother do anything or will ever watch me do anything.

I watch him after the game, before he dresses quietly, gets on the bus, waits for his teammates, calls home to recite the numbers of his evening. Watch him before he becomes a boy again in his striped shirt, his jean shorts hanging below still-pudgy kneecaps. Watch him before he lies down in the cramped one-room apartment, keeps his mouth closed in case of bugs. Watch him before I hound him again, asking for meaning, getting one-word answers, before he hits the weights tomorrow, working too much, working without smiling. He is perfect right now. He is playing a game and winning, and he is being admired because he deserves to be. And that is a happy thing.

The Winning Streak

SOMETHING HAS HAPPENED.

The LumberKings are good. Not just showing potential or getting there, but the bully of each new game, the better squad on the field. Other teams do not want to play them. I know because when the coaches are chatting in the bowels of the stadium before games, the opponents, guys Tamargo knows from somewhere and some time, say, "We don't want any piece of you boys right now."

In the first week in August, the LumberKings win seven straight games, most of them beat downs, the kinds of high-scoring contests that make casual fans actually like baseball. Twelve runs from the home team, doubles that come in bunches, players hopping out of the dugout again and again to celebrate, Brad gleefully hoarse in the PA booth by the end of the night. What has changed?

A lot of things have changed.

For one, Cerione, Danny's main competition in center field, is on a hot streak. And the team, as a whole, is better. In truth, it's a stretch to think of this group as the same team. Say all you want about figuring out how to win together, but the figuring out has been a complete overhaul. The bullpen is brand-new, a stable of big, bullish prospects throwing ninety-five, easy. The core pitchers who have survived all season, Erasmo and some others, watch the newcomers warm up each day, smiling and then wincing. Wilhelmsen and Medina, with his gap-toothed smile and vicious sinking fastball, haven't lost yet.

There are so many new faces that I've stopped trying to introduce myself when players arrive to replace guys I'll never see again. Slugging first basemen and balletic Venezuelan infielders and even more outfielders who have shown up to fill the hole that Kalian Sams left when he was demoted and ensure that Danny doesn't start every game. Betty and Tim and Tammy and Joyce are scrambling to keep up with the name changes, programs out, fingers pointing at players, then paper, then back again.

But as August rolls on with heat and tumult, the way I see it, this is Hank's story now. He has wrested control of the narrative or at least staked out a place in it. His name is known. When Betty gives him candy, it is no longer a grandmotherly gesture to keep him occupied through aimless innings, it's a fan's tribute: You deserve these strawberry suckers, you special, special boy.

I am in the bleachers going crazy with adjectives.

He is stooped. He is noble. He is weathered. He is squat and thick and strong. He is serious, always serious on the field, because there is a job to be done.

He is stealing adjectives from pages in my memory, from *The Kid from Tomkinsville.*

Old Dave, the catcher. Nobody's dandy. The sturdy, brown-eyed figure behind the mask.

Hank has been batting sixth, occasionally even fifth. He has benefited from being unknown. I've never seen him get a hit off anything other than a straight fastball, but that's okay because there's no scouting report to announce his secrets. He still swings at the first or second pitch, either puts the ball in play or fouls it off and gets up hacking again. They are formidable hacks. And he's being treated like a formidable figure, addressed by teammates as an equal. He no longer has to bargain with the strength coach, fresh off a star playing career at a tiny college, promising that if he throws Hank batting practice, Hank will return the favor to keep the coach in playing shape. And he no longer has to suffer the ultimate indignity when the strength coach is busy, lowering his voice and asking me to pitch to him, trying not to get mad as I bounce timid lobs at his feet.

As Hank's season is beginning, his teammates are exhausted and scowling.

"I feel like shittiness is contagious," Vinnie Catricala says over the card table in the locker room. "So, like, if we're in this really shitty place for half a year, we're bound to catch it."

As a very literal example, he describes an effort to move out into the community, hitting the local pool before practice. A kid shit himself, and Vinnie was forced to swim away from the turd like everyone else, the current of his flailing only pulling the loaf closer. He refused to go back, ever. Pool-shitting happens in everyone's hometown, but here, in an August that feels drab and endless, the anecdote becomes unforgivable.

"You know, it would be one thing if anyone gave a fuck," another player chimes in. "Pack the fucking stadium one time. Watch me play. You don't have anything else to do. We're the main draw."

I wince and put a card down, look around to see if anyone is silently deriding my move. There are levels of acceptance that one strives for around a team, some proof of deserving to be attached to the core group and its unified purpose. Anyone who serves a function is accepted, and who doesn't want to be functional? The Jimmy John's sandwich delivery staff has, with their punctuality, earned universal acceptance and can walk into the locker room at any time, face a wall of unabashed, enormous, nude bodies, and be welcomed with thanks, even a tip. Dave can come in, look at the lineup card, ask politely for pregame interviews, wave his hand awkwardly in hello and good-bye, then retreat back into the world of the watchers. Any Mariners employee in town for a progress report is, of course, welcomed with a respect merging into fear. And there are two reverends who enter each Sunday, one with an approved English sermon, the other with the exact same sermon in Spanish. They're trained volunteers with Baseball Chapel, serving an almost uniformly Christian population of players, so they are perhaps the most necessary of all. Indeed, many fans saw me popping in and out of the clubhouse early in the season and, before Betty set them straight, assumed I was some sort of junior minister. Why else would I occasionally wear collared shirts? Why else would I deserve a place in the sweaty, cement-walled inner sanctum? I never tried to explain my place inside, because it felt like all I did was show up, tolerate being stared at, stay so insignificant that nobody could find cause to kick me out. And I know that my only qualification to make me different from the longtime fans is living outside of Clinton—not a player, not a coach, just an alien allowed in for being unfamiliar.

It's hard to defend fans to players who have no real reason to know them. Because sometimes I think that as much as anything the players' most prized possession is their sense of exclusivity. When you haven't reached the identity that you want, that you need, when every failed at bat is a reminder that you probably never will, when *Baseball America* identifies the Seattle Mariners as a team that has only managed to produce one legitimate big leaguer out of their farm system in seven years, it has to be nice to occupy a space where most people aren't worthy to trespass. Anybody they see should be either in service of their improvement or unworthy of their acknowledgment.

For most of the season, I assumed that all the white-haired guys who showed up in Clinton for a day, watched, spoke with a few players, and left in rented Buicks with Illinois plates were scouts. That they shared a purpose, that of the critical observer. I hadn't seen an older man who moved with any sort of authority do anything except judge. But one man stood out despite the snowy hair, warm-up pants, clipboard. I saw him hold Danny's shoulder tenderly after a bad game, promise him with feeling that they'd talk soon.

His name is Jack. He is a grandpa, and when he leaves Clinton, he heads up to his lake house in Wisconsin. His grandkids join him, and they go tubing. That's the kind of story that he likes to tell the players, the kind that makes them smile and say, *"Man, tubing."* Jack is a sports psychologist, one of a tiny wave of innovators who slowly gained acceptance in locker rooms during the 1990s, despite the unmistakable New Agey whiff of their philosophies. Still, he seems out of place, and his acceptance is an uneasy one. All the coaches played at a time when there were no Jacks, when nobody patted their shoulders, made them promises. Jack brings kindness, something akin to weakness. Jack does the thing that everybody who watches wants to do.

When Jack leaves, Danny goes through his mantras of self-care.

I am a good hitter, he tells himself.

I am going to succeed at what I can control and not worry about what I cannot control.

I am in a calm, settled place, and good things happen in that place.

He can get more specific:

I will hit a double today.

I will feel good each time I step to the plate.

Even if yesterday was a bad day, I am not a bad player, nor am I a bad person.

Sams is doing the same in Everett, Washington, both tagged as guys with potential, getting into their own heads and stalling their own progress. This is the kind of fragility and resulting gentleness that makes the clubhouse so off-limits. This sweet man, this hand on that shoulder, these quiet, hopeful repetitions of mantras to make a young boy calm down—all of it is completely unexpected. Unwanted. It's disturbing, far more wrong, I think, than the steroids I've never seen but everyone figures I'm looking for. Everything else I see daily is a confirmation of what I've assumed. The sometimes focused, sometimes jocular, often homoerotic lives of athletes. Boredom and weight lifting and porn and tobacco and makeshift contests of strength and Bibles with Post-its in them. It's vivid, all of it, but unsurprising. Not as disconcerting as a shaved and muscled stud scheduling time to remind himself that he has some worth in the world.

Today, I stand with Hank while he suits up, and we watch Danny from a short distance as he whispers good things. Hank is talking about Sams, calling him sensitive, not as a direct insult, but kind of. Hank always seems proud of himself when he talks about Sams now. They are no longer roommates, and Hank is no longer a sidekick, because Hank has won, still relevant in this place, in this moment. And all the while, since the day he was drafted, he has had to supply his own belief.

According to his doctors, Tom Bigwood was the most pathologically hopeful person they'd ever treated. These weren't local doctors who knew Tom well. By the end, he had to be driven to Iowa City, where I live, and given experimental, aggressive treatment in the state's biggest hospital. There he would wait his turn, doubled in pain, smiling at the strangers who seemed frightened of him. And then the doctors would call him and say, *Tom, this isn't good.* Or, *Tom, there won't be any stopping the pain.* Or, finally, *Tom, you will not live. No, nothing is for certain, but it would be a miracle if you weren't dead next year.*

He smiled like someone who didn't know better than to smile. That's why, his sister-in-law thinks, they took her aside and asked her, *Does he know what we said? Does he realize? Does he understand?* If he didn't, it was because he chose not to. They left the hospital with Tom making bright announcements in the waiting room that he would be healthy soon, that the next time these strangers saw him, he would be cured.

Everything clicked in at a certain point, of course. It made his death like a flash fire, like a trip-wire boom, because he refused to build up any glum, nihilistic shell, preferred to not be dying until he un-ignorably was. That's when he started asking about the bricks he'd been promised. Those to be purchased in his name and placed by the stadium entrance. *How long does it take for brick to fade away? How long does it take? When will my brick be gone?* He couldn't walk much at that point and it was winter and there was still ice everywhere. His sister-in-law couldn't take him around the empty downtown as a reminder, point out all the brick that was there when he was born and would be there, it was certain now, when he died.

She reassured him. Brick is one of those things that if you leave it, if you are content with it, it will stay. And in front of the entrance at Alliant Energy Field, there is proof of that—low-maintenance permanence. There are so few rules. Just don't clean the brick too often, that will begin to chip away at it. If you take a powerful pressure washer and force the clean, the brick will start to disappear. But that's not hard to not do. Don't let too many feet kick at the brick, if it can be helped. Brick is better looked at than stepped on. There will be snow on the brick, yes, and then there will be plows scraping the snow off. But, still, Tom's brick will last. The only real way to destroy brick is to do so intentionally. To pull it from the ground and haul it to the dump. To blow it up to get to the dirt below.

Tom wanted to know if his brick would be safe if the team was sold, if the stadium was remodeled for something newer. That answer, probably, was no.

Hank still fields questions from me and everyone else who is not too intimidated to ask him: *When do you think you'll quit? What do you want to do for a living someday? Will it be cool to say that you were once room-mates with Nick Franklin?* On paper, or actually on a computer screen, his own career is almost untraceable, just a couple of links to his name and his stats, no pictures, no comments below discussing his progress.

The smallest of athletic footprints, followed by tabs about an amateur boxer named Henry Contreras, a high school wrestler, an immigration lawyer.

But in the real and present mid-August, Clinton, Iowa, Hank is hitting well above .300, the only LumberKing with that kind of productivity to his name. Sure, he hasn't had many opportunities to fail, but numbers are irrefutable. On the other hand, Nick has been scouted and sort of exposed. I haven't seen him get a fastball for a strike in a month. I've seen him get frustrated, jumping out at changeups, pounding curves into the ground. His average in the .270s now. And his chase of the franchise home run record, which had a month ago seemed almost too easy, has stalled at twenty-two, one away. He is upset about it. He is just generally upset. Fans tell him he can do it, tell him they're sure he will make this season something memorable, but that doesn't make him feel better. Quite the opposite. As Nick stays furious, as the fans want him to know that they believe he will win, an inevitable question keeps pushing through the tension: Why should anybody give a shit?

The corn is starting to bust from its husks. Combines like giant spiders have already started to pluck and grind. Soon nothing will be growing. Soon this season will be over. Soon some of the splotchy teens who work the concession stands at the park will be suited up playing high school football, slipping through an early snow on a Friday night, and plenty of people will find just as much a cause to root for them as they did for Nick.

And for the players, what's winning in Low-A compared with going home? The Latinos, for the most part, rarely stop playing. They might get Christmas with their families, but Erasmo is already preparing for the Liga Paralela, a season of games throughout the fall in Venezuela. The best American players, like Nick, are beginning to find out about fall ball assignments. They will go to the Mariners' Arizona complex for a tournament that lasts a month. If the LumberKings don't make the play-offs, they'll get a few weeks off to go to the beach in whatever sunny place they're from, to have all the sex they promise they'll be having, to see all the friends they sometimes tell each other about. They have already hit the calendar, pointed out that if they make it to the championship series, a laughable idea, they'll get two days between seasons, not enough time to go home, maybe not even enough time to get over the happy hangover. To win here, in this town, at this level, wouldn't be worth the sore legs.

It's almost sweet, the *I-wanna-go-home* sentiment of the players. It sounds like sleepaway camp, me and the other coddled boys waiting in line to call our parents and mewl with protest. But these players are meant to care, that's the whole idea, the simplest foundation of this place they inhabit. They are the select few people whose job it is to want to win, not in the metaphorical sense, but really to score more than someone else. Reminders of the importance of this role are rained down on them daily from the front rows of the stands, from people the players don't know but who seem proud to know them.

I feel good about this, boys. We're gonna do it this time.

The players can only nod or ignore it, pretend five feet of distance is insurmountable as long as they are on the field and we aren't. It seems as if, now that there's a play-off race, they hurry to the dugout faster, sign less of what is reached out to them. But then there's Hank, strutting in his catcher's gear, giving a thumbs-up or sometimes even a verbal response. Oh, the things I let myself think about him. He is, by virtue of his patience and work ethic, a part of this town. Having seen so much, having lost some, he appreciates the value of a win. And if the Lumber-Kings keep winning, if they win out, he will stand with Tim on the pitcher's mound holding up the momentarily gigantic wooden trophy like it could be twenty years ago.

With the game scoreless in the second, Hank cracks a skidding rocket down the third-base line. He takes off in his sped-up slow motion, ballooning out around first and not stopping, determined to get double. We rise, of course, and cheer him on. But he pulls up lame somewhere between first and second. He keeps trying and still slides in safe, though his slide is more of a wincing belly flop. There is a collective groan, for him and what he must be feeling and for us having to lose him. He pulls his face out of the dirt, contorted, sees everybody watching him.

In the grand expanse of a fully realized athletic career, Hank's injury is not worth mentioning. It's a tweak, for sure, not a break or a tear. It means maybe a couple weeks of limitation. But this isn't a career. This is an extended audition. And these couple weeks might be Hank's last. This season could be over by Labor Day, and it only just started for him.

The intimacy is stunning. We are close enough to see the lines stretching across his dirt-speckled face. We can hear him breathing. We can hear a repressed gasp escape as he reaches down his leg. BJ bounces across the infield toward him, medical fanny pack shaking in rhythm with his steps, and we are silent. BJ prods, nods, like, yeah, that does look painful. After a while, Hank limps off the field, and Ochoa already has his helmet on, ready to replace him. Ochoa's wife claps and points so their infant son can follow her gaze, see his father. The rest of us muster an ovation to honor Hank's pain or Ochoa's presence, depending on who is listening and how they want to hear.

I think I've always been drawn to endings like a slow walk off the field. Lou Gehrig and his farewell speech of thanks at Yankee Stadium, the way my father would recite the whole thing and I would be the microphone echo behind him, a tradition that is so morbid in retrospect but that felt so warm then. That last line of *Bang the Drum Slowly*, as the two of us man-blubbered on the couch: *From here on in, I rag nobody.* Tammy and Tim went down to South Clinton for the first round of demolitions, watched with their arms crossed as wrecking balls cleared away homes deemed clutter. Because somebody should at least be a witness. Tammy brought flowers. She told me that the people watching their homes fall said thanks because she was there. They told her it's a shame that not enough people want to witness things end, and she said, "I always do."

I'm driving Hank and his new roommates home. Hank has lasted through three different living situations. Now it's two pitchers and an outfielder. Two of them are new, and so they ask the questions that Hank used to ask as we pass the factory: What is that thing? And then the follow-up questions about the smell and the smoke, the patches of green-gray blankness outside the fence that look as if something was once there.

"It's open all night," one player observes. "You can see it shining, always."

"Maybe that's why nobody shows up to our fucking games," another offers. "Everybody's locked inside there."

I'm asked nasty questions, as a representative of the civilian population. What is it about these people and this place? Do they know that the field exists? Do they not even have the extra cash to spend six bucks on a ticket? Also, not to sound like a dick, but are there more, you know, retards in this town than in most? Are the only people in the stadium the people unfit to work?

We pull away from the factory and hit chain-store row. Somebody yells, "Walmart!" and so we stop. I am still trying to think of an answer that doesn't sound like pleading.

"What about the percentages?" I say. "If a thousand people show up for a game here, that's one in twenty-six."

And then, like a grade school teacher: "So think about the math. What if one in twenty-six people in New York showed up to a Yankees game. That would be like half a million people at every game."

It's not the best analogy. It stinks of both condescension and desperation, a difficult pairing to achieve. And the math is wrong. I'm reminded that I haven't gone on the road as far east as Dayton or Bowling Green. In Dayton, eight thousand people show up. Every night. Enough people so you can't tell individuals apart. You feel like a professional, the way you should.

But what about the underdog? And suddenly it's an argument. I am the anti-Dayton side of the argument. Fuck Dayton, a place I've never been, a bland and mid-grade semi-urban sprawl, with its burgeoning tech-sector opportunities and its proximity to that great metropolis Cincinnati. Fuck those eight thousand Reds fans who hardly have to travel at all to see the future prospects of their real favorite team. Fuck the lumping together of major-league and minor-league interests. Fuck expansion. Fuck progress. I want to scream "*Fuck progress*" at the players and make them realize that they are included in that fuck. For bleeding-heart romantics like me, and for Joyce and for Tim, and for Tom Bigwood, who none of us in this car has ever met, the existence of these not-quite-talented-enough ones, their constant play in stadiums away from the real spotlight—that is comfort like quiet rain. We can see them small and weathered and doomed and stuck, too, the players. There should be camaraderie in that.

"Don't you think it's more meaningful for these one thousand to come see you here?"

I say it at their backs, pushing through the Walmart doors. Hank is limping noticeably. I can hear him groan a little when he puts pressure on his right knee. He is tired. He is too tired to defend the underdog just because he is one. Why does he have to be the underdog all the time, anyway?

We head to the frozen-food aisle. One game this summer felt intense, the players are saying. It was a Sunday afternoon, hot as hell, but there were packs of guys all around the bleachers, drunk and cheering the way guys should. I think they're referring to that day when the work floor at ADM got to 137 degrees and workers got off early. "Why can't people come out like that all the time?" the players ask.

Ryan Royster, new competition in the outfield, says, "Why should a place have a team if nobody wants to play there?"

I don't say anything else.

In the Indian Village apartment, the only wall decorations are ripped-out magazine workout routines, showing men's abs with suggestions written on them in red, all capitals. Somebody's Bible is out on the coffee table. Empty cans are mostly in a garbage bag hanging off a doorknob, but some have spilled over, constellating across the carpet that covers every inch of the floor.

One roommate, a normally gregarious California pitcher who lost today, accepts a jumbo pizza from Domino's at the door, sifts for singles to pay, and trudges to his room saying that he might be dead by cheese come morning and, if so, fuck it. The rest of us drink a little, throw empty cans in the vicinity of the hung-up trash bag. We go outside to piss in the patch of grass between apartment blocks, face the black of the meager surrounding woods. There is a bathroom in the apartment, but something isn't quite right with the flusher, and there's a moldy smell, and, whatever, they'll be gone soon, better to piss outside into blackness than fix things.

Hank balances a bag of frozen green beans on his knee and asks for someone to remind him when it's been twenty minutes. He closes his eyes. He will play through the knee injury. I will stand with him after every game, BJ pushing down and asking where it hurts, him nodding at almost every spot. It will feel heroic. I will be proud to stand over him, asking, like everybody, if he'll be okay.

Yes, he will say. *I'm fine.*

He will say things that I think even he knows are hyperbolic, that he got out of a movie. *Just tell me I can walk and I'll play,* that kind of line. But, damn, it works.

BJ will look severe and say, with more pathos than I've ever heard from him, *That's a man right there.*

Teammates will walk in. *Hank, you all right, brother?*

He will say, *Sí, sí, sí.* Or, *You know me, too dumb to quit.*

Everybody will tell him, *We need you,* and what is better than that?

I ask him if this is some homage to his father, and he says, come on, stop reaching, he just wants to play. But it's hard not to inject a parallel into his set-jawed stoicism. Hank here, playing on a knee that makes noises when he moves, his father, whose knee is shattered, lying on a couch outside L.A. in a full-on metal leg brace. No matter what happens with this season, Hank, limping less than his father, will be climbing trees in Pasadena with a chain saw, doing his part with the kind of resilience that the un-resilient like me inflate toward godliness. And it's not just me. We all lean out at him from the stands, try to think to ourselves that if faced with similar pain, we too would conquer it. That's what he's doing, conquering. And *conquer* is a nice word, full of options, full of power. Hank feels powerful, even as he limps.

In a week when a foul ball cracks his thumb, reaggravating an injury from last year, never properly treated, Hank will again refuse to come out. He will be told that consistent pressure on the thumb means it might never heal right, but then he'll be asked, what's the point of full thumb mobility when you're retired? And he'll shrug, say he wants to play.

I'm not sure what it takes to throw out the first pitch at a LumberKings game. I think you're supposed to pay for the privilege but some are given a break. I've seen children do it for their birthdays, bouncing the ball over the plate as Brad calls out, *"Curveball, steee-rike on the outside corner!"* I've seen the employees of a local insurance company all get a turn, and old men just retired, and the mayor, and eighteen-year-old newly enlisted marines paraded around their hometown before shipping out, while recruiters challenge fresh teenagers to pull-up contests in the parking lot.

Tim is throwing out the first pitch before the final home game of the year. I know he didn't have to pay. His pitch will be in Tom Bigwood's memory, a cause deserving a free pass. Tom Bigwood never got to throw out a first pitch. When he finally got up the courage to ask, he looked in the mirror and decided that he didn't want to be seen unable to get ball to glove, standing ashamed and greenish and ghostly in the place he loved most in the world.

"Why?" I asked his sister-in-law as she showed me pictures from the little shrine in her kitchen. "Why never ask until . . . ?"

"It was one of those things he always wanted to do," she said. "But time kept passing and he'd get nervous and he wouldn't ask and then it was too late."

He wanted to see a major-league game, preferably the Cubs, but by the end he would have accepted the Cardinals. And he didn't. He wanted to travel somewhere, sometime. The last nights before he died, he was yelling in pain for a while, but in those minutes when he could say real words, he told his family that he never sat in the Lumber Lounge. He just realized that. He sat in the same seat he always sat in, by third base, looked out at the people sitting above the right-field wall, thought, *I bet it's nice out there.* But he never went. And he couldn't remember why.

She said when the season started again, he'd sit out there.

He looked at her and shook his head and said no.

Tim has been drinking all day, first to dull the magnitude of the occasion, then at a certain point, I think, to heighten it. I find him wandering between the concession stands and his seat, high-fiving people he knows and people he doesn't. He's wearing his old Roadkill Crew tank top and the 1991 Clinton Giants championship cap the same age as his shirt. We hug, and then my shirt is wet because he's crying. He says he's sorry for the crying, and then he thinks about it and says, "No I'm not."

I realize I've never seen him throw. I've never seen him run. I've never seen him swing, not even kidding around with one of those toy bats in the gift shop. And I've never heard him talk swinging, either, unlike so many others, Matt and Derek and Ryan and all the guys at away games whose faces blend into one guy who was once great and has since let himself go.

"I'm gonna throw the ball up," he says. "Like I'm throwing at heaven."

I say nothing.

He says, "I'm gonna throw it up so Tom can reach down and grab it."

We stand for a while. He sways and I think about how hot it is, how the air has stopped for the last part of the summer, no current on the river, no drift to the smoke. I look to Tim and try to see if he's kidding. He's not a God guy normally. He believes in fate, I think, karma, trying to be good, but this place is the closest thing he has to a church on Sundays. I've never heard him say "heaven." I've never heard him speculate about the future, only inflate the past. He cannot actually think that a cancer-ravaged hand will reach down and grab an official Midwest League ball, a call of *"Thanks!"* echoing from the clouds. If it were me, I would be mortified at the thought of thousands of eyes casually on me, throwing a ball so strangely high that it makes people look at their feet and wait for it to be over.

"He'll get himself one last ball," Tim says. He hugs me again, weaves away.

I can feel the nerves in the stands with the Baseball Family, watching him. Is he at the point of good drunken openness or the point past it? Is he embarrassing to watch alone, standing, without the support of the voices of the group? And will people know what this is for? Will the players? Danny remembers Tom Bigwood, and maybe Hank, too. They were here when Tom was. Or maybe they don't remember. But he was so memorable. Still, has anybody reminded them of the man who used to sit in my seat?

From the PA booth, Brad announces Tim as a "great fan," and those who know him say, *"Woo."* He says that Tim is here to honor the memory of Tom, another great fan. I see some people nodding. There is a scattered clap. It is so quiet. Tim waves like he's the queen of England and toes the rubber of the mound. He winds up, long and slow, like a grainy film clip of a greatest-generation star. And then he keeps his word.

It's an awkward, halting toss, throwing his body forward as hard as he can but angling his arm up toward the sky and the idea of Tom. I want the ball to hang longer than it does. At least it makes it up over the stadium lights for a moment, feels like something out of a bad movie, a guilty pleasure. But it falls fast and hard. Hank is waiting at the plate as the honorary catcher. He's in his crouch but isn't sure what to do. He follows the ball as it lands a good fifteen feet in front of him on the grass. He watches it bounce once, then roll, then stop. He walks to pick it up.

The two meet for a moment, a photo op for Betty and anyone else who cares about this. I imagine that Hank can smell the booze on Tim, in the tears and the sweat that he is not bothering to hide. They shake hands, and Tim steps forward, puts his arm gingerly on Hank's shoulder. Hank lets him. Tim is ushered away.

"Win for us," he slurs over his shoulder.

Hank looks unsure. "Okay," he says.

What Is Left Behind

BOYHOOD IS FOR SAVING THINGS. That's the way I always understood it. Give everything meaning, reach out to touch all objects you pass, then pile, then hoard. Eventually, somebody will tell you that it's time to cull what you have saved, make the tough decisions: If the words have faded off the front, then it's no longer identifiable and should be disposed of. If two parts must be re-glued, then the sum of those parts is null. There is only so much space.

It was cars with me at first. I was a nonverbal, barely mobile toddler, one who inspired worry, was brought to developmental psychologists, where I remained disappointing on the office floor. That is until Matchbox cars were brought out. I pointed at the cars—*Toyota, Mitsubishi, Honda Civic*—animated by what I knew. Cars had faded for me by the time I was five, I think because I grasped that they were fundamentally ordinary, a new one parked across the street every day, something that any fool could know, own, drive. I watched my father watch games, and I dedicated myself to faithful knowledge of baseball, not so much how to play, but how to understand it holistically. The peculiar language, the ever-present past, most of all the way it could be quantified, the sheer amount of information generated in any given inning that somebody bothered to mention. On the 1991 New York Yankees, a terrible team twenty games out of first place, I knew that Steve Howe, former coke addict, rehabilitated his career and his teammates claimed in interviews he drank eight cups of coffee in the clubhouse before each game, more than anyone they'd ever seen. He was, thus, a "real character." Scott Sanderson won sixteen games, but he lost ten. He was an all-star that year, for the first and last time. Matt Nokes had twenty-four home runs, and I had one Matt Nokes rookie card.

There's a ball in my parents' house, never used, bought at Macy's right before a Pat Kelly and Andy Stankiewicz autograph session that, to my great surprise, was sparsely attended on a freezing November morning. The ink from both utility infielders faded off that ball because we kept it near the kitchen window. It is a pointless trinket now, just a baseball with no dirt on it. Which doesn't really matter, because who are Pat Kelly and Andy Stankiewicz? Pat Kelly coaches a team in Australia, which almost sounds like a joke. Stankiewicz is a roving instructor for the Mariners. He came through Clinton, and when I said to him, "You're Andy *Stankiewicz*," he looked way too shocked.

My father had a Mickey Mantle rookie card as a boy in Brooklyn, and his mother threw it out, a piece of maybe false family trivia that used to enrage me on behalf of both my father and Mickey Mantle. At my grandmother's apartment in Bay Ridge, I stared at her, wary, unable to comprehend how someone I was supposed to love could be so heartless toward the most important piece of cardboard ever in existence. Only when she fed me did the suspicion evaporate, and I remembered to love her.

This is a benign anecdote, one consistently proved so by the slew of people I've met whose fathers had a similar prized possession, whose clean-happy immigrant grandmothers also failed to recognize their significance. These stories take on a natural progression, moving from childhood pain into something funny, an adorable revelation bolstered by an adult self-awareness that suggests the appropriate order of a boy's life. To care so much is a phase, one that men are supposed to look back on after women change them into something more sensible.

It is why adjectives like *cute,* at best, and *quirky,* and even *sad* sometimes feel most appropriate in thinking about Joyce. There is wonder, reverence even, in her saving, not family heirlooms, but objects related to memories of a game. That wonder is necessarily pathetic, powerless, especially because she is a woman remembering the exploits of boys and I have absorbed the idea that such remembering needs to have a penis attached to it. But I love her reverence, too. I love it more now that the season is almost over and mourning for something I didn't know I cared about has begun to sting my throat and spread hot through my torso. And yet I feel as if I'm supposed to pity her still. She is embodying boyhood, and that doesn't make sense.

. . .

"Do you hold on to things?" she asks me when she meets me at the door to her home, one story, four rooms, a few blocks away from the stadium. It is a *heavy* question. I begin to stammer. She assures me it's not a big deal, she just wants me to be ready to understand when I walk into her place for the first time. She invites people in sometimes, like her father, and they, well. She goes silent.

She looks down. She rubs her hands together in small circles and says, "It's cluttered in here, that's all I mean."

I walk into her TV room, and it is not cluttered. It is packed, yes. A fire hazard, probably. It smells of yellowed paper and cat piss, or something generally catty and sour. But clutter implies a randomness that Joyce will not allow. She smiles. She tells me she has a system. She snatches a box of index cards from an end table right by the front door. The cards are stiff, well stored. They're color coded, each written on. She tells me it helps to have a guide to her things, her home.

I didn't want to come here, perhaps because everybody I ever told about Joyce said, "Get in that house; the place must be a gold mine." I knew that she would be open and she would be proud, and no reaction that I might have to her collection could come close to approximating what she thinks it deserves. She will present it as more than it is. That's the reason to go. It's not like I haven't heard the term "cognitive dissonance." I don't find Joyce sad. I don't think I do.

Her cat is matted, of course, nearly dreadlocked. Obese and almost twenty years old.

The light is dim all through the house, of course.

And there is one recliner, of course, angled at the TV, her shape permanently outlined in the cushion. There's a couch to the side where I will sit. It feels un-sat-on.

There's a LumberKings cozy. A LumberKings ashtray. There is a channel on the TV in the background that you have to pay extra for, all baseball, all the time. The volume is loud, a man with a voice like Dave's but deeper is announcing the next hour of programming, a countdown of the nine best left fielders of all time, certain to cause some argument, certain to be a *whole* lot of fun.

"Did you turn this on for me?" I ask.

She looks at me funny. "No, I just like to keep up on who they pick. This morning it was second basemen. Can you guess who was number one?"

And then, before I can answer, "Oh, of course you can."

She walks into the dining room. She says, "Look." I do.

Baseballs.

They are everywhere.

From the door frame to the wall on the left side of the room, interrupted only by windows. Then floor to ceiling on the far wall, then mixed in with photos and cards down the right side. There are no spaces. This is a room three-dimensionally wallpapered, an effect that could almost seem futuristic if it wasn't, in fact, the opposite. Each ball is in its own clear plastic box, the kind you can buy in bulk at Walmart for three bucks a pop, which, multiplied by 889 pops, is a lot of money invested in protection and display. But she has paid for the overall effect. It works.

"They all have names on them, the baseballs," she says, because I've lingered in the doorway, too far from any one ball to discern what makes it different from the others. I walk closer.

Danny is on the left wall under the window. Fourth row from the bottom. Big *D*, big *C*, lots of practiced squiggles in the middle. I ask her to point him out because he's gone now, finally moved up to High-A, hanging in the purgatory of being just removed from our reality, still vivid, more vivid because he's ours to remember how we will. That's when she starts looking at signatures more closely, Joyce tells me. Once the signer is gone. She runs her fingers across clear plastic, moving her lips silently, the box of different-colored index cards in her left hand. Old men in libraries, scholars or grandfathers or wizards from Disney movies, come to mind. Kindly experts, all. She stops her finger on the ball she was searching for, and we both crouch to look at it closely, as if it would now reveal something new, something that had lain dormant until Danny's departure.

On his last night, Danny stood in the tiled, open shower room, naked and still damp after everyone had gone home. He faced the mirror on the wall and held a teammate's hair clippers, the kind used mostly by Venezuelans to sculpt shapes along the sides of their heads. Danny put the machine on the most extreme setting, shaved everything onto the tiles, cropping military close so that his ears stuck out more than usual and he looked four years younger, an unintended consequence of catharsis.

It was his most obnoxious display of defiance the whole season, perhaps his only one. I wasn't there to see it, because no one was, but I smiled at this blunt, obvious gesture the next morning. Some of the team stood in a circle around what he'd left, stuck to the floor that's always a bit damp and soapy. Some people laughed, maybe impressed. Some called Danny a dick or a faggot or, worse, a loser. The clubhouse manager pushed forward to look, muttered, "Fuck," went to get his broom and his mop, and proceeded to wipe.

"I'm happy for him," Joyce says as we look at his name. "I didn't think he was going anywhere. He promised me a bat at the end of the season. I wish I got to say good-bye."

"I think Danny was a little fed up with the team," I tell Joyce. "He cut all his hair off and left it on the floor of the clubhouse."

Joyce smiles, then looks serious and says, "What did they do with that hair?"

I feel my back straighten up, flinching away from her and her implied desire, both together. The sun sneaks through the slats in her blinds, which makes me all the more aware of her efforts to keep light out. Sun fades ink; ink takes priority. Joyce, I'm pretty sure, just made a gesture toward a hair doll, moving her interest into the realm of the desperate and bodily.

"Oh, just teasing," she says. I laugh too quickly and too loudly, and then she does the same.

She is funny. Do I let myself acknowledge that? How does she see the way I see her? How does she see herself?

She did ask Danny for everything but the bodily—a hat with a note scrawled on the brim, a broken bat, a whole bat. A jersey if he could manage it. A printed picture of him, signed. His address or his parents' address so that the give-and-take of possessions and sentiments could become potentially infinite. So where is the line? Or is there one at all? There has to be one, a defined place to separate dedicated from cartoonish. These are questions that have been lurking all season, growing louder as I have become more invested in the investment around me. Joyce is the most overt manifestation of fanhood because of all that she keeps, as if she's been waiting for somebody to say, *Prove to me that you care about the team,* so she can bring the person to this place, her home, say *look*, make it clear.

I can't think of fans of film or literature who are anything other than harmless jokes or harmful monsters, nothing in between the lovable drunks in *Major League* and a murderous De Niro watching Wesley Snipes with a loaded pistol in his lap. When I tell people about Joyce, they inevitably think of Susan Sarandon's character in *Bull Durham.* They say, "Is she beautiful? Does she give them a good time?" As though the only role she could possibly occupy in the minor-league ecosystem is that of a warm, wet, willing place to land for the night. Beyond that, what can she be? Plotting something, maybe. Or just lonely. All I know is that I don't want this season to end in a few days. And it's not just for narrative reasons. It is the feel of being swaddled in a collective compulsion. It is a haze, a high; it is an attempt at beauty. I like to say "we." *We* need to win this one. *We* have got a shot. *We* deserve this. I feel not lonely next to Joyce. That's what I know.

I miss Danny, too. I do. And I have saved his texts, along with Hank's, along with Erasmo's. They make up the only digital correspondence that I keep when I clean out my in-box full of my mother's "How's the anxiety?" and my girlfriend's "Why don't you just come home?"

I wrote to Danny, "Good luck in High-A! You deserve it!" He wrote back, "Thanks! God bless!" That was at 12:13 p.m. yesterday, stored and verifiable. I showed it off in the bleachers, let the coos lap over me. What a nice boy. We will miss him.

Joyce has Danny cataloged on her index cards under year 2009, also year 2010, a ball for each season. If he "retires," the nice way to say he's been released, and Joyce hears about it and has the time for editing, he will be reclassified, officially finished, no longer something to highlight, still on display, of course, but annotated with disappointment. If Danny makes it to the majors, he'll be prized with the other elite, like Mitch Moreland, a 2008 LumberKing just moved up to the majors. He's Joyce's former favorite player, only a few years older than Danny. They played against each other in the Midwest League, paths crossing for half a season before Moreland was promoted. Joyce cheered them both at once.

I ask Joyce if she thinks Danny will ever be a ball to show off, one asked about.

"No, probably not. Almost definitely not. It's not his fault, it's just—"

There's no nice way or even a definitive way to end that sentence.

We sit on the floor, and Joyce explains her organization to me. I notice an old IBM word processor in the corner, collecting dust. There's a printer next to it with the perforated sheets of paper that you need to rip apart. She follows my eyes.

"Oh, it's a computer," she says. "Do you want one? No, you probably have one. Do you know somebody who wants one? I got it for free."

It has to be twenty years old. She got it for free because some office closed or finally upgraded to a machine that didn't rely on floppy disks. She got it because somebody was going to cart it off to the Clinton County Landfill, but thought, *Joyce might keep this; there's no point in discarding something that may still have some function for someone.* And she won't get rid of it without being sure that somebody will take it up. Still, she can't use it. She won't. How could something that plugs in and can thus be unplugged, its fancy blinking cursor disappearing, have a place here in this museum where nothing is deleted, nothing turned on or off? I glare at the blameless machine, then realize the absurdity of it, then realize the powerful contagion of Joyce's perspective, her ability to make an out-of-date computer feel both useless and futuristic.

We stay sitting cross-legged on the thick brown carpet for what feels like a long time. I scrape my heel back and forth, watch how the groove I'm making stays in place, how it will linger until another foot walks over it. The conversation moves back to Nick, of course, who has now tied the home run record. If he breaks it, Joyce says, hands fidgeting, fingers gripping thick carpet, ungripping, gripping again, it will be history.

"Well, of course," I say. Anything that's over, after all, is history. At monthly Baseball Family meetings at the local Pizza Ranch buffet, in the off-season, the talk will be all, *I saw Nick,* never, *I see him.*

She grins, a pretty, symmetrical flash save for the one dead tooth off to the left, a detail that I omit when I describe her to anyone who hasn't seen her, because it means rotting, because there is no connotation to rot other than the obvious ones. She knows I'm just messing with her. She means history with a capital *H,* as in one for the History Books. And she has assumed the task of writing this history as it happens. In her red notebook that she keeps next to the balls and pens in her red bag, she has begun the myth of Nick Franklin. It's the story she told me about months ago, but now Joyce is bringing in all of the other figures from her wall who are also a part of it. Mitch Moreland is important because he got to eighteen home runs two years ago. Joyce thought he would break the record, or at least she says she did. It's fun to throw Moreland into any storyline because it adds a certain optimism. Moreland is part of a major-league play-off race now. I just dealt for him in my fantasy league, giving up a relief pitcher and a middle infielder for the power of his bat. He is beyond this place, but still available. That's what Joyce likes and I do, too, looking at her. She's claimed a piece of whatever Mitch Moreland was and is and will be.

"Do you think he knows about Nick?" she asks. "And the record?"

"I dunno."

It's difficult to try to weigh Nick's presence outside this place. It's difficult to remember that before I started coming to every game, I had no idea who he was. That when I first looked him up, I got a bunch of blogs saying, Decent potential, solid all-around skill set, but they overpaid for somebody untested and unseen. Of all the names read by scouts and coaches and nerds and hopeful players and hopeful fathers, how much does his name stick out if you're not looking for it? There's another guy in the story whose name I don't remember. He got to nineteen home runs in Clinton, before being sent up, so Joyce and Tammy and Tim say his name to me as if they were old friends, but he hasn't done anything since. Gac, it's Gac. Ian Gac. She points me to his name, second row of the back wall, not yet retired, not yet made it. He's a backup in North Carolina somewhere, she thinks. He'll retire soon.

It's the last series of the season, on the road in Burlington, and Joyce isn't here. She's at the Wild Rose, on blackjack duty, hands moving mechanically through the deal. She never has a moment to cross her fingers the way she'd like to, to close her eyes and hope. She took a risk and used her last vacation days for 2010 betting on as many play-off games as possible. But now the LumberKings have lost two in a row, making last-place Burlington look like a team to fear, shrouding what seemed to be an almost certain play-off bid in doubt. Now there are two games left, and the LumberKings need to reconfirm that they want more. If Joyce were somebody else, she would feel betrayed. Nick has been hitting miserably, has been sulking about it. After every game, Joyce has leaned over the railing and yelled, "Next game is the one, Nick," occasionally followed by "Nice butt!" to cheer him, which never works.

She needs to get to him one last time, but she hasn't been able to. Nick's parents arrived here for the last games, strolling through the stadium, recognized but aloof, intimidating to all of us who chase their son. When all the games are over, they will drive with him to the airport and fly him home, and he will become all theirs again, a bored teenager under his parents' old roof, never mind the remodeling of the home under that roof, making his new bedroom so big that the old one became a walk-in closet.

His parents are in the front row in Burlington as Nick stands in lefty for his first at bat, twisting his hips, getting comfortable in the box, the same way we've seen him do it hundreds of times. We go silent in the bleachers and watch him. Burlington fans haven't shown up to this penultimate game, because it's cruelly hot and the Bees are the worst team in the league. It's just some kids, a few old couples who put players up in their spare bedrooms, and Dancing Bobby, standing in his same spot above third base, gyrating violently to every hitter's walk-up music. The Clinton voices—Brad, Derek, Tim, Erin, Matt, the mailman, his wife—drown out the hometown fans.

We watch a pitch delivered low and outside, but it's a fastball and Nick swings, a bit late. The crack of the bat is weak and hollow, lost in the breeze, but the ball rises toward the fence. The left fielder trots back after it, glove up, and our eyes follow him. The wind is blowing out. The ball hangs for a moment, as if indecisive.

Then it disappears. Then the left fielder is looking in his glove, finding nothing. Then the umpire is running out toward the fence looking for evidence of a baseball in play. Then he's windmilling his right arm as if he were riding a mechanical bull, the motion that means home run.

There's Nick Franklin, somewhere between first and second, stopping for a moment, confused, before flashing a quick grin, then returning to a face that suggests none of this is that big of a deal. There's his fist up in the air, the way he's seen people do it on TV. There's his father, standing up in the front row, pointing at him in a manner that would seem accusatory if he weren't so proud. There's his mother, waiting to see his father's reaction and copying it.

There are Brad's thick, damp arms around me, and there are our torsos, jumping, or more bobbing, along with the six other Clinton fans who somehow coalesce to feel like a mob. There are the screams of *"Finally,"* of *"He did it,"* of *"We did it."* There are Brad's words over all others, *"The wait is over,"* and even though it wasn't a wait that most people knew was there until it ended, those words feel true.

There are the teammates, realizing soon enough what they need to do, spilling out of the dugout to embrace Nick. There's Hank at the front of the pack, grabbing his roommate around the torso, lifting him off the ground. There's my mind focused on the shot of Yogi Berra and Don Larsen from the 1956 World Series, the one my father used to show me, or Crash and Meat from *Bull Durham,* or Dave and the Kid from Tomkinsville, the way I imagined them as he read aloud, the squat one supporting the graceful one, an instinctive and unforced intimacy that I always wanted so badly.

There's the mob dispersing too quickly, Nick waving once at his parents.

There's Hank, trailing the crowd back into the dugout, face returning to blank. This might be the last professional baseball game he ever plays. And then what? Hank disappears into the dugout. Some country rock starts up from the speakers. Dancing Bobby begins to dance again.

There is the moment ended.

Nick's father calls his agent, and I hear him: "Yeah, it happened." And I hear the fuzz of the agent's happy yells, the quick hang up to facilitate the spreading of this achievement. I call Joyce, reflexively, though I know she isn't home to answer and doesn't own a cell phone. It rings twelve times and disconnects. I call again and it's the same. Her answering machine is full. She doesn't like to delete.

The first record breaker I ever read about was a Transylvanian man who created a machine that looked like a tommy gun and allowed him to smoke eight hundred cigarettes at once. There was a picture of him, mid-achievement, in a *Guinness* book that my brother bought me as a birthday present. I was aware, even then, that he looked like a stereotype, angular and oily, black pants, black leather jacket. But I stared at his face. It was ill, pale, depleted. You could see the sweat on him, even through the mass of people surrounding him, congratulating or asking why. He was gaunt, frightening, but he was proud. He stood the way I wanted to stand, exhausted in the pursuit of something worthwhile, certain of an achievement that could not be taken away until someone even crazier broke his record.

And when my brother snuck me a hit off his poseur cigar, I sucked it down with the eagerness with which one begins a marathon, a first burst toward ecstatic pain. And the nausea that came instantly with no ecstasy attached only made me look at my brother as more amazing, capable of achieving something I couldn't, even though that thing was awful. That was a small moment, one with no real heroes, nothing to make it important. And yet I think of the Transylvanian stranger, of my brother smiling, because it is my foundation for hanging importance on something so arbitrary. I think of myself, the strikeout record holder of the twelve-and-under division of a tiny Little League, the plaque that came with such an honor, the row of gold plastic trophies that I *never* let my mother throw out. For the last time, Nick has allowed me to inflate his moment, snatch it, mold it, make it connect to me somehow, and extend far beyond the thirty seconds that transpired between when the ball hit his bat and the team all wandered back to the dugout. Brad is leaning forward and calling to Nick's parents: "We haven't seen someone like this since Dick Kenworthy set the record back in 1961. Kenworthy is a legend, and Nick will be, too. I didn't know if I'd see it in my lifetime. Your son is in the books, sir."

Steve Franklin gives him a short handshake, looks past him.

Dick Kenworthy got a decent amount of space in the paid obits section of *The Kansas City Star* in April. Facts were established to define the triumph of his life and the details of his death. He went to a better place, obviously. While in this lesser place, he was a high school sports star, then he won a AAA MVP in Indianapolis, then he played six seasons on and off in the majors. He had three sons. His father, Roscoe, a farmer, outlived him. There was no mention of Dick Kenworthy as the fifty-year home run record holder in Clinton, though in the online version of the obit a Clinton fan has added that detail in the comments section.

Joyce was a toddler when Dick Kenworthy hit those home runs, and I imagine her chubby, sunburned body, her face with no dead tooth, perched up on the tar roof of the shed across from the stadium, pulling an oversized T-shirt down to cover her knees. Or maybe the team was on the road, who knows? Maybe she wasn't aware of what she missed, not like now. Last year a guy named Kyle Russell hit twenty-six home runs playing for Great Lakes. And a couple years before that, there was Juan Francisco, who hit twenty-five for Dayton. They just happened to not be LumberKings. Who are these people? I don't think they've made it yet. I've never heard of them. And nobody *ever* cared this much about young Kyle's home runs in Great Lakes, a fifteen-year-old team catering to a tri-city area of 400,000.

The more you care about something, the more you are set up to look foolish. I have tried to live by this basic truth, pushing toward nonchalance and irony. Because there are always others, less invested, who will look at you with withering contempt. That's why the players never express empathy. Or even excitement. That's why the culture of baseball is still Tamargo speaking in low, unsurprised tones, speaking as though ready to be disappointed. Tamargo is nearing sixty and has been disappointed. Disappointment is his routine. His quiet refusal of joy is earned. He has a limp to go with his tone, and a failing heart. But his players simulate his tone, even as their bodies are all youth, all hope. The gruff quiet is stifling now.

The game lulls, just as every baseball game ever has lulled. Matt fills the silence with his excoriations of the team's lack of effort. Brad looks nervous and agrees as if he wishes he didn't have to. Everybody is so fucking serious. Everybody wants more than what is happening. Especially me. It's a minor-league baseball game, for Christ's sake, and even Dancing Bobby's face looks grim while his hips thrust. I walk up to the Franklins, put my hand on Steve's shoulder.

"Congratulations," I say.

Nick's father gives a clipped nod and says, "Thanks. It was good to see him take that pitch the other way. He's been pressing a little. But I knew he'd do it."

"We're proud," Nick's mother reiterates. There's nothing else. They look at me long enough to let me know it's my cue to leave.

Hank hits a single in the third inning to give the LumberKings a lead.

But then, in the seventh, he tries to force his way into the play that will be remembered as the difference. He gets a throw in from the outfield and tries to catch an advancing runner he has no chance at, skidding the ball past Mario at third, letting another run score, giving Burlington a lead that they won't relinquish.

He sits in the dugout and stares out at the field, that most romantic pose of failure.

Two men are sitting silently in the bleachers, black sneakers, khaki pants, white hair, clipboard. These are talent evaluators from the Mariners, in Iowa to take what may be their last look of the season. One is called Toughy. He is expressionless, writes a lot. After games, he shakes players' hands, tells them, "Good job, son," often regardless of what transpired on the field. The players say thank you, wary, and that is the end of the interaction. On another day, in the bleachers of another stadium, Toughy told me that it's hard to evaluate a player's character in a place like Burlington or Clinton because what you're seeing is so far from being a simulation of the conditions that he'll face at higher levels. When he takes notes here, he has to focus his eyes on just the body. Arm angle, hip rotation, the power pushing out from a boy's thighs. Because you cannot judge his relationship to pressure, his immunity to being overwhelmed, when nothing around him is overwhelming.

"We want it," Brad says sometime around the eighth inning. "We want it more."

He looks to me for agreement.

"Yeah," I say, surprised at how easy I say it. "Looks like we do."

But whether or not the want was ever there, the results aren't. Six to four Burlington. Nick Franklin strikes out to end the game, walks off, and doesn't look up at us.

In a Mexican restaurant next to a Taco Bell, we find out that the Lumber-Kings grabbed the last spot in the play-offs. Despite their losing streak, the LumberKings managed to blow it less than the Beloit Snappers. We're eating enchiladas. Dave is clicking refresh, refresh on his Black-Berry, updating the Midwest League scoreboard every couple of minutes. Brad has been monologuing about how he doesn't want to back into the play-offs. I've already gotten a call from Tim saying just about the same thing. Dave, the most professional one here, says don't be ridiculous. You get in how you get in. Something as concrete and awesome as a play-off berth can't be judged on sentiment, whether things *feel* right. He admonishes the table with his eyes, continues. There's a system in place. If you make it, then you earned it. And by that logic, the LumberKings did earn it, and so we all did. Because after Dave's final refresh, the results are there, Internet-voiced and thus true. Dave raises his BlackBerry up like a chalice, gives a whoop before catching himself and saying, knowingly, "It ain't over, folks."

I go to meet the Franklin family in the lobby of the Pzazz! FunCity for a celebratory talk. I have been deemed by the parents to be an adequate instrument to record their son's moment of achievement. The four of us sit right outside the Boogaloo Cafe. It's packed for Labor Day weekend. Nobody notices us, none of the families, none of the gamblers or the tweens streaming in to ride bumper cars. My notebook is out, my eyes reverent on Nick, and that is the only signal that something worth noticing might be happening.

Finally, a little boy tugs his father over, stands at Nick's shoulder.

"Are you a player?" he asks.

"Yes, he is," Nick's mom answers.

"Cool," the boy says, and Nick says nothing and the boy leaves.

"The Clinton people think Nick's really special," I say to the parents.

"Oh, I know it," his mom says.

"It's good for them to have him here," his dad says, and Nick says nothing.

It's time for the origin tale. His mom begins, well-rehearsed. This day, this glory, can be traced, she tells me, back to the yard behind their house in Florida. Nicky would run back and forth through the grass, as though there was always a throw to beat. Debbie sat reading on the porch, looking up occasionally, and once when she looked up, honest to God, she saw the little guy executing a perfect pop-up slide. She asks if I know what a pop-up slide is, then explains before I can answer: when a player is running full speed, then folds his legs to slide feetfirst, but as soon as his heels hit the base, he uses his momentum to raise his body, as though a reanimated puppet, standing in one fluid movement ready to run again.

"Nicky was three," she says. "Maybe four. No, definitely three."

She was raised in a baseball family. Her dad played in the minors. Her brothers starred in high school. She married a baseball man, who always said that all his sons would play the game right. Her eldest son pitched for the University of Florida. But she felt a new excitement with Nick, her baby boy, something heightened, hallowed from toddlerdom.

She keeps going.

Nick was a freshman on his high school varsity team, all of five feet nine inches and 120 pounds if you were being generous. The scouts were there to watch his older brother pitch. Nick was catching, just for kicks. He threw the ball down to second a couple of times, stung the shortstop's hand as he caught the throws. The scouts all wanted to know who that was, where that arm came from. The parents had to tell them, *He's fourteen, fellas, you're going to have to wait.* Everybody chuckled.

I'm pretty sure I look bored. Nick's mom is leaning farther forward, disappointed with my boredom. His dad's arms are folded the way they always are when somebody isn't fully appreciating what must be appreciated. But the memories that make any one boy unique blend with the memories of every boy who is unique in the same way. Looking at the Franklins, I think of Danny, the first long talk I had with him, when I began with "How did you know—" and he was ready to finish my sentence for me. "How did I know I was gonna be a baseball player? Well, my parents sent me and my brother away to camp for a week. My brother's older than me, but he cried and cried. I didn't even notice that I was gone. I ran all day until the counselors got worried." And then he smiled, so I felt compelled to, and that was the end of it. Nice and tidy. The boy born to run and not be scared, so he did and he wasn't.

Tamargo shuffles over holding a whiskey on the rocks, clinking it, watching the ice cubes bob. He nods at the parents.

"Sorry to interrupt," he says. "Nick, you've got to go."

"Huh?" Nick says.

"Well, I mean, congratulations," Tamargo says, and then he smiles a bit too late. "Double-A. Shortstop broke his leg, so, you know, it's time."

The Franklin parents look to each other, and their son looks to them for how to react to this moment. The parents decide to stand and hug in celebration, but Nick holds back.

"JT, we've got play-offs," he says.

Tamargo looks at him the way one might look at a small, unhousebroken dog. "I know," he says. "We'll have to manage without you. Congratulations."

More emotions move through Nick's smooth, symmetrical face than I have ever seen on him. They move in pulses, surprisingly easy to identify. There is indignation, then pure anger, then fear, then a forlorn sadness, the kind you see on children tired at the mall, silly and heartbreaking all at once.

He sputters out, "B-but," before catching himself, straightening his posture, looking Tamargo in the eye, looking his father in the eye.

"I want to say good-bye to people," he says. Nobody responds.

"I should be able to say good-bye to people," his voice higher than I imagine he wanted it.

Of course, he is told.

So Nick Franklin wanders the city of fun, and I trail him. It is a sitcom montage, his expensive loafers dragging on the tacky carpet with a dollar-sign pattern, lights flashing, people together at blackjack tables, restaurant tables, Nok Hockey tables, and he, the self-obsessed, just slouching by them all. Harry Nilsson should be playing or Tom Waits, the kinds of men I put on the jukeboxes of Clinton dive bars before driving home, musicians Nick has never heard of and would describe as providing both no rhythm and no fun.

His teammates are scattered everywhere, and he is determined to find them. At the sports bar, some pitchers who know they won't be throwing for a few days are drinking, watching opening-week football highlights on TV, laughing. Nick walks up, stands at the edges of their conversation, tells them he won't be able to help them in the play-offs. "Congrats," they say, and, "It's about time." Because it is. They shake his hand, raise their bottles to him, turn away. He stands unsure and then moves on. At the velvet rope security check before the casino entrance, he's stopped, underage. He must lean over the velvet rope, yell to his teammates at the tables, Dwight sucking down a cigarette at the bar.

"I'm leaving," he yells.

They wander over. There is the same process. Well-wishes, bottles raised, turn away, silence. Somebody blurts out, "Yo, Morris just won three hundred dollars at blackjack," and Nick manages a "Whoa, crazy." This moment isn't enough for Nick. He doesn't say it out loud, doesn't say anything out loud, really, but this send-off isn't worth remembering.

All of Nick's gear is still in the visitors' locker room at the stadium, so we have to drive over. The lights are off. Teenage interns, Nick's peers, are carrying blue recycling bags full of Bud Light bottles out into the parking lot. Men with caked, patchy hair and sole-less shoes wait for them. Burlington is right behind Clinton with Iowa's second-highest unemployment rate. The Franklins look at their own shoes walking past. I do, too.

"Well, doesn't this place look different now?" someone says.

I take a quick detour up a ramp into the bleachers, stare out to left field, the spot where Nick's record breaker disappeared over the wall, but there's dusky shadow from the woods behind and nothing is recognizable.

A guy my age with red hair and a round face, perhaps actually on salary, opens the clubhouse, flicks on the lights.

"You've got about ten minutes to get your stuff together, so no rush," he says. "Congratulations on the play-offs."

"He set the home run record for Clinton," Nick's mom says.

"*Mom,*" Nick says. There are nervous chuckles.

"Yes, I think I heard that," the red-haired guy says.

Nick picks up his jockstrap first, not yet washed, shoves it quickly into a bag. Then some Under Armour, his glove.

"Your bats," his father says.

"I *know,*" he says.

He grabs his hats instead, four different ones. Special breast cancer awareness hat with the pink brim, black hat, gray hat, green hat. All of them adorned with Louie the LumberKing, with his beard and club and rippling muscles, his maniacal grin. Nick stacks them neatly, gives a quick tweak to the brims. He looks up. He seems to be trying to weigh the nostalgic value of these items that have become instantly useless. He grabs the gray cap because it's newest and cleanest. He could wear it at home, to a party, something.

"You want one?" he says to me. It is generous. He is offering me an item that was once his and thus must be worth something. But I hold back and feel a strange pride in that, maybe because his eyes have been hovering near tears for an hour, because he is just a nineteen-year-old boy packing up a dirty jockstrap, missing friends who he didn't quite realize were his friends until now. I have an overwhelming desire to add little exclamations to whatever pain he is feeling. As though I, as a representative for everyone who has felt small near him, deserve that. I will not run to reassure him.

"I'm good," I say, and he shrugs, tosses the remainder on the ground. I could tell him that Joyce would take each one. Tell him that if he wrote a message on one of them—*Great knowing you! Miss you! Go LumberKings!*—the hat would remain pristine and displayed until long after he played his last game of baseball. And I should say something. I'm aware that I should. Any of his hats is a relic of a day that some people will think of as important for a long time, certainly longer than Nick will. Joyce can have it and treat it with more respect than has ever been given a hat. But I say nothing. Stubborn. Jealous, maybe. Or protective. Because I think he will laugh at the notion of Joyce's care and I'll feel compelled to laugh with him.

"Nick's a real teammate," his mother says as we head back to the hotel. "Now that he's been here, gotten these guys to the play-offs, he wants to take it to the end with them."

"If they were going to make him stay here, I don't see why they couldn't let him finish it," his father says. "This is another reason why he should've been up and out in June."

This is the party line, but there is something else to it now. Dad is being defensive not only of the brand—"*Franklin, Est. 1991*"—but also of the boy. Nick Franklin will miss this place, even if he is too much for it, even if it is baseball purgatory. Nick Franklin in his loafers, with his strut, with those fast hands, wants nothing more right now than to play the game for two more weeks the way every kid is told one should play it, the way the highest-paid stars claim to play it and the way we choose to believe they do. He wants to win a championship and then share that with those who won with him. That shouldn't be shocking, but it is. It's the first time I have ever watched him behave with the motivation that everyone projects upon him, and now, after he has stumbled into this moment of purity, it is being snatched away.

Can I pity an athlete? In the lobby of the Pzazz! FunCity, can it feel tragic for ten minutes that Nick Franklin is having no fun?

I have a habit that's more than a habit. In the morning, over coffee, I find the most contentious stories on ESPN.com and skim the content, rushing to get to the comment section, usually numbering in the thousands of individual opinions, always alive, generating new responses each second, sometimes freezing my computer with the speed of the virtual conversation. I love the voyeuristic tingle of reading the homophobia ever present on-screen, sure, and the racism, too. But more than that, I'm drawn to the general, frantic certainty that all the comments coalesce to create. One voice of divisive yet unifying fandom, a shared belief that these athletes are of the utmost importance and thus should be worshipped until the moment they fail to live up to the worship and reviled ever after.

When professional jocks are quoted as complaining, I particularly revel in the responses. In between "fuck you, you boston c*cksucker," and "your mother likes to suck on ARod's bitch tits!!!!" there are moments of raw hurt, profane and misspelled versions of the same implied question: *How dare this person who lives the life that I want complain?*

Nick Franklin is young and beautiful and rich and sometimes cold. And when he is not cold, I admire him for the capacity to be polite to somebody as insignificant as me—somebody born with middling fast-twitch reflexes—in a way that I never would anyone else. He is leaving a place that he never particularly wanted to come to, jumping up two levels to be the youngest person on a team where guys have a legitimate shot of getting a late-night text saying that they are wanted in the major leagues. Hank Contreras is up in his room right now talking to his girlfriend on her work break, planning an off-season of labor next to his father, who is gentle and does not ask things out loud like, *When are you going to start life?* He considers AA to be a goal so barely reachable that he refuses to say that he deserves to be there, with a livable wage and extra legroom on the bus, a chance to get called on to be a third-string, last-minute substitute for one day for an injury-ridden major-league squad.

But Nick Franklin is small right now, and alone. And he doesn't want his parents hovering near him with hugs and reminders. He doesn't want the plane ride in a few hours to somewhere else. It is simple, manufactured nostalgia, that silly thing that I feel all the time, that thing best felt by the young who don't have enough moments strung together to remind themselves that there is something more important than the place being left. It's that swell of crushing emptiness that makes the insignificant seem anything but.

He says, kind of to nobody, "This was a good team."

There are all kinds of things wrong with this sentence. The team still is, so if he has decided to label it good, it remains so. Though maybe, to read him cynically, the idea is that the team was good until he left it. Which is kind of true. But how good has this team been? Seventy-four and sixty-five, ten games out of first place, a four-game losing streak to end the season, benefiting because the winner of the first half of the season is also leading the second half and one team can't take two play-off spots. A general apathy toward all these facts. And Nick himself, in his last at bat today, record already in hand, two outs in the ninth, had a chance to help clinch the play-offs, but he struck out on three pitches.

I think of us in the clubhouse a couple of days ago, before he trotted out to the field, last to make his entrance, as always. He was alone except for my half presence, casually shining his cleats. I asked him if it would be hard to leave this place—friends, fans, his older, midwestern girlfriend who he met after a game in Peoria, Illinois. He told me, "A little." Leaving is hard, but you have to look at it as moving on. And the girlfriend, she was a perfect Single-A girlfriend, he would remember her fondly, but a AAA girl would be something else entirely. Leaving, he said, is almost always improving.

But not now. He doesn't think that right now. Everything means so much right now. Half a year of not so many years was lived here. People loved him here. He lived with roommates here, shared rented TVs with four other guys, rode in the back of shitty cars like mine to dive bars, was served illegal drinks by smoky-voiced bartenders who told him they liked his fancy diamond earring, that it made him look like a rap star. He will not be loved like this anywhere else. Not really. Maybe if he becomes a major-league superstar, he will be known to the nation, the world, but it will be a diffuse love, and, anyway, that situation probably won't happen. He'll probably be a mediocre big-league infielder for a decade or so, make more money than I'll ever see, the kind of money that could buy Alliant Energy Field and all the riverfront property around it, everything in town that isn't a factory. He'll probably fuck women in clinging dresses who have waited for his team in the marble lobby of hotels much grander than the Pzazz! FunCity. He'll probably do commercials for local car dealerships. He'll probably have a kid, and all his kid's friends will be jealous of the father he lucked into.

This is likely to be the last time he will be a record breaker.

Joyce has all of Nick's remains in hand for the first round of the play-offs, half brag, more of a good luck charm. There's a pair of his socks, ripped and unwearable, still with his sweat in the fibers and stadium dirt from a dive that must have been magnificent behind second base. There's an armband tossed to her after a home win. And an old hat, and a jersey, and a bat that he splintered, his branded signature still intact on the barrel, the imprint of his fingers still visible in the pine tar smudge. She is overshadowed, though, by Derek, who has his sleeves rolled up to his shoulders to expose upper-arm flesh that is nothing but pale and doughy except for his tattoo of Nick's signature, just like the one on Joyce's bat. Just like the one seen a lot of places. Go to eBay, type in "Nick Franklin Card." The number of results fluctuates from day to day, but the pool never dries up. As I type, a window on my screen displays 287 items, most of them with a picture of his face for sale, all of them with his name. You can get a plain old card, with his signature unraised, obviously a printout copy. That'll run you ninety-nine cents. There are limited-edition cards that cost eight bucks, and cards signed by Nick Franklin himself—authenticity guaranteed—those can get up to eighty bucks. There are stranger items for sale, pricier and more specific, sold by those with Joyce's proclivities but without her belief in anti-commerce. Some guy from across the river in Illinois got his hands on a real-deal lineup card from last month, got the players who might be worth something to sign over their printed names—Nick, Vinnie Catricala, a fourth-rounder named Max Stassi from Kane County. They're worth a hundred dollars when bundled together.

"I've got him on my *skin,*" Derek says. "And it hurt like a bitch, but it's never going anywhere."

His fiancée has started coming to the games with him again but still rolls her eyes when he mentions the thing. She doesn't get it at all. Why should she?

Joyce says, "I wouldn't have the nerve. I don't like needles."

She smiles, then looks down. She rummages in her bag for something, doesn't find it, stops.

After the season, I still go to Joyce's house every month or so. She shows me her things and I like her excitement and she likes that I like it. We sit down and watch TV, and the cat paces. Usually, she's picked up something new to show. Sometimes she has a present for me. A Louie the LumberKing fridge magnet. A little holiday card on which she's written nothing but *125 days until opening day!* Sometimes I get her presents, too. I was on vacation with my girlfriend, wandering through a consignment shop in geriatric Florida. I found a mini-bat in the back of the store, hidden in a pile of children's gloves, left sneakers with no right, a Frisbee dedicated to the fire department of a town I've never heard of. The bat was faded. There was half the face of a mascot I couldn't recognize. It was dated 1991, made the year Clinton won, the year Nick Franklin was born, the year Joyce started working at the casino thinking she'd someday leave, a collection of coincidences that mean nothing but still comfort me because there can be a pattern to things if you want there to be.

I tell Joyce a story, and then it becomes co-authored. Nick Franklin went upstairs to his hotel room alone before he and his parents drove away from Burlington, up 61 to Clinton, packed his clothes by midnight, slid out past the industrial sprawl in the early morning. He told his mother and father to stay put, leaving them to tell me all the bullshit things that they thought I needed to hear—how grateful the family is for the chance, how all Nicky wanted to do was be part of a team. He left to find Hank. Nick stayed up there a long time, just the two of them talking, his parents looking at their watches in the lobby, his father finally bolting to the parking lot to let the rental car's A/C run for a while.

"It must have been like talking to his older brother," Joyce says.

"They really get close here," she continues.

"I bet he thanked him," I say, not knowing. But Hank was so important to him.

"I bet he said, 'See you soon,'" she says. "That's what they say to each other because it's nice to hear."

We go on like that, batting one-sentence proclamations back and forth, making the scene, off-season archival baseball footage on the TV in the background, unwatched for the moment.

Their phones were buzzing, neither of them picking up. Finally, an embrace. Maybe an exchange of a token. That must have happened. A wristband or a piece of paper with a note on it, something for Hank to keep.

We sit in her dining room, where nobody dines. My allergies are acting up because of the cat. The carpet isn't helping, neither is the lack of airflow, windows never opened, vacuum never sucking up the things hidden in the cracks. I sneeze and my eyes are beginning to water, streaks of defensive tears running into the creases between nose and cheek. She looks at me, hopeful, head cocked, eyes ready to empathize.

"Are you okay?" she asks. "I know, it's a lot."

I'm not exactly sure what "*it*" is. I think "*it*" might mean the end of a season, the talk of Nick now gone. Or maybe it's the experience of looking at all these names from all these season, stacked floor to ceiling, trinkets of the past looming over us in the present. I want to be really crying for her. "I can't wait for opening day," she says. "I don't like this town as much in the winter. It seems like there's less people every year."

I will be going to spring training next year and Joyce won't. She asks me to take things for her. She asks me to take the stories she's written to those she's written about. She has Nick's story ready, not just in her omnipresent red notebook, but typed up in a nice bold font on a nice clean sheet of paper. She'll put it in a blue envelope for me, with polka dots. She bought a big pack of polka-dot blue envelopes. She uses them for the players who she thinks will have a lot of mail to sift through. The ones who have become public property, no longer glad for attention. That is who Nick Franklin is now. She's happy for him. She just wants to be remembered for her part, her shadow waiting by the fence to get signatures, her voice above all the others, her collection. And so Nick will get a blue polka-dot envelope from Joyce, different from the envelopes of all the other people who want to know him now. And there will also be a blue polka-dot envelope at the Texas Rangers' spring-training facility, too, on a Santa Claus–sized pile of letters, a copy of the tale for Mitch Moreland to sign and send back, his signature confirming that he knows she saw him.

Something Climactic

THE HOT TUB IN THE BLEACHERS of Veterans Memorial Stadium in Cedar Rapids is empty but on, bubbles crashing into each other and fizzling out. The hot tub is perched over the left-field fence, meant to house parties of young, drunk fans who want to be seen. Right now, though, the most noticeable presence in the stands is the small but vocal Roadkill redux, all of whom have driven an hour and a half and will be driving the same again home at eleven on a work night. Joyce is here, of course, irked at the tepid home crowd that seems willing to only give lackluster claps during the deciding game of the first round of the Midwest League play-offs.

The most effusive I've seen Cedar Rapids fans was during a softball home run derby held before the national anthem of a game in July, entered by weekend warriors in specially made T-shirts repping autobody shops, custom decal services, divorce lawyers. I watched the field, heard kinetic noise behind me that did not fit what I was watching. I leaned on the fence behind home plate with Bose, the strength coach. We glared at the men on the field and laughed uneasily. They were enormous.

"Look at these pussies," Bose said to me. I let my voice get cold and condescending, too, like, What kind of void are these clowns trying to fill getting one last afternoon of cheers? These local monsters could hit, though. Softballs like ostrich eggs went flying as far as a baseball can when the Nick Franklins of the world swing right. Each hitter was cheered with fervor, especially Scott, the best, who scowled in his bright orange uniform and had a collection of manic-grinning women holding signs in his honor. Terry Pollreisz sidled up next to us as we watched. The last time he hit in a game was during the Nixon administration, but he sounded young and blustery and personally invested in the thought of being unintentionally shown up by another guy's success when he said, "Hey, I'll tell you something. I went in the office before the game and saw the staff freezing softballs so that they'd fly farther. So don't get too impressed."

We sneered and I wondered if Scott knew, if mammoth Scott was complicit in the lie of his greatness or if he hadn't been told and thought that all the distance was supplied by his body that was no less than a pro's. It didn't matter. He was worshipped and people who cared about him were there to see his staged exploits and to wave their glitter-glue homemade signs as he posed with his plastic trophy.

Now the crowd energy that Scott basked in is absent. The real players are out limbering up for a crucial play-off game, and they are met with near silence, children's sneakered feet running, the crunch of nacho chewing, the collective chuckling of people killing time. Erasmo is bouncing in anticipation on the top step of the dugout, jacket on even in the sticky heat. He is pitching tonight, what is surely the most important performance of his life by the metrics through which we are taught to look at team sports. This is a make-or-break game for a team on which he is a crucial member. Winners of this league get rings with gems in them and a write-up in the hometown paper of a place that is not their hometown. Erasmo, after a life's training, has never actually pitched in a game like this, one with consequence, with a community of fans' and teammates' expectations resting on him, not just his own or his family's, desires that aren't actually tied to teams or victories. "Hey," yells one autograph seeker who has wandered to the front row, the loudest voice in the stadium. "Hey, hey, hey, hey," until Erasmo turns to him. And then, "Who the fuck are you?"

I've been reading pamphlets and interview transcripts from the Clinton Corn strike, saved on microfilm, converted into PDFs by a few loving hands. Not much documenting the conflict has been saved in Clinton, because why would there be? In the historical society's illustrated history of the town, there are a few pictures of angry-looking picketers with a caption saying, "Many claim that today's economic problems in Clinton are a direct result of that strike," but that's where the story ends.

In state historical societies and university libraries, Clinton is defined, if at all, by two moments. There is the invariable blurb about the lumber and the millionaires, such happy and unexpected facts, and then a jump right to 1979 and 1980, the years taken as the town's last stand and a metaphor for an entire part of the country, an entire way of life.

I have a copy of the document that Clinton workers wrote to remember themselves, forty pages of reassertion that this place is important. "A Year in Our Lives" is the simple title. Of course I flip right to the page with the pictures of proud, organized protest taking place in the stadium, no players on the field, just workers. I look for Bill and Betty and Tim and Tammy in the pictures, as if they'll be where they always are, by the third-base line, maybe even laying out free candy for the strikers to take home. I don't see them, though they were there, somewhere, I think they've told me that. Or maybe I'm looking at them, but I don't recognize who I'm seeing.

It's the best crowd I've ever seen in Clinton's stadium. Every seat is full in the photographs. And there are signs. Nobody in Clinton thinks to make signs now, not for Nick Franklin's record-breaking home run, not even for a play-off win. In the pictures of the protest, all the signs say the same things, printed on the same flimsy white scrap wood with the same stenciled lettering that you see on the "ADM Poly Is Not a Good Neighbor" signs today in south Clinton. But these aren't hidden in the neighborhood that nobody goes to. These say, "We Stand with Local 6."

Three thousand people filled the stadium. It was Labor Day, 1979, and in the thirty-one years since then nothing has remained the same except for the skeleton of the stadium. There were union representatives on the field that day. Men from the Teamsters and the United Automobile Workers as well as from the national offices of the Grain Millers Union. The crowd paraded from the stadium down to the foot of the factory, arms raised in the pictures, flags waving, American flags, Iowa state flags, homemade banners to represent the Labor Congress, and then back to the stadium for prayer. They seemed to believe, from the language in the news clippings and personal recollections, that they would win, that they had to. And even a year later, when no more protesters flooded the stadium, when many had left town, when they had definitively lost, the newsletter for the struggle asserted a refusal of the ending: "Personal differences divide the community we formed with one another. People are feeling burned out after the long, hard, bitter struggle. But a faithful remnant remains. And we shall overcome."

It makes sense to think about the Clinton Corn factory that would become ADM while I'm in Cedar Rapids because ADM has a facility here, too, its smell mixing with the similar but softer odor of the Quaker Oats plant. What's different, though, is that ADM doesn't feel so omnipresent here. Maybe because it employs 500 out of 125,000 in the city. Or because, like in many other American cities, just not in Clinton, the plant is situated off a highway here, kept to the very edges of town. Or because the Teamsters established a local at the plant in the 1950s and the industry in the town has remained unionized ever since, no ire-filled arguments in the local paper, no lawsuits, no signs. Even the trains full of product sliding past the stadium don't sound so *heavy*. You hear them if you want to listen, but they do not force you. And when I drive by Cedar Rapids with my university friends we all say, "*God*," and hold our noses, but really the smell doesn't seep into everything, or at least it doesn't bother me so much. Cedar Rapids, to all who have traveled from Clinton, is sneered at. A rising economy, a booming population, uniform suburbs full of new homes. Yeah, there was that flood a couple of years back, but the new stadium looks just fine.

For the Clinton faithful who have traveled here, for me, Hank embodies that feeling as he stands waiting for a pitch. He limps every time he walks now. Even just standing in his half crouch in the batter's box, he winces. The bat is loose in his swollen hand, resting on his broken thumb. The bases are loaded, too perfect. James Jones is on third, ready to sprint. And Kevin Mailloux, Nick's replacement who was the home run leader in rookie ball, but who obviously no Clinton fan likes, he's on second. Catricala is on first.

A fastball bores in on Hank's hands. He swings and groans. The ball makes a pop on his bat, skids hard toward the hole between shortstop and third. My body tenses along with Betty's and Joyce's next to me. It looks as though the shortstop will get to the ball. Maybe he takes a bad route, but the ball slides under his glove, into the outfield. Everything is moving. Jones scores, Mailloux scores. Hank hobbles around first, ecstatic pain on his face.

Another run scores in the first, and the LumberKings don't need anything more. Erasmo, as he always has, does his job. His arm has been worked this season nearly twice as much as any year in his young life, and though his stuff is in no way electric—his fastball barely reaching ninety, his curve limp and flat—he does his job. He gives up an early hit in every inning, loud ones that quasi-excite the Cedar Rapids fans, but each time a couple of lazy fly balls or a double play ends their chances. In what could be Erasmo's last performance as a LumberKing, he turns in a game that looks exactly like so many of his others. Seven innings, a lot of hits that amount to not much, no walks, two runs, and then he's up on the top step of the dugout, jacket on, grinning a little. He is right there to see and he's hard to notice. Joyce notices.

"You're the best, E-mo," she yells to him, and in a movement so small but so big he turns, smiles, nods once. She lists his accomplishments this year to everyone around us, him, too, easily within earshot. His ERA, his wins, his all-star selection, how few people he walked. All the numbers that only he and she and I remember.

In the clubhouse, after winning the first round of the play-offs, guys are happy and cheering, and then they turn their attention to sandwich orders. Tamargo is napping in his underwear with the door to the manager's office left open a crack. Hank is on the trainer's table tensing his body and trying not to yell.

Freeze this. The light is shitty. The room is cramped. There's a radio on somewhere playing honky-tonk rock, Seger into Mellencamp into George Thorogood, and somehow no player has thought to drown it out with vibrating beats from his portable speakers. BJ is looking through cupboards and coolers that have already been emptied, trying to find enough tape and enough ice. Other players are standing, waiting for treatment on blistered hands or sore knees, but they all come after Hank. There is one table in here, and it's occupied by the number five hitter, the game winner, a crucial man.

BJ is leaning in and saying, "You can't play."

And Hank is saying, "Bullshit, I'm fine."

And BJ is saying, "I know you want to. But you can't run. You can't throw the ball to second."

And Hank is saying, "You all need me."

And BJ is softening, saying, "Of course. Of course we do. That's not what I mean."

I am hanging by Hank's shoulder. His pain is wonderful to me, brings with it soaring thoughts of *If this guy can last through this, then I can . . . then we all can . . .* Fill in the blanks. Or don't. It is a feeling better undefined. But by now Hank doesn't want to mean what I want him to mean. He doesn't want to be hurt. He doesn't want to be flailing against inevitability. He wants real things, like no pain and a contract beyond September.

He keeps playing against Kane County in the second round of the play-offs, but the pain only increases. By the time a foul ball bounces off his right hand, hitting the spot that is already fractured, leaving him looking more stunned than writhing, there is a fatalistic quality about him, intrigue already waning.

"That must've stung," Betty says in the stands.

"He'll be fine," someone responds. "He ain't in Afghanistan or anything."

That comes up a lot. Tough game out there, or those boys must be hot, or they can't catch a break. Hey, they're not in Afghanistan.

True. But Hank's gritting his teeth and trying hard to live up to the maxims of war movies and recruitment officers. He doesn't get a moment to limp off, giving a little wave to tell the fans he will keep trying. He plays through the inning without much notice of his obstinacy. Then in the dugout, he's told he's done, he can't help with anything as banged up as he is. He doesn't reappear for the next inning. This moment that didn't happen is his last moment as a player in Clinton, Iowa.

It feels as if the winning should end when he leaves the field, with how clutch he's been, how he's muscled himself into the center of the story. But the LumberKings coast to a 6–2 victory, easy, even with Ochoa's two strikeouts in Hank's stead. I'm almost annoyed about it. And then the next game, the deciding game. The LumberKings all hit; the bleachers are pandemonium. They win easily.

Hank limps to the mound to make a gesture at celebration with his team. They have done it. The thing that they worked for, the vague collective goal that they shared since April has arrived, though Danny's gone and Sams is gone and young Nick Franklin has moved way beyond. Still, without them, without Hank, the LumberKings will play the Lake County Captains from Ohio for the chance to be champions.

Everybody gets really drunk in Ohio. After a seventeen-inning game at home, the LumberKings winning on a wild pitch, bringing every player off the bench, falling all over one another at the plate when it was all over, a crazed exhaustion has settled over the team. Every pitcher who has pitched in this series knows he is done for the season, free to turn his attention to the hotel bar. The coaches will be returning home to wives and families soon. To grandkids, for Tamargo. To crosswords in the morning and then all day long nothing, for Pollreisz. To the grain farm and the gun shows for Dwight. No matter what the team does, this season and its frat-house, band-of-brothers conceit, the same one attached to every season, will end, and there will be boredom for five months, a lot of half promises about finally retiring before the inevitable report to spring training come February. So they're drunk every night. And then there's Hank, who will not play an inning here and who knows that. Who took a ten-hour bus ride for no reason other than to watch, no better than me and Brad and the other Clinton fans who carpooled from the Alliant Energy Field parking lot. He is alternately sullen and manic, looking to get numb with anyone at any time. Everyone feels a little sorry about how things panned out for him, so plenty of people oblige.

We stay at the bar until closing, drinking shots alongside middle-aged women with bleached, coarse hair. The women survey the tables with glassy eyes. They have seen ballplayers come through this place before. They don't admit that they were waiting for some to show, but that is a distinct possibility.

"Are you pros?" one asks.

"Fuck yes," Hank says, fast.

"Who do you play for?" she asks.

That's when the mumbling comes in.

You wouldn't have heard of us. Minor-league ball. Still pro, though. Clinton. Iowa. LumberKings. No, not Lumberjacks. LumberKings.

It's the usual caveats, spoken all at once, too quick to be a convincing defense of anything and ultimately an indictment. The pros they want to be wouldn't have to say anything. But these women don't care. The boys are young and strong and proud enough to defend themselves. The women sit close, and their hands are grazing forearms soon, then foreheads, then legs.

"Let me tell you all who you are," one says, slurring a little.

We let the implied depth fade into the jukebox, and she points around the table. *Pitcher. Pitcher. Pitcher.* She's spot-on. She gets to Hank, and I see him flex a little, his white T-shirt stretched thin. She studies him, the calluses of his hands, his pronounced cheekbones and broad body. *Catcher,* she says, and he smiles. Then she looks over him, back toward the pitchers, elegant, tall even when sitting down. Catcher means the same for her as it does for everyone else. Identifiably middling.

She gets to me at the end of the table. I let myself think, as she pauses, that I blend in. I realize how important a nod of belief would be from her, validation that I'm better than all those people who buy these guys shots and have their pictures snapped next to them just to prove that their proportions are the same. The validation that I am not like those fish that ride on sharks, valuable to the ecosystem only with my need to be attached.

"Camera boy," she says at me and giggles. Everybody giggles. I didn't even know there were camera boys. I say that out loud, trying to keep my tone from moving into anything but a smirk. Hank shoves me, playful and satisfied. Someone is less than he is.

The players watch the women watch them. Phones ring, the women look, hit silent, and slide them back into their purses. The players say they're competing for the championship. They say, *Maybe it's been mentioned in the paper.* The women ask if they're going to win, and the players say, *Definitely, without a doubt.* Everyone at the table likes that certainty. Bose is the most physically impressive of these guys. As the strength coach, he works out all day. And he is twenty-four, grown, fully filled out. The women think he's the team's star power hitter, and the players let him have that. They stifle laughs as one woman, a little too old to be his sister, a little young to be his mom, looks at him with pickled eyes, whispers something, leads him to the men's room on precarious heels.

Hank is smiling, and then he isn't. He says he's tired. I follow him to the hotel lobby. He sits on a stiff couch that approximates leather.

He picks up a newsletter advertising the tourism gems hidden within Lake County, Ohio, highlighting an arboretum, two scenic rivers, and Gildersleeve Mountain, just waiting to be climbed. He makes almost comical expressions, raised eyebrows or down-turned lips, as though considering the merits of each option. As though he is just a salesman in town for a few extra days or a father who wants to show his children everything worth showing as they drive across America. But he will not go to any rivers or mountains or arboretums. He will go to the bar or Chipotle across the street, and the field. He will sit and wait until it feels as if there wasn't a beginning and there won't be an end to all his sitting and waiting.

The glass doors at the front of the hotel slide open. Nick Franklin walks in. The room doesn't stop at first. It seems as though he should be here. Why not? But then Hank says his name and Nick smiles, and everyone realizes that there's been no Nick Franklin for almost two weeks.

His parents are with him, dragging hastily packed suitcases. There's a high school girl standing next to him with long, curly hair, a tan that isn't fake like the ones you see in Midwest bars. She is wearing big sunglasses, and she is frowning. It looks like the beginning of a teen movie, the check-in scene before all the hilarious vacation pandemonium, except for the ring that Nick is wearing, from when his team won the rookie ball crown last year. It's the kind favored by gamblers or grandfathers, meant to be worn on old, gnarled hands, not the smooth digits of the baby of the family. I've never seen him wear it before. Nick trots over to Hank, sits down next to him. The girl hovers above the couch and waits.

"I heard y'all needed me," Nick says, smiling.

Hank says yeah.

Other players wander over, and Nick shares his epic tale. He was down in Florida, just chilling, giving himself a deserved break. He was on the beach with this girl, not his girlfriend, just, whatever. His phone was ringing, but he wasn't answering. Finally, it rang a few times in a row, and he picked it up out of the sand, saw it was the number of the front office in Seattle.

He lets the fact that it's common for him to receive front-office calls sink in. Then he goes on. He was told, We need you back in A-ball. Nick said, Huh? The bosses said, Go help them win a championship. You've got a flight booked to Ohio in three hours. They toweled off and ran to his Escalade. He called his father. His father said, No time to bring the girl home, not in traffic. Nick looked at her and said, Yo, wanna fly to Ohio? The team will pay. She thought the whole thing was cool, and so here she is in her flip-flops, sand still between her toes.

He's different. No, he can't be. It's been eleven days.

His shiny blue shirt is open down to the middle of his chest, showing off the lines tracing his pectorals. He is rubbing his ring like a cartoon villain or like Gollum or just like John Tamargo. And look at how pressed his jeans are. Look at the shoes, his white Honey Bear loafers that were too much for going out on a Saturday night and are certainly too much for checking into a Comfort Suites with his parents. He sits, space on the cushions between himself and his teammates. A scene begins to unfold the way you would expect it to, the imparting of knowledge from the player who has been where the others want to go. Hold for grizzled wisdom. Hold for youthful reverence.

But the scene isn't right. The promised land in this conversation is Double-A. The real promised land isn't even promised. And Nick isn't speaking to the myth, the power, of the place—Jackson, Tennessee. The players are nothing special, he says. No different from in the Midwest. Maybe a little more consistent. Otherwise, he's not sure what the big deal is. He shrugs. It was easy.

His father interrupts, tells his mother to take the girl upstairs, says, "Why don't you ladies get settled in?" They oblige.

"Hello, men," says Mr. Franklin. Everyone says hello.

Finally, someone non-Franklin speaks.

"How'd they let you back?"

Nick shrugs. It is not for the players to discuss, though they know that something odd happened since there isn't supposed to be any roster adjustment once the play-offs start, unless there are unforeseen injuries. Tomorrow, Kevin Mailloux, twenty-four, a surprise slugger only when playing in rookie ball with fresh-meat teens, will go on injured reserve, and Nick will take his place. Mailloux's parents will drive down from Canada to pick him up from the last professional baseball locker room he'll ever inhabit. He is more temporary than he thought.

It's not that everybody who isn't good enough is compelling. Because, man, that's a lot of people. And to see them walk away is a series of mini-tragedies, each a failure worth honoring at least. I want to say that much. So few will ever know what it is to play in the majors beyond a couple of garbage-time at bats in September for a team long out of contention. Just because I know Kevin Mailloux's ending, just because he has made the decision to be identified as a ballplayer until eventually his jersey is taken from him, doesn't mean that something enormous isn't happening when he walks to his parents' car, all his clothes and his bats slung over his shoulders like the most muscle-bound, hair-gelled train-hopper you've ever seen, nodding a silent good-bye.

There's no chance that the LumberKings can lose. That is the consensus. Gone is the bunch of underachievers or lovable try-hards depending on who is talking. Nick Franklin is back. The team re-earned him. And how could they lose with him when they won without him? Now that they've overcome so much? I don't know what has been overcome. But I know that the tingle of group hyperbole is palpable. The clubhouse now is the rollicking, unified Eden that I tell Tim and Tammy it's always been.

"How are they?" Tim asks over the phone, all day, all night.

"They're good," I report like a babysitter. "They're excited. They want to win."

I imagine Tim closing his eyes on the other end of the line, seeing their want.

"Yeah, they want it," he says, before hanging up.

Brad, who drove Erin and me nine and a half hours from one end of the Midwest to the other in a groaning red Impala because he would not miss history, confirms that assumption.

Look at them. Look at how much they want this.

But what about those other guys, the Lake County Captains? They must want it too.

No disrespect, but they don't want it like we do.

There are many reasons. The Captains only moved here eight years ago. They play in a stadium that is antiseptic in its brightly colored, state-of-the-art functionality. And look at the place, all this shine, all this investment, and there are more empty seats than at a game in Clinton. There is nothing to see in Lake County but easy, fast, smug success and a lack of tradition.

To come to this conclusion, we must discount the fact that the Lake County, Ohio, economy has plummeted, a real rust-belt bust, not a slow Iowa erosion, something both present and not present at the stadium. Present in the empty seats, not present in the forceful cheer of the huge, furry mascot and the new Jumbotron. There is no tradition of under-doggery here, that's the issue. No lineage of wanting more, of needing, for once, to win. They are not playing for anything, just playing.

Brad and Tim have faith not only in the talent of the players who happen to wear their home team jersey. They have faith in their collective character, in their thought process, in the purity of their motivation, one vaguely akin to Clinton's own. But the enormous valley between the competing perspectives has never been more apparent. No matter how excited the players get in the clubhouse during the championship, it's excitement born of casual pragmatism—if you make it to the championship, you might as well win. It feels good to win, and I'm sure the Lake County Captains think the exact same thing. The concept of players who want to win not just because of an always honed instinct toward success but for some greater sense of legacy, is a fiction. It's the type of player that everybody assumed would show up, the same assumption as last year and the year before, and before that. The type I read in books about made-up players chasing made-up crowns. And so a collection of always new faces with no allegiance to one team can meld into a continuous narrative. It is a necessary lie.

The players, boarding the bus from the hotel, beating on the seats in front of them, giving the bus driver some new Eminem track to play, about overcoming both pill addiction and the haters, include Clinton as one of the things they overcame on the way to earning the title of champion. An empty town that they won in spite of. The fans see Clinton as one of the reasons they made it.

I'm hanging over the outfield railing before batting practice. Joyce isn't here. That is all I can think of. This is where she should be. This is the space she has made hers. Her vacation days have run out. She made it to every game before the championship and knew, as she pored over her LumberKings calendar, that she wouldn't have enough days to give if they made it all the way. It had seemed so improbable. She thought about rooting, secretly at least, for the LumberKings to lose with dignity in the conference series so that she would be a part of the almost and wouldn't be left out of the end. But that wouldn't be right.

The players don't ask about her. They're concentrating. The only man standing with me before game four is old and stooped and smells like birdseed. He has a round face that I imagine was once handsome. His jeans are sliding down off narrow hips.

"You know 46?" he asks me, meaning the man behind the jersey number.

James Jones. "Yes."

"I need him. Hey, 46!" But Jones is already through the door into the outfield, trotting bat in hand. He turns and says, "I'll get you after."

The man doesn't respond to Jones. Then he says to me, "You know 3? He's worth getting, right?"

Nick Franklin. "Yes."

Nick Franklin is already through the door, too, and is in no mood to turn.

"I only have two hours," the man says to me. "My name's Cal."

Cal doesn't like baseball. He never cares to watch the games. They take too long. And he doesn't want to get invested. But the stadium is pretty and smells nice, and it's walking distance from his house. And he's one of those people who got laid off—auto parts, bound to happen—and his wife is sick; well, she's been sick for a while, but now it's all he can think about because he's home all day. So he gets two hours, after he tucks her in for a nap, to get signatures, to snag batting practice home run balls, bringing a bagful of souvenirs home every evening. He tells his wife that it's a matter of persistence, that you're catching people before their full development, and sometimes, if you wait long enough, the objects they leave behind can make the retriever rich. They probably won't, he acknowledges that. Still, it's nice to collect things that might someday have more value than they do now.

He shakes my hand. He says he hopes this is worth it, and doesn't explain.

After he moves off, unwilling to wait until the end of batting practice today, I begin to think that I imagined him. That he was some combination of oracle and ghost. And then I'm stilled by how fictional or necessary or profound anyone can be here, a hologram or an illusion rippling in too-hot air. Part of me thinks that Cal, stooped, maybe-real Cal, is the most honest person I've met all season, a man who defines things simply as what they are, braver in the face of the aimlessness of reality than I will ever be. The players are still taking swings. I call Joyce on reflex. I call to tell her that I'm watching Nick Franklin take batting practice again, leaving out the part about how rusty he looks, fouling balls off the cage, like he's starting over as someone new.

Faith has begun to waver a little since Nick showed his rust. His first game in Ohio, he batted second, swung hard, never made solid contact. He went hitless with two strikeouts, and the home fans who don't know anything about anything began to laugh and say, "Why's a scrawny, overmatched kid batting second?" Brad tried to explain to the rival fans what Nick had done this season, but when you looked at him out of context, the embellished facts felt like outright lies. The LumberKings lost that game, down 2–1 in a best-of-five series, one away from elimination yet again.

Tom Wilhelmsen finally pitched a bad game for that second LumberKings loss. His year is over, and so he's next in line to drink himself stupid with Hank. And me. We take shots, split pitchers, like friends. A round of good whiskey shows up. The waitress leans in, points down the bar to Ted, the general manager, sitting alone. He raises his glass in tribute.

"You've been fantastic, boys," he calls out.

There's the awkward raising of glasses in return, that too-long silence when Ted could invite the players over or the players could invite Ted. None of them know each other well enough to do that. Everyone looks down. Ted is paying his own way to be here, staying alone. Nate, his assistant general manager, is here, too, with the whole family, wanting to see a championship that belongs to him and doesn't.

"Good guy," Tom says, looking at Ted, not sure if he means it.

We start talking about Nick Franklin.

Voices are lowered. I am glanced at. Sentences are ended with sudden silences and jerks of the neck toward me. Even though they are drunk

and unhinged, even though we are sharing some basic bar stool camaraderie, the ballplayer is schooled not to talk about any issue that matters enough to get him in trouble. Nick Franklin is that issue.

Hank's voice is working to not sound betrayed, just impartial.

"He thinks he's big-league now. Once you leave, you come back and
you're not one of us."

Is it that tenuous? Well, how could it not be? If the connection, the
brotherhood, the shared triumph and despair, is a hurried fabrication,
it should end swiftly and arbitrarily as well. What is shared is a sense of
wanting and of injustice. Nick wanted to move up, and then he did, so
there is no bond left.

I look at Hank. He is both himself and not. Or he is not the person
I saw before. He is just there. I have ascribed so much to him. I have
rooted for his success because he needed to be rooted for and I needed
to feel as if I noticed beauty previously unseen. I have made him tragic
because sometimes I think he is, but also because it makes him so worthy of attention. He is bored. Somebody is playing piano. There is a
bachelorette party. The bachelorette, in her plastic crown, stumbles past
us toward the bathroom and back again.

"I want to get a ring," he says, down into his beer, a reminder. "That's
what is important. That's what we're here for."

I am tired. I accept the platitude.

Chris, the bus driver, has let me crash in his hotel room, and so I end
up sneaking in late, tiptoeing and brushing my teeth to cut the booze,
fifteen again. He likes to fall asleep to Fox News at high volume, so that
is what I fall asleep to. Pundits are screaming. People are accusing. *Take
responsibility.* I hear that phrase clear enough. *I'm sick of you,* voices
assert, back and forth in a contest of apportioning blame. There is ter-
rorism in this world. And famine, too. There are godless people with
sinister intentions. Chris knows this, worries, talks about it often. I say,
"Uh-huh." I agree with nothing he says, but I think we're scared in the
same way.

Chris worked in restaurants for thirty years, which fed both his type-A
personality and his drinking. But about a decade ago, he decided no
more drinking, and because he decided, it was done. It's about personal

responsibility. That's why he likes driving ballplayers. Bird-watchers and family reunions and tour groups that travel east to see the leaves change, they all tip better, but they are not en route to a job, not working, always working.

"It's about personal responsibility," he says. "If the players come to me saying, 'Chris, I left my stuff in the clubhouse, drive me to get it,' I say, 'Son, it's about personal responsibility. It's only a mile and a half. Walk.'"

I wake him up screaming in my sleep, and he says, "Good goddamn, boy. You know why I never dream? I was having bad ones and I just said to myself, *stop.*"

I was dreaming about hands around my neck squeezing me like a bat.

We're both up, and we go to Cracker Barrel for eggs.

In the stands, Captains fans who remember Brad come over to say that they recognize some of their own—at the park early, always loud, always knowing the count, the score, the inning. Brad gives a serious handshake, says likewise.

The talk turns, naturally, to who likes who in the grand expanse of all leagues and teams. Well, all the Cleveland teams suck. Brad tells them he roots for Chicago teams, but not the way he roots for the LumberKings. He tells them that he's been the PA announcer for LumberKings games since he was seventeen, waits for them to be impressed. They ask how big the town is. Brad says, "Not too big, not too small." They chuckle. They ask how their own PA announcer is doing. Brad says, "Doing okay, but he's a bit busy. Needs to learn to let the action speak for itself." Brad tells them all the players who have come through Clinton whose names he's spoken. The same list I was led to the first day I came to Clinton.

We talk about LeBron James because this is the summer of his treachery, when he left his native Ohio to go live a flashy life in Miami, thus bringing into question his own values and the state of society at large. Brad says, with real empathy, "That must have hurt."

"You know it, brother," says one Captains fan.

"Nobody likes to be left behind," Brad says.

"You know," says the fan, "I had my suspicions. Everybody called him the savior, called him the king and our hero, like he was some great guy.

But I knew it. Look at him now. We were tricked. Underneath all the good things we thought about him, he's just another nigger."

Brad and I are silent. I focus on my curly fries, afraid, I think, of seeing the casual grin on the fan's face. He goes to take a piss eventually. I lean into Brad, say, "Jesus Christ, what kind of fans are these, huh?"

Brad says, "What?"

I say, "The *n-word*?"

Brad says, "It's hard. With what that man did to his hometown . . . It's tough to say how hurt you'd be."

And then, "Things are said when somebody hurts you."

Brad is a good man. In the time I've known him, I've seen only that. He is open and he is loyal. He takes a pleasure in speaking the names of all the players who arrive in Clinton, wishes each one well. Brad admires a guy like Erasmo for his sturdy build and serious face, for the effort he always puts forth on Clinton's behalf. But if Erasmo lost the championship game and gave a terse postgame interview, too tired and disappointed to be polite, would Brad just listen as an opportunistic racist called him a spic or another liar from some south-of-the-border shithole? It's the flip side of adoration. It's supporting a guy so much, investing so much in the hope for his success, that it feels reasonable to be personally hurt by his failures. To hate him and flail against the talent that you feel he is wasting. And rarely, if ever, does a fan know what a player will feel when a game is over. What he cares about and what he doesn't. Where he sleeps away from all the eyes. No matter if Erasmo ends up loved or reviled or just forgotten after this season, he will be on a bottom bunk in the jungle in a month, and then home to Rivas, sleeping in a house that his money helped fix.

But not yet. The LumberKings squeak out a one-run win to stay alive. Brad exhales like a cartoon portrayal of the wind. The series is 2–2. Tomorrow will decide it.

Nick Franklin makes loud contact in the first inning. Brad screams, grabs my forearm. The ball dies in center, caught easily. He is the only LumberKing in the first eight batters who doesn't strike out. The score is tied at zero through four innings. Brad is squirming. Pastor Ray Gimenez is, too. He's from the Bronx, was a star second baseman for the Clinton Pilots in the 1970s. Like a few other players before him, after his career fizzled, Ray came back to Clinton, where people still knew him and remembered his talent, where jobs were then easy to find. He made Clinton home, and now he roots the way he was himself rooted for. Ray started an outreach shelter down the street from the stadium. At first seldom used, now its forty-eight beds are filled every night. He brought some of his boarders to the game to root. The men with Ray are cheering, they're appreciating their nachos, but they are not the Roadkill Crew. I have no memories of the Crew at away games. I wasn't there. But I assume, believe, that they were more imposing than what is here now.

Tim calls me.

"Buddy," he says. "Buddy, can you hear me?"

As though there should be a deafening roar cutting through our connection.

"Do you see any Roadkill T-shirts in the crowd?"

"I don't think so. Can't see everybody."

Nobody stands out. I see lots of hats with bald eagles on them. Lots of work shirts from jobs still held down or from past lives, the name tags impossible to read from afar. Tim tells me that anyone who was ever in Roadkill, or who ever met and loved Roadkill, has been waiting for Clinton to return to a championship. There was an agreement, never stated, but felt. When the LumberKings were in the championship again, they would all be there, that's what they'd do. Something so shared, so imprinted, couldn't be forgotten.

"Yell it," Tim says. "Please. Yell, '*Rooooadkill*,' nice and long, the way I do it. They'll hear it and they'll know."

Brad hears through the phone, says he'll yell with me. Brad likes tradition.

"*Rooooadkill*," he begins. The word hangs, wavers, disappears over the field.

He does it again and I join in.

"*Rooooadkill*," until these clueless Ohioans turn and look at us like, *Who howls mournfully into the crevices of a stadium? Start a wave at least.*

Nobody stands to respond. The only person, no, the only thing that moves toward us is the mascot, a ship's captain cum enormous purple furry beast. He has taken our yells as some sort of taunt pointing out

how slow this scoreless game has become. He bounces over, pantomimes a challenge for a fight, pinches the tip of his snout to show that
we smell, turns and shakes his furry ass in Brad's face.

I hold the phone to my ear for a while and don't have anything to say
to Tim.

I can tell that he is alone. Nobody is clamoring to speak over him in
the background. Tammy might be with Dan, watching to make sure
he doesn't sneak out for cigarettes with that bad heart. She will try to
care for him during the times that he is still in Clinton. She texted me
earlier: *Cheer loud for us. Tell them we're sorry we couldn't be there.* Betty
and Bill must be at home, Bill sick again, confused, not at all the man
who took driving shifts in 1991, who drank with umps, who sometimes
mustered a yell of derision at the opponents that got chuckles from a
whole stadium section. And Mailman Matt, who screams until he cannot breathe. And other Crew members: Eileen and Gary—him working the twelve-hour at ADM, her listening to the radio, arms folded.
And Tom, dead. And Joyce's friend, I don't remember the name, dead. A
bunch of others dead or moved, a job lost or a home or a cancer battle.
That is how life progresses. It shouldn't feel remarkable, shouldn't wield
the vicious sting of tragedy, but it does.

Medina gives up a run in the fifth, and the possibility of the Lumber-
Kings not being destined to win, or losing in spite of destiny, begins to
feel very, very real. We need a rally. Hank is on the top step of the dugout. He begins to warm up, rotating his shoulders in circles, twisting his
torso so that his eyes are looking at us in the stands for a moment, and
then back again.

I grab Brad and point.

"He's gonna be the hero," I say.

"I knew it," he says. "If it should be anybody, it should be him."

We rise to cheer. He tips his cap. From somewhere in the stadium,
far away but still booming, our answer finally comes. *"Roooooaaadkill."*

None of that happened. It is too clean a fantasy. There is no way that
it can be true. Hank is on the disabled list, officially, irreversibly inactive.
Nothing, not him wanting it, not me wanting it, not the team needing
it, will make the right thing happen. Erasmo will not play tonight either.
He pitched a few days ago, and he is being monitored, 151 innings this
year, thrown by a body that is still growing. It doesn't matter if he is the

best chance at winning this championship for Clinton. He has a future now. It has been decided. He is worth protecting. He is better than this place. Joyce would be protesting if she were here, *E-mo, put in E-mo.* But after four more innings he will no longer be on this team. Already he isn't. Joyce is on blackjack tonight, dealing to friendly faces as they lose and lose and win and lose again.

I haven't been sleeping, not well anyway. And it started before I was draped over Bus Driver Chris's couch fighting to squeak out much-needed rest over the high-volume punditry on TV.

Isolation. And failure. And heat. Thunderstorms that shake the house and the bed, lightning that sounds like something being ripped. The loss of a game is not like the loss of anything real. Not like the loss of life. Not like the loss of big, loud words—innocence, belief, desire, childhood. My father texts along with Tammy now. He is listening to the game on his computer as if it is a game that I'm playing in, the way it used to be, because this is important to me, so it can be important to him, too. He is rooting. We love to root. That is what we do together. All those seasons after my brother when my father didn't miss a Yankees game on TV, and I passed by his room every night, lit only by the screen glow, and I joined him to watch and yell. His shoulders were rounded when I went home this summer. It is to be expected. An old man shrinking, a son surprised.

The LumberKings score one in the sixth, but so does Lake County. And the Captains score another in the seventh with bloop singles and a bunt and an error by Medina, scoring to soft cheers, the whimper of small ball. Now it's the ninth inning, so slow and fast all at once that I don't even realize until I say, "Wait, is this the—?" Brad says, more sighs, "Yeah." Then he whispers, "Nick's up this inning."

There he is, going through the rhythms that all Clinton baseball fans have subconsciously memorized. Feet spread, leaning back on his hips, rotating, a looseness that he has worked very hard to achieve. He taps his bat on the edge of the plate, settles in, and we rise. A lanky closer I've never heard of stares him down, winds up, throws.

Nick likes the pitch. He steps forward. He swings.

It's not that I like happy endings. I think I like sad ones better. There is more to talk about, more value, somehow, when there's failure. And Tim and Joyce, Betty, Brad, everyone—no matter if they're smiling, they're almost always talking about losing, the humor within it, the effort behind it, how close it came to being not losing. I used to map my maturity by how I took in baseball. At first, the win was everything. Ends were only acceptable when those that I wanted to win won. Then everything was redeemed. There was no point to doing or watching, or being read a story, if it didn't end in victory.

But he held that ball. And the game was over.

Those Russell boys can't be beat.

Thump-thump. Thump. Thump.

That was the sound of the happy crowd in John R. Tunis books, the sound of fervor.

I told my father that the thump-thump was like a heartbeat. He smiled and said yes. He held a hand to my chest.

"Thump-thump," he said. "Still alive. Thump-thump."

At a certain point postpuberty, it's satisfying to doubt, to deflate and mock the certainty with which we were told games matter. I could go to games in high school, sneer at the fat drunks with high-and-tights who looked so serious during the national anthem, as if they were doing their part by watching a full nine innings. I could laugh with friends about grown men in replica jerseys, an adulthood that we would never have once our band got its break.

But mocking is the last thing I want to do now. I like that it feels as though I'm surrounded only by people who never took pleasure in saying fuck you to those who thought they knew better. As Nick Franklin swings, he believes fully in how infallible his talent is, the way his whole family believes, the way everybody around him has always believed. He hasn't ever doubted what he's been told he is. His father can sip whiskey while telling me with a straight face, "Nick's just always been a free spirit," because it's such a lie that it comes with no fear of repudiation.

And in that willingness to believe, maybe Nick is like Tim, who should be here, a part of this. Tim, who has spent all of his adulthood watching with his parents, sharing in the value of their presence in this town that needs people, good people, to stay. They are a whole family intact, believing in the same things, occupying the same space, something as unbelievable and comforting as any perfect season I've ever read about.

A year later, I'm in Venezuela, on the tallest mountain above Caracas, and being up so high, I am no longer scared. I wander, cold at such altitudes, awash in fast Spanish that I can't make sense of. And then I hear soft, southern English as I sit on a rock to watch the bowl of a city below.

"Praise God, that's a view," one voice says. And then a bunch of others: "Amen."

The leaders of the voices are baseball chaplains, taking a church youth group from South Carolina to tour a land beautiful but not quite yet saved. They come for a month each year, and then some stay longer, getting rides into the jungle to lead baseball players in the right kind of prayer.

The extent of the faith is so stunning, and the fact that through thousands of miles and testy governmental relations, cultural and linguistic barriers, the same fidelity to notions of progress and winning and God translates so seamlessly. I'm alone in Venezuela, or I'm surrounded in the Midwest—it's all the same content. It's not so much the God-ness that is important; it's how well that dogma fits into what is being sold.

The potbellied white pastors shake my hand and bless me, look over the sprawl of Caracas, and tell me about the character of the ballplayers they've met in Venezuela. How they had a devout quality to them that made everyone in their hometowns yearn to be better, how that quality transcends the circumstances into which they'd been born.

It's amazing when you bring people a game and a God to keep them good, how well they will respond.

So sure.

And when the Mariners re-sign to house their Low-A affiliate in Clinton for another three years, the Baseball Family is happy, but they expected it.

There will always be baseball here. Show teams a good place full of good people, they'll want to be a part of it.

And when the census numbers come out after the season and sum up another decade of losses, there is a rebranding of this fact.

We lost less than we thought we would, which is like gaining.

Stubborn, happy belief. Even if it's forced at times, it is constant—a cement foundation on which everything is supported. I drive and drive, and then I sit with and watch people who've never said outright, *I am unhappy.* Or, *This isn't worth it.* I don't know what people are really feeling, what they want to feel, but I love the surface of it as I find myself longing for what was maybe never really there. I'm awake gasping most mornings before the sun comes up, that invisible hand, again, gripping me like I'm a bat and it's the ninth inning. When I close my eyes, fail to sleep, open them again, all I want is to see Tim dancing with his mother during the seventh-inning stretch.

In Lake County, the center fielder is moving back, worried. I lose the ball for a second in the moon, which isn't full but I imagine it to be. Nick is watching as he rounds first base, betraying no emotion. The center fielder's name is Delvi Cid, a Dominican kid who played a couple of years ago in a complex just like the Venezuelan ones I will visit. But tonight, he is the Ohio home team's long-legged hope to catch Nick Franklin's drive.

Cid stops right at the warning track.

He waits.

He taps his glove once, watches the ball drop, catches it, tosses it in.

We sigh, all the Clinton fans. I'm sure Tim is screaming at home and on the casino floor Joyce is begging them to let her put the radio on. Nick Franklin got under it, and now the game is almost over. He swung too hard. It was a pop fly, nothing more.

"It's not over," Brad says. "We want it more. We deserve it."

"Twenty years," he says. "We've been waiting."

And then there's another fly out and a strikeout, so fast, so matter-of-fact, that it feels as if we were robbed of watching the conclusion to this season. And then the last strikeout victim is throwing his bat in disgust, and the LumberKings have lost.

Hank walks alone and Nick walks alone and Erasmo walks alone back to the visitors' clubhouse. A bunch of Lake County boys collapse on the mound and wait for their trophy. There it is, the same one Tim held those years ago, still simple and wooden. Still smaller than you'd like it to be.

Ride Home

BRAD IS WHIMPERING. He is a very big man who cries like a very small child, and nobody knows quite what to do with that. Perhaps it's the volume of his emotion that allows me to, for a while at least, ignore my own. But, yes, my body is slumping, my cheeks a little wet, my eyes stinging. We are in the parking lot, and we can see the Captains sprinting out of the home locker room in various states of champagne-doused undress, tackling each other in the small patches of grass in between walkway and parking lot, giggling, shouting, coltish in a way that would be adorable to both Brad and me had we not already decided to hate these young men.

Earlier, I walked the second tier of the new, empty Classic Park stadium, watching the two-dimensional fireworks on their not-quite-jumbo Jumbotron. I called home, and my father picked up and said, "Where are you?" He sounded far away. He was. He'd been listening to Dave's broadcast online, or trying to, but the signal got fuzzy.

They lost, I told him. I'm not sure how I'm going to get home and they lost.

I went to the visitors' locker room. I moved into the center of the crowded, square space, the steam resting on the tile walls, settling in the dampened blue carpet. Hank didn't shower, because he didn't work up a sweat. He has his jeans on already, a black undershirt clinging to his torso with no dress shirt over it because the season ended exactly thirteen minutes ago and pointless rules, like wear a collar to represent your team with pride, ceased to apply. BJ asks him if he wants ice, for the hand, for the leg. He says no, no more, not this season. BJ shrugs. He's busy.

Pollreisz is shirtless and sagging, moving around the room, smiling, clapping shoulders, shaking hands, saying all the things that a man deepened by experience is supposed to say to those who still feel acutely. Matt Cerione throws his bats into his locker, and the crash, the sound of wood on wood, makes everyone realize how hushed it had been. He yells, *"Fuck,"* and slams his palms against the wall, kicks at his chair. He is roundly mocked.

"Easy, Slappy," Catricala says, and laughs. "It's over."

"Can anybody tell me what the fuck we're doing here?" a big, jovial reliever says, laughing before he finishes his sentence. He wraps a towel around himself, walks to the showers whistling. He stands in a clump with his teammates, shoving each other, slipping on sudsy tiles, in violent, naked contact, the way they've been since April.

In the parking lot, John Tamargo is ready to leave. His enormous SUV is waiting. He'll drive home to Tampa, taking a halting, leisurely route, sleeping in quiet, starchy motel rooms, feeling the hours alone. He looks maybe impatient, maybe nervous, waiting for all his players to file onto the bus. Brad is standing near him, and Tamargo is trying his best not to acknowledge the sounds of how much this hurts him. Brad takes a quivering breath, then a more stable one. He holds out his hand to shake Tamargo's.

"Thank you for a hell of a season," he says. "We'll all remember this one."

Tamargo nods, mumbles out something like, My pleasure or Happy to do it.

"We've been waiting a long time," Brad says.

"Yeah," Tamargo says.

They will never speak again. Tamargo boards the bus for a second, lifting his tired catcher's legs up the stairs, facing the group that's no longer his team. They all look up.

"All right," he says. "Hell of a season."

He waves one short, thick arm and leaves. The players laugh.

I hound him for the last time until we're standing by his car. I don't want him to leave without any ceremony. I want some acknowledgment of all that's happened, though I'm not sure what has happened. He looks at me like I'm Brad.

"Wow," I say. "It's crazy that it's over."

"Yeah," he says. "Seasons end."

I ask, "Where to now?"

Home. Sit on the couch for a month or two. Eat breakfast late with his wife. See his grandkids, watch them scoot around in the dirt. In late November, he will go to Venezuela and manage a pro team there for a pretty decent influx of extra cash, dodging riotous, beer-throwing fans, standing in cold showers. Maybe his family will visit. They'll go to the beach. Then spring training. Then repeat.

He gets in his SUV, honks once, drives away.

I am not the biggest intruder on the bus ride home. Ted wanted to ride with his boys, to be among them, not above, let them know that he appreciates their work. He even canceled his flight home. He is not some suit. He is in cargo shorts and an old, torn shirt. He is built like a stuffed bear. He played football and baseball in college. He still loves buses that smell, packed tight with exhausted, gaseous men, and he will display that now, before it's all over. Yeah, he sits in an office, but he does it for moments like this.

The players have found something to focus on in the post-loss hush, so they lean heads together and whisper viciously—*we bust our asses all season, this guy makes money off us, and now we have to double up so he gets a seat?*

I'm in the crosshairs as well, no longer with anything to give, a ride or adulation, just a person who wants a piece of their space, wants to watch their movies and watch them sleep. I don't deserve what the players deserve. Everything they have done for me, for the fans, the team; all they ask is two seats on which to spread out one sore body. The simmering indignity of six months has finally boiled. Ted Tornow sits alone in the front. I sit opposite him, next to Dave, the only one on this bus not practiced enough in the art of the manly rebuttal to tell me no. Ted pulls out a bottle of Crown Royal and a pile of crumpled clear plastic cups. He pours, tells everyone around him to take one. Dave, laptop out, says, "In a while, I have to finish the game notes." Ted says, "*David*," and Dave sighs, takes a cup, sips. The whiskey has been sitting under a stadium seat for hours and is the temperature and texture of cough syrup. It burns.

Erasmo is in the back with the Latino players that ever-flank him—

Ochoa, Mario, Noriega, Medina, a couple of others. They are laughing quietly. Even after a whole season, a team that has, by all accounts, jelled well remains segregated. The Latinos sit with each other and talk about places and games that only they know. This is only a fraction of the year's baseball competition for the Dominican and Venezuelan players. In their lives of repeated tryouts and shuffling allegiances, the only constants are each other's presence and the very real sense that every performance is as important as the next. How could this one loss, then, be the end of anything? There are no ends until nobody in any country pays you to swing or throw.

A collective decision has been reached in the back, and Ochoa, the oldest and least accented in his English, walks forward as spokesman. He stands at the front of the bus, deciding what authority figure to address. He speaks to everyone who might have power—BJ, Ted, Pollreisz, Bus Driver Chris.

"We have decided," he says, "that we should watch a Spanish movie for the last bus ride."

Silence.

"We haven't watched one all year. And it's not fair."

It's not so much that somebody says a definitive no, there just isn't a yes. And when the American players start yelling, *Bullshit,* no fucking way that the last bus ride will involve the crooning of Marc Anthony in *El Cantante,* no older man feels like entering the fight. Subtle anger mounts. No malice is expressed, nothing directly racially inflammatory is mentioned, but the subtext is thick and choking. Only eight or nine men on this team are here on a temporary work visa, and they are always in the back with the engine vibration and the bathroom piss stench. And the look on Ochoa's face, the faces of all his friends standing up in support, suggests an inflated importance placed on Marc Anthony's eyes-closed angel voice, the feeling of this as a first and last stand. The American players shout over him.

BJ starts shouting, too, at everyone.

"Oh, just shut the fuck up, majority rules."

Catricala jumps up and pops in an American action flick. Ochoa is told to sit down. He says no, even as he begins to walk back to his seat. He turns to yell again, but his legs keep moving away from what he's yelling about.

"*Bullshit!*" Mario Martinez yells, and Noriega echoes him unintelligibly.

I spot Erasmo in the farthest-back seat of the bus, watching closely, not participating. He leans into Medina to teach him one more thing—this isn't worth it. Also, keep smiling. He won't sleep during the bus ride. He will stare out the window for ten hours, occasionally tapping Medina on the shoulder, pointing out the window, happy to be able to explain something to someone newer than he is to the middle of this country.

That is an extra-long truck, that bright thing with a fountain in front of it is a casino, that smoke is coming from some factory somewhere. This is Ohio. Now this is Indiana. Do you know what comes next?

He has learned a lot. He has aged.

He will, when we leave the bus at dawn, shake my hand as I try to position my body for a hug.

"I'll call you soon," I will say.

"We'll see," he will say. "Facebook is better. I will be working."

I'll stand near him for too long in the clubhouse, until he nods at me, then jerks his head toward the meager pile of his possessions waiting to be packed, my cue that I am in the way of his moving forward. He will fly to Rivas alone early in the morning, see his mother, father, sister, grandmother, grow restless, will go to live in the Agua Linda dormitories in November. He will e-mail me periodically: "I am here. It is good. I am working." I will see him at spring training in Arizona, thinner, more muscular, walking with an adult composure so different from how he was when I met him.

"No more Clinton," he will tell me, standing by the practice fields, new sunglasses reflecting the desert sun, arms across his chest, smirking a little.

"Double-A?" I will say.

And he will allow himself to say, "Maybe."

"Triple-A."

"Hey, come on."

"Major leagues."

"I'm gonna do it," he will tell me, a blatant period to our last conversation. "Soon. That is the goal. You can see me on TV."

He will turn his back, talk to a frightened, eighteen-year-old Venezuelan pitcher spending his first week in America, looking at Erasmo the way I used to look at my brother. He will point at the English bulldog that belongs to the visiting Orange County family of another pitcher, in town to watch their son.

"*Feo,*" he will say, and go so far as to do an impression of the dog's underbite. His new friend-fan will laugh. He will look at ease, an ease that has been earned by nothing easy. I should feel happy for him, but I won't because of his disinterest, because I will be one of the people that he very obviously has moved past. I will put my hand on his shoulder, feel the heat and the swell of fifteen extra pounds of muscle, no baby fat floating on top. He will give a small shrug. I will wish him good luck and he will say, "No luck."

The players haven't eaten since three o'clock this afternoon, and that was peanut butter and jelly with mealy apples for a locker-room lunch, scarfed down with one-bite adrenaline before the game. Now there's no adrenaline, just anger. Anger exacerbates hunger. We must stop.

Ohio rest stops look like pods, something extraterrestrial, all circular, all uniform. There are no lights on in any stores. We pile out anyway, find nothing open but bathrooms and vending machines, return to the bus, then repeat fifteen miles down I-80. It feels like a dream where you wake up still inside that dream, wake up again, same place, quick relief, and then the realization.

Fuck. Fuck. Cocksucker. Fuck. Bullshit.

It is a chorus of irritation. What kind of shithole rest stop is this? Shithole state? Shithole life? I think that the furious fake questions are exacerbated by the fact that just a couple of hours ago there were bright lights, there was a mini-Jumbotron, a trophy, even if this team didn't win it. It feels as if something should be open in honor of these circumstances—God, or at least the owner of a roadside Quiznos, should be aware of this fact, should know what tonight is. These are near champions. And me and Ted and BJ and Dave—we're the guys who hang around near champions. How can that not be enough to get a sandwich?

Everyone is a little boy now, cell phones out, searching for service, wanting to tell moms and dads and girlfriends that we're somewhere in Ohio and that everything sucks. Wanting to hear kind, patient lies in return. Soon the bus is loaded, ready to try again. BJ does a head count. No Nick Franklin. BJ curses. Pollreisz gives a little smirk that I think is meant to suppress anger. The players' eyes are hard. Nick comes walking out of the glass doors, pauses to send a text under the two floodlights still on at the front of the building. The whole bus watches him, breathing into the glass separating him from us, but he doesn't notice. Or maybe he does. I lean too close to the window watching him, my forehead touching the grimy surface. I wipe my breath off the glass and watch him adjust the collar of his shirt, opening it one more button. I have my notebook out. I try to conjure adjectives to encompass him, an exercise that is just forced disappointment after six months. And it's not particularly unique, the effort to sum him up. It's the job of a whole slew of people, those who watch and laud and critique and brand the Nick Franklins of this small world.

Slick. Indifferent. Cold. I tilt it the other way. Statuesque. Ripe. Flawless. I angle the notebook away from Dave, but he isn't looking anyway. He is quantifying the season online already. He is archiving everything that happened with all of the men on this bus, the numbers they will leave behind. Nick sees, finally, the eyes on him, begins a trot.

I will see him running next March, not an easy trot but an almost sprint, legs still spindly enough to look like a suburban boy scooting through the yard in a Cheever story. He will be running from his former agents, left behind in the trajectory of his career and relieved of their charge of him on a rainy Orlando afternoon while Nick's mother spoke to them of opportunity and Nick lingered in the back of their office crying. I will be standing next to his former agents in Arizona as they watch him on the practice field, scowling and relaying the story. Mid-sentence, they will take off in pursuit of Nick as soon as the team breaks for lunch, running with the limp of the formerly athletic, now stiff, bound by loafers and slacks. I won't know what they're hoping for if they catch him, just a reprimand or maybe a last negotiation after the fact. They won't get anything. Nick will make it to the safety of the locker room, where nobody is allowed unless invited, and he will wait them out, wait me out, too, for an hour while I sit in the parched parking lot, running my hand across the chrome of his Escalade.

The next day, I'll be the one running to catch up to Nick as he walks with his new agent, a representative of the Boras Corporation, the most hated, feared, and successful sports agency on earth. I will introduce myself to this new agent, his eyes hidden behind sunglasses. I will ask him, foolishly, if Nick has said my name, mention, foolishly, our time in Clinton as though he might say, *Wow, what a season that was!* I will ask to talk to Nick again, maybe sit down with the two of them. He'll say Nick's busy, not just busy for me, I shouldn't feel bad. Everything anybody has to say to Nick now goes through this man in front of me, I will be told. He will reach into his pocket to look for a business card and say, "Whoops, all out," will pat me on my shoulder, and say, "Have a safe trip back to Iowa."

"Fuck, Franklin," somebody calls from the back of the bus. "It's cool. We weren't just sitting here waiting." Nick glares toward the face behind the voice, obscured in semidarkness, and he begins to yell, or maybe it's grunt—furious, guttural exclamations, almost unintelligible but with a clear message.

I don't want anger to be the only thing felt now, because this is a bus full of people who shared something. The something isn't exactly clear, and maybe the something isn't much, but it existed, didn't it? And I want to be somebody who has gathered momentum with everyone else toward a collective crescendo, who watches all the way through to its end, invested. Invested in a moment that becomes impossible to erase as Dave writes down the last stats that will exist always, somewhere in a Google search, for anyone looking to find.

Nick sits near the front, speaks to BJ as if he were a hallway monitor.

"I wanted a snack."

He's gone from teammate to mercenary in a week and a half. He was tearing up in the lobby of the Pzazz! FunCity, remember? I saw it. I tell myself that. He was crying because he was connected to these people, and now, since he left and was asked to return, just the fact of being asked has reminded him that he is different, that he is alone.

My phone rings and it's Tim. I hear the choking slur of drunk and grieving together as soon as I answer.

"Hi, Tim."

A pause. "Hi. It's Tim."

I know where he's sitting, his couch, brown and soft. I know the black cat is nuzzling his leg, pawing at the loose fabric of the Roadkill Crew '91 tank top that I know he's wearing. I know that the TV is on mute, the radio is on, Dave's postgame report long over, leaving behind the crackling horns of music older than Tim himself, but he always did like the sound of older things. I know that next to the TV, there is a shrine to the former members of the Baseball Family, a compact, well-maintained vigil that never goes away. That picture of Tom is there, from near the end, strangely thin, the brim of his LumberKings hat making a little shadow on his face.

We apologize to each other. He sighs into the phone. He asks me what the bus is like, how everybody is. I tell him quietly, hand over my mouth, that it's a deflated and silent bus. I use those words instead of "angry."

"Poor guys," Tim says. "They came close."

"I thought they were going to do it," I said.

He breathes into the phone for a while and says, "You know, maybe the better thing is to lose."

I'm not sure what to say.

"Winning is easy," he says. "It's a . . ."

He trails off, takes a halting breath, begins again. "It's a lie."

I try to think if I agree with him.

"I wish I could've been there," he says. "Not because it would have done anything, but, you know."

"I wish you could've been there, too."

"Did I ever tell you that I was on the field with the players in '91?" he asks. "I was on the pitcher's mound holding the trophy."

He continues for a while, and I say nothing to interrupt.

"Where are you guys now?" he says when the story is done.

I look over Dave out the window through a small slit in the curtain. Shimmering black highway, the darker black trees alongside the highway, headlights like flames as cars pass us. We are somewhere.

"I don't know."

"When will you be home?" he asks, and I'm stuck on that word. Home. Clinton isn't, not for me, certainly, not for anybody on this bus except for Ted and Dave, who hates that fact. But I don't think "home" means Clinton, not as Tim is saying it. Well, it does, but it's also a feeling or just an end point, someplace to stop.

"We want to be there when the team gets home," Tim says. "All of us. The Family. They deserve to have us tell them thank you."

His voice is still shaking when we say good-bye, but he will call everyone, rally them even if they're sleeping. They'll be waiting. He promises. I tell him that he is a good guy for doing so, surprised at how serious it sounds when I say it, how much I want him to know that I think that. He tells me to hush.

There is an oasis in Indiana, an open one, made for sleepless truckers.

The players wait in a line that pushes out the door of the McDonald's. Teenagers in their uniforms and official drive-thru headsets stumble through orders, slipping, bumping into one another, not expecting so many big, demanding young men at one in the morning on a Monday. It is Monday, isn't it? Hank is standing in line with some others, trying to reconcile the day, the time, the place.

Hank limps his way forward, grimacing a little, but still going, his perseverance now directed toward a bacon double cheeseburger. It's the twentieth, he announces, which everyone kind of knew, but still. No, wait, it's morning. It's the twenty-first. Some of his teammates groan because they have training that they are both honored and obligated to be attending in a couple of days. They will not go home. They received word of the next mission from Tamargo, relayed from the front office on high—pack up for Arizona, Puerto Rico, Australia. This is good, ultimately. The longer you live at home, the less chance to be forgotten. Hank will fly into Burbank. His father will pick him up in the work truck, take him home. He will sleep in his old twin bed, under his old posters and old trophies. It will feel as if he never left, as if he won't again.

When I visit him in January, I'll be around for his only baseball-related activity. We'll drive to Pasadena, where Hank teaches his game to the uncoordinated children of wealthy families whose gardens his father tends. He'll lob them batting practice in a cage that his father helped build in their yard, as nice as the one he used in Clinton. He'll let himself have fun, get intense, turn each lob into an important pitch, turn each day into a pennant race, and they will love him.

"We get taught by a major leaguer," they will say to me.

He will force himself to correct them.

Hank gets his burger and returns to the bus. He eats with his head on the window, and as he bites, his reflection gnaws his own face. I impose thoughts into his head, about home, family, girlfriend. She will be his fiancée soon. Maybe that's what he is thinking. Maybe that's what tepid McDonald's in an Indiana rest stop, a throbbing ankle, a thumb where you can push the bone chips around, makes any person think about.

He will tell me about his proposal sitting outside the Comfort Suites in Peoria, Arizona, drinking watered-down hotel lobby coffee. He will sound more sure than I've ever heard him, saying that the team should be ready to give him a chance, that the only thing he'd heard thus far at spring training was "Boy, you earned it." And his girlfriend, now his fiancée, she knew that, too. She knew what he could be, and she was happy to let him have a last good shot at it.

"I'm not going back to Clinton," he will tell me, certain. "If they send me back there, it'll be to back up Baron, and I'm not doing that again." It's time to move forward. He is a man. He has a life to live. He'll tell them that, he promises.

I will leave Arizona that night and for a month scan the Web site for each team in the Mariners system, looking for his name, finding it nowhere. I will Google search for some recognition of the end of his career, and find nothing. He kept his word. Faced with a return to a backup role in Clinton, he went into the office, said I deserve better, said I'll quit before I go back. The team said they understood. He was free to go.

But when I see him for the last time, it will not be in a starter apartment with his future wife or leaving class as he tries to finish his degree; it will be in Sioux Falls, South Dakota, where he signed on to catch in the American Association of Independent Professional Baseball, unaffiliated with any major league organization, dotted in random places with fields spanning a continent—Amarillo and Gary, Indiana, and Winnipeg. Hank will be finishing up a pretty solid season, not playing the last two weeks after getting concussed in a home plate collision and having to wait for the team's volunteer doctor to return from vacation and confirm that diagnosis.

We will get hammered drunk in an apartment that looks like his old Clinton place, the only difference being that Hank is now the youngest of his roommates, so they all drink legally, and a lot of them smoke a lot of weed because nobody cares. We will chug until I feel as if I'm choking, then crush the cans and play a game where you try to fling the empties into a small trash bin without looking, Coors Light splattering on wall-to-wall carpet. An outfielder from Massachusetts will tell me about his time in AAA, describing in exquisite detail how nice the buses are, how far the seats recline. An infielder will pass me a blunt and tell me he was offered $100,000 by the Yankees but turned it down to go to college. Got hurt, got high, flunked out—I'm half-listening because I know the end. They will both tell me that Hank was such a goody-goody when he got here, the way many freshly released are, still used to important eyes watching them. They will point at Hank now, chugging, his hair hanging over his eyes, newly long, his fledgling beard wet.

They will, Hank included, describe themselves as warriors or at least as those born to compete, to be a part of this thing. This thing, the game, it can validate all. Hank is still telling the story of himself, a man quietly suffering but not quitting, never that. I've driven six hours diagonally across Iowa to find him in a new place just like the old place. He is treading water in his own myth, Hank, who is still worth watching, worth remembering for some, for me.

John R. Tunis wrote about the end of a baseball career, and to me that used to mean the end of a life. I remember his images of an older body gone loose, slackened, and wrinkled, doubled over itself on a wooden bench, unable to move for a while to pack and leave. I tried to sit like that, perfectly still, heavy, to show when I was anxious or afraid, depressed and unable then to put a word to the feeling. And that's how I explained to myself the way my father sat after his son died and I saw him feel the loss, silent but loud. I made the pose understandable.

Erasmo has forsaken McDonald's and gone to get a gas station hot dog, showing Medina, his new sidekick, how all the condiments are hidden in little drawers beneath the rotating grill, a crucial detail of American life. Men in camouflage hats buying Skoal and energy drinks, women with tired eyes over by the magazine rack, they all watch the pair of foreigners. Erasmo doesn't notice, or he does notice and doesn't care. He is so used to being watched.

Soon the new home page for the LumberKings will be up—Nick Franklin tracking a home run along the left side of the screen, Erasmo opposite him staring intently into Hank's catcher's mitt along the right side. Erasmo is one of the two worth being a reminder of a season that was good, almost great. After next season, he will be replaced on the

Web site by a couple of other pitchers, each hard-throwing and new, but for now he is the one to see.

The rest of the drive is drunk and loud, then hungover, nearly muted. The bus smells like freshly opened cans of cheap beer, then smells like burps, then just staleness. Chris keeps us at an even sixty-five, always in the right lane, and we drive straight, no bathroom breaks, until it feels as if we're not even moving. Ted keeps passing around whiskey, pounding plenty of it himself, until he is drunk enough to announce that, goddamn it, these players did all the work, he shouldn't have a seat by himself while they're doubled up. Their bodies need space. He stands up, says, "Take my seat," not to anyone in particular, just to the whole back of the bus, and he goes to sit on the stairs at the front, still holding his Crown Royal, wincing as his back seizes when we hit a bump. He raises his plastic cup to the men who, after tonight, are no longer his charges and, under their quasi-shared corporate umbrella, never really were.

"To you fellas," he says. "You played your hearts out for us. You deserve to be comfortable."

A movie with a lot of car chases is still on, and nobody is watching it. Pollreisz does his crossword and I help. Next to me, I think I hear Dave listening to the clips of some of his best calls from the season, happy ones that he has saved—his announcements: *"The LumberKings are going to the Midwest League Championship!"* And, *"Ladies and gentlemen, your new home run king, Nick Franklin!"* Some of the players read, mostly the Bible or books about how to win at blackjack. Some talk low into their phones, all the same answers to what I imagine to be the same questions—*not sure where I'm at right now, not sure when I'll be back,* then the only certainty: *we lost.*

First light happens in Illinois.

"Almost home," Pollreisz says.

We pull onto Highway 30, past the air freshener factory, past the plastics factory, past the gravel roads that turn off into the corn. And then we're in town. Past the Wild Rose. Joyce just left after the late shift, didn't get to hear any of the last game. Past ADM, pumping. Past the trains and the trucks, moving in and out. Past the blank, still-matted patches of grass where houses had been, where men protested three decades ago and lost and never protested again.

The players are already packing, some standing in the aisle, bouncing on the balls of their feet, ready to move, ignoring Chris's pleas for safety. They're planning to go in and out in five minutes, what they hope will be the last time they ever see that locker room, leaving nothing behind.

The sun has been rising behind us, like we're driving away from it, trying to preserve this night. But at Sixth Avenue North, we turn, drive the last block to the clubhouse heading east. The sun, orange and pink, climbs out of the river. It's morning.

The bus pulls up to the clubhouse, and they're all there. Tim kept his word. There are maybe twenty people in a tight group, squinting up at the tinted windows. They begin to clap as the bus slows, then stops. Tim, in the front, lets out a wolf's howl, maybe mournful, but reverent, too. Betty is next to him and Tammy and Bill, the whole family that is a part of this place, something close to mortar.

Joyce is here, running on no sleep, LumberKings sweatshirt over her casino vest, notebook out, folder full of the pages of a story just begun, Nick Franklin and his home run chase. Cindy is here, her husband still in Afghanistan, and Julie, her son at a base getting ready to go, neither one worrying in this moment. There are others that I recognize, peripheral members of the Baseball Family, clapping in unison. And others that I've never talked to—the ladies who sit behind home plate, the hecklers from the top row, the Indian doctor and his daughters, lost in and in love with this ultimate assimilation. Brad, who beat us back to Clinton and parked here to wait.

All of them clapping and giving thanks.

I don't think the players know what to do with this.

They hop off the bus gingerly, wade through the adoration and the brightness off the river. There are twenty feet of pavement between the bus, which is theirs alone, and the locker room, closed off, full of their smell and their possessions. Twenty feet of interaction with everyone who wants to tell them what they mean. Betty hugs. Tim slaps backs with a familiarity both earned and not. Children scramble around legs. Joyce reaches out her pen and paper and balls and hats, anything to hold a last drop of inky permanence.

I hear one player whisper to another, "I bet that bitch is gonna ask for your sweaty underpants," and then there are some kind *shut ups,* and some chuckling that I choose to read as apologetic, not just uncomfortable. Because she would, I think, and not in some sexual fantasy, ringing his sweat out into her LumberKings coffee mug, but because anything can be saved and can be made worth saving. And nobody will care as much about his underpants as this small group of people do by this stadium in this town by this river under this sun.

"This was almost the greatest season," Tim says.

Brad begins to weep again, reaches out for fellow fans to hug.

"Nicky," Joyce says. "Nicky, I wrote a story about you."

Some of the players pause. Hank stops, says thank you to Betty, to Tim, says good-bye, signs a ball for Joyce, says, "Hold on to that now," with a smile. She will. I watch him limp into the locker room, and he is, for the last time, everything I want him to be, head proud and erect even as his body fails, his injured catcher's legs never resting, old Dave from the books my father read to me, Bruce from *Bang the Drum Slowly* when he let me stay home from school and watched with me, each born to crouch and born to lose with symphonic beauty. Hank is just a guy moving back to his teenage bedroom. Failure is only romantic if it's not really failure.

Nick Franklin moves quickly. He silently accepts a shout of "We thought we'd never see you again!"

And then, "You're gonna make it."

And then, "I'm gonna tell everyone you were here, after you make it, when we watch you on TV."

And then, "Did you like it here?"

And then, "What happened to your Facebook account? I can't see it anymore."

Brad says, "People will remember this one for a long time. This was a great one to be a part of." He claps my back like I'm part of it, too.

I walk over to the front of the stadium to find Tom's brick. I rub my thumb across his engraved name. It costs $75 for one of these, $150 if you want a duplicate for your mantel. Just print out a PDF of the form from the LumberKings Web site, mail it with a check. Those are nasty and unimportant truths. Brick never fades, that is the thing to think.

Another year happens.

The corn is all harvested, and the husks decompose into the soil.

Joyce gets certified to work craps. She celebrates her twentieth year at the casino. She is the oldest dealer on staff and the bosses take her to dinner for that.

Bill gets sicker, and Betty says, "Well, getting older happens."

Tammy and Dan are having money problems, the trucking life bringing a less steady paycheck than he had at ADM. He ends up chasing a job to North Dakota, hauling dirt for an oil pipeline, living in a town that barely existed a year ago. She waits.

Cindy's husband comes home, and he doesn't like crowds. He fishes a lot and does not talk about Afghanistan.

Every month, the whole Baseball Family meets at Pizza Ranch to talk about this season and other seasons.

Alliant Energy Field, formerly Riverview Stadium, is renamed Ashford University Field.

Flavor Flav opens a fried chicken restaurant in Clinton, a decision so strange that it makes national news. At a theme night in a hipster bar in my college town, a guy with thick glasses and an ironic Pocahontas braid says, "Thank God somebody's bringing a little *flava* to one of Iowa's greatest dying cities." I laugh with the rest of the crowd. The chicken joint closes, and the building stays empty.

South Clinton residents, the ones left, file a lawsuit against ADM for ruining the ground and air and light, everything. They say, Our dogs are dying off. They say, The sides of our houses are turning green. They say, Everybody is sick. Look at our trees, they say. They are dying. Trees don't just die in bunches. That is not progress, they say.

A new season starts, new faces on the field, a new name for the stadium, new manager. Tim gives his howl and then speaks about how perfect this moment is, another perfect beginning to a season just like all the others.

On a hot, hot day, Joyce and I ride the gravels together. There are back roads through every mammoth, thousand-acre property, with occasional street signs identifying the intersection of 307th Street and 265th. There isn't a pattern. Or maybe there is, we just don't know it.

We get high, and that makes the logic of the gravel road grid system even more incomprehensible. I get giggly, and Joyce looks at me like someone she never expected to get giggly.

"Where *are* we?" I say.

"I don't know exactly, but I know where we're going," she says. "At least it's not night."

Her pipe is copper and shaped like a baseball bat.

"Isn't that great?" she says.

I grip it between my thumb and my index finger, moving them in little circles so the bat waggles.

Creedence is playing, drums like a horse trotting. We pass some horses. They are the color of tanned skin. I look at their legs flexing even as they're just standing there, and I think stoned thoughts about how *vain* they are, horses, just standing there, useless, flexing all their muscles to look pretty, a cowboy version of a Pomeranian.

"Look," I say. "Horses."

"Mmhmm," she says.

She tells me stories. She talks about her friend, using only a first name, as if I know her, so I say, "Uh-huh," as if that were true. They used to drive the gravels together, not to baseball games, just to nowhere, driving until one of them realized something and said it was time to turn around.

"Like that game," I say. "The one where you swim until one person gets scared they won't make it back to shore."

"I never played that," she says. "I saw the ocean once. In Texas. I lived in Texas."

"I never played either," I say, maybe as some sort of apology, although it's also just true. "I was always scared of things like that."

Her friend, whose name I don't remember, is dead now. "She was older than me," Joyce says. She used to know the way better. Or guess better at least. She found the oldest tree in Iowa. It was in a field, all alone, next to a red house, with a copper plaque that said "This is the oldest tree in Iowa." They stopped and walked over, touched the bark.

They found a cow's skull once, half buried in the dirt by the side of the road, when they stopped to take a piss. They picked it up and let the soil spill out of its eyes. They put it in the trunk.

They stole corn, like Robin Hoods of the ethanol era, the friend standing lookout for the sight of a tractor or a dog, Joyce wrapping her hands around the ears until one felt plump, ready, then snatching it off with an expert yank, running back to the car, laughing, thinking, When was the last time a single hand touched a single ear of corn on all these acres?

Joyce doesn't go as far now, just south or west to baseball games, Quad Cities, Cedar Rapids, Burlington, always a destination. Together they used to go north until they could feel the weather change, but cars feel smaller and dark feels darker when you are alone.

We are alone. We keep the windows open to let the smell of earth in and the combined smoke of old weed and Pall Mall 100s out. Tire on gravel sounds like part of a Creedence song and I say that and Joyce says, "*Doesn't* it? I've always thought that."

We pass a river with an old Indian name and creeks with no names. We pass trucks headed the other direction, toward I-80, and from there toward Clinton, to drop the corn off at ADM, to be heated with burned coal, beaten to mush, turned to fuel and candy and potato chip bags. We crank the windows up when we feel the ground vibrate, the first signal of the trucks, because they kick up dirt and it will seep through open windows, settle on the dashboard and in our lungs. And then the trucks are gone, we are calmed, the air clears, the windows open again.

We finish the pipe and drink Cherry Pepsi until we stop coughing. I get that leaden, impenetrable kind of stoned sleepiness. I feel her glancing at me as I close my eyes, force them open, close them again.

I wake up because we're no longer moving, perched on the unfinished banks of a man-made lake. There are backhoes on the new hillside, idle for the day, paused, frightening with all those teeth.

"Where *are* we?" I ask.

"In between Clinton and Davenport," Joyce says, looking at the water. "By a lake."

She walks into the muddy, tall grass by the shore, and I follow her.

"I wonder what was here," she says. "Under the water."

I give a stoned drawl in response: "*Lots* of stuff, probably."

We look at the skeletons of soon-to-be lakefront vacation homes, identical and clustered. We smoke cigarettes on the hood of her car, then get in, keep driving. We talk about baseball, and we talk about driving. She talks about how, when you drive eighty miles an hour down highways, you can't see anything, you miss everything between where you started and where you end up. What a waste. I tell her, a bit guiltily, that I speed, but I don't want to. Going slowly makes me nervous, but I regret what I'm missing. She tells me she understands. We are about to hit the end of the gravels, come right up on a four-lane highway like a burst of fluorescent light that will shoot us down to the stadium in Quad Cities, another game, a mostly new crop of players with names she is still learning.

"Oh, *look*," she says and stops the car.

There's an old, once-red wooden building next to a nonoperational farm.

"That's Buffalo Bill's ranch," she says.

I don't say anything, because it seems dubious, a landmark hidden off a road with no name.

"Sometimes you'll see people touring it, the ones that know about it," she says. "People take care of it still. They keep buffaloes right there behind the house."

I want to see, and so we drive up. But the field behind the house is empty, browned in late-summer heat. I sigh and I wish it weren't such a loud sigh. Joyce says they must be inside, the buffaloes. She promises they exist. They're magnificent, huge and antique. She's sorry that I didn't get to see them, but they were there, somewhere, hidden from any casual passersby. So remarkable and so close to us. They were there. And now we both know that.

ACKNOWLEDGMENTS

I should start at the beginning. Thank you to Ted Tornow, Nate Kreinbrink, Mitch Butz, Dave Lezotte, Brad Seward, and the rest of the LumberKings staff. Thanks for letting me into the front office, for allowing me to watch you work, for believing in the value of a project documenting the team you run so well. John Tamargo could have kicked me out at any time, and didn't. I truly appreciate his kindness. Thanks to JT, Terry Pollreisz, and Dwight Bernard for letting me be a part of the clubhouse and imparting to me at least a fraction of your combined century of baseball knowledge.

Of course, thank you to all the players on the 2010 Clinton LumberKings, with special thanks to Danny Carroll, Henry Contreras, Nick Franklin, and Erasmo Ramírez. You let me get to know you when you had plenty of other things to do. Thank you for sharing your stories with me. You are some of the most talented, dedicated people I have ever had the privilege to know. I wish you all the best. You deserve it.

So much of my Clinton experience was shaped by the fans, a group unlike any other I've ever met. Thank you to Joyce, Betty, Bill, Tammy, Tim, Eileen, Gary, Cindy, Julie, and so many more, as well as Sue Bigwood for her words about Tom. To be welcomed into The Baseball Family was a gift that I never anticipated. I am grateful to have sat all those hours with you and to be able to call you my friends. Outside of The Family, so many helped me get to know Clinton: Mike Kearny, Bob Soesbe, Bob Krajnovic, Ed Broderick, Jennifer Sherer, Charlene Bielema, Tony Davis, Lydia Hallbach, Steven Ames, Heather Bahnsen, Gary Herrity, Rev. Ray Gimenez, the volunteers at the Clinton County Historical Society, the list goes on and on. Thank you all for your time.

The amazing generosity that people showed me during my research didn't end in Iowa. So many people made my travels in Venezuela possible. Thank you to Jose Manuel Plata Ramírez, Juan Carlos Hererra, Alba Tirado, Sara Jiminez Molina, Luis Linares, Reny Bernal, Arturo Marcano, my gracious Tinaquillo hosts Ana, Luis, Justino, and Arnaldo, the staff and players of the VSL Mariners at Agua Linda, the scholars at the Venezuelan Baseball Hall of Fame in Valencia, and many, many kind strangers. I, quite literally, would have been lost without you.

Thank you to my teachers, without whom I would also be lost, though perhaps less literally. First, to Amitava Kumar at Vassar College, for telling me I was a writer and then telling me to shut up when I disagreed. And to my professors in the Nonfiction Writing Program at the University of Iowa. Thank you for teaching me what this genre really is and why it is important. John D'Agata, there are so many ways in which you helped me grow as a writer. I will just say a simple thanks and hope it can suffice.

The best gift that the University of Iowa gave me was a group of peers and friends who also happen to be some of the best young writers in the country. I can't mention everyone, though I should. Kristen Radtke, Mary Hellen Kennerly, Angela Davies Stewart, Lina Maria Fereira Cabeza Vanegas, Chelsea Cox, Ariel Lewiton, Inara Verzemnieks, and Mike Lewis. Thank you all for being so smart and willing to take time away from your own work to make this manuscript better.

I would also like to thank my editor, Keith Goldsmith, and everyone at Pantheon. Keith, thank you for the opportunity, the support, the shrewd and thorough edits. And thank you to my agent, Victoria Marini, for finding me and staying with me, for being a great reader, advocate, and friend.

Finally, my family. Thank you to my parents and my brother Pete for being kind, funny, and smart, and making me aspire to those qualities. And to Ottavia: I am so lucky for everything that you are. I love you.

ABOUT THE AUTHOR

Lucas Mann received his MFA in nonfiction from the University of Iowa, where he is currently a Provost's Visiting Writer. His essays and stories have appeared in or are forthcoming from *Wigleaf, Barrelhouse, New South, Columbia: A Journal of Literature and Art,* and *The Kenyon Review.* He lives in Iowa City, Iowa.

A NOTE ON THE TYPE

This book was set in Minion, a typeface produced by the Adobe Corporation specifically for the Macintosh personal computer, and released in 1990. Designed by Robert Slimbach, Minion combines the classic characteristics of old-style faces with the full complement of weights required for modern typesetting.

Typeset by Scribe, Phiadelphia, Pennsylvania

Printed and bound by Berryville Graphics, Berryville, Virginia

Book design by Robert C. Olsson